HONOR BOUND

HONOR BOUND

Race and Shame in America

David Leverenz

RUTGERS UNIVERSITY PRESS

NEW BRUNSWICK, NEW JERSEY, AND LONDON

Library of Congress Cataloging-in-Publication Data
Leverenz, David.
Honor bound : race and shame in America / David Leverenz.
      p.   cm.
   Includes bibliographical references and index.
   ISBN 978–0–8135–5269–9 (hardcover : alk. paper) — ISBN 978–0–8135–5270–5
(pbk. : alk. paper) — ISBN 978–0–8135–5331–3 (e-book)
   1. United States—Race relations—History.   2. Racism—United States—
History.   3. National characteristics, American—History.   4. Political culture—United
States—History.   5. Shame—United States.   6. Honor—United States.   7. Social
values—United States.   8. Race in literature.   9. Race relations in literature.   10.
Literature and society—United States—History.   I. Title.   II. Title: Race and shame
in America.
   E184.A1L466 2012
   305.800973—dc23

                                                              2011028829
A British Cataloging-in-Publication record for this book is available from the British
Library.

Visit our Web site: http://rutgerspress.rutgers.edu

Manufactured in the United States of America

To Anne

CONTENTS

ACKNOWLEDGMENTS

Among the many people whose conversations and e-mails have provoked fresh research and rethinking during the last eight years, I'm particularly indebted to Joanne Braxton, Bill Hardwig, Jonathan Holloway, Evelin Lindner, Deborah McDowell, Susan Petit, Vivian Pollak, Stephen Rachman, Andrew Reynolds, Riché Richardson, and Malini Schueller. I'm especially grateful to Ed White for conversations about Benedict Anderson and for alerting me to Article 11 of the 1797 treaty with Tripoli. Bertram Wyatt-Brown generously read one of the later drafts and gave me detailed commentary on each chapter. Gordon Hutner's astute assessment of an article draft for *American Literary History* persuaded me that I should write a book instead. The book benefited from stimulating audiences at the American Literature Association's conventions in 2007 and 2010, a University of Florida symposium in 2009, the Human Dignity and Humiliation Society's conference in 2009, and the Modern Language Association's convention in 2010.

Leslie Mitchner's enthusiasm for the project has been crucial, and she sent the manuscript to just the right reader, whose report pushed me toward clearer framings. Her own page-by-page reading of a penultimate draft gave me innumerable pointers and suggestions, such as changing Samuel Huntington's "quiet desperation" to "noisy desperation." She has been an ideal editor. Thanks also to Marilyn Campbell, Katie Keeran, Marilyn Schwartz, and Lisa Boyajian for their helpful expertise. Kate Babbitt has been an exceptionally careful and resourceful copyeditor. She improved every page, and she made me improve almost every page. Finally, thanks to Rachel Nishan for careful indexing.

More generally, conversations with Steven Feierman have sustained me for two decades. I also thank the Gang—Diana and Richard Brantley,

Mary and Jim Twitchell, and Elise and Rod Webb—for many evenings of candor and raucous humor, and some shared adventuring too. Elise suggested a tempting title, "Talking Smack in America: We Are Not as Idiotic as We Used to Be." Among our four wonderful children and their spouses, Nell Rutledge-Leverenz gave a keen reading of an earlier, much lengthier introduction, and Jim Marion suggested my subtitle. Conversations with Nell, Jim, Allison Rutledge-Parisi, Elizabeth Parisi, Tim O'Brien, Trevor Rutledge-Leverenz, and Shannon Kenny sparked many ideas about race and recent politics. Elizabeth, a creative art director at Scholastic Press, and Tim, who is an internationally known illustrator, designed the cover, both for love. Check him out at obrienillustration.com. He said the title should simply say "Race: It's Complicated."

As my dedication implies, Anne Rutledge remains my chum, my soulmate, and my anchor to practically everything. Until the book was accepted, I wouldn't let her read any of the drafts, because she would have derailed my fitful momentum by spotting all the faulty transitions and imprecise phrasings. When she read what I thought was my final draft of the introduction, she flagged problematic phrasings in every paragraph. Unfortunately I only took most of her advice. Throughout she has been my skeptical sounding board for ideas and some fifty or sixty titles. She also keeps reminding me that life is about living, not just books.

HONOR BOUND

INTRODUCTION

In 1959 Bo Diddley experienced what he later recalled as the most humiliating moment of his life. When he and his band were playing in Las Vegas at the Showboat Casino, one afternoon they jumped into the hotel's swimming pool. Immediately all the white people climbed out, and an attendant put up a sign saying "Contaminated Water."[1]

Fifty years later, Barack Obama became the forty-fourth president of the United States. Grudgingly or enthusiastically, most white people seemed to accept an African American as their nation's leader. Yet anger at his "intrusive" agenda erupted soon after he took office. There's some evidence that Obama's presidency sparked such contempt not only because he has defined himself as black but also because many people think he's a Muslim.[2] The alien religion augments the alarm so frequently associated with the familiar race. Many of those who want to "take our country back" or "restore honor" have said that Obama is African, not American. Except for the most bigoted of the protesters, overt racism no longer seems acceptable. Nevertheless, a black man is in the White House, and fears of a contaminated country helped to swell a roar of Just Say No.

Such fears seemed normal to white people in 1959. Now they animate only an impassioned fringe, or the fringe of a fringe. In the last fifty years, most white Americans' fears of racial contamination have clearly declined. A young black man can hold hands with a white woman or take her to the prom, even in southern towns, and not get lynched. In 2007, when Don Imus called the Rutgers women's basketball team "nappy-headed hos," he lost his radio show, though only temporarily.

Yet in housing, in schooling, in jails and prisons, in access to money and privilege, barriers to black people remain entrenched. Extraordinary progress toward equal rights, equal educational opportunities, and workplace integration has obscured the continuities. Obama has made it to the top, but over a third of all African American males have been in trouble with the law. In some inner-city neighborhoods, 70 percent of young black men have been labeled felons, usually for drug offenses. Racial branding still has a fearful intensity when it targets poor black people, especially poor black men.[3] As Bill Clinton said in his second inaugural address, "The divide of race has been America's constant curse."

This book explores the past and presence of that divide. My focus on fear, honor, and shaming offers some new perspectives on an old, shared problem. I argue that in the United States, the rise and decline of white people's racial shaming reflect the rise and decline of white honor. "White skin" and "black skin" are fictions of honor and shame. Americans have lived these fictions for over 400 years.

The history of relations between white and black Americans has been a story of progress and recoil. The Civil War brought the most dramatic progress, and the recoil lasted almost a century. The civil rights movement brought major progress in schools and at work. The recoil has lasted forty years, especially in suburban segregation and backlash politics, thinly masked as charges of "socialism," or giving "our" money to "them." Obama's election was a third instance of real and symbolic progress. Then came the Tea Party recoil. The reaction time may be getting shorter, and explicitly racial attacks now can be countered. But white fears of contamination have a long half-life. Many African Americans as well as many light-skinned Americans still presume that white means honor and black means shame.

My subtitle could have been "The Uses, Causes, and Consequences of Racial Shaming by Americans Who Think They're White." I use "Race and Shame" partly to give it more zing and partly to imply an intimate bond between the two words. As noun and verb, shame gives race its negative meanings, because light-skinned people use shaming and humiliation to make race feel like shame. The two states of self-perception become equivalent, except for those who can claim whiteness, which confers honor as well as dominance. Such shaming carries its own shame, since it springs not from prowess or goodness but from white people's fears of losing superiority. These fears aren't usually acknowledged. On the receiving end, racial shaming often produces anger, not shame. Usually, at least until the last sixty years, that anger had nowhere to go.

To make my arguments I cast an unusually wide net, from ancient and modern cultures of honor to social, political, and military history to American literature and popular culture. Sometimes it may look as though I'm trying to make ducks and cats and horses walk the same straight line. Yet I believe the straight line leads right back to honor as a key element in American racial formations. The book's interdisciplinary reach tries to show that white honor has prompted racial shaming and humiliation in many ways at many times.

This book doesn't consider how people branded black have tried to shame people who think of themselves as white. Among Latinos, Native Americans, and Asian Americans as well as African Americans, rage at being labeled inferior has a long and varied history. Malcolm X's speeches eloquently tried to reverse racial shaming. Partly because that history is more familiar, and partly to keep the book within publishable length, I focus on the dominant group's constructions of race and honor. Surprisingly, that focus encourages some long-term optimism. If I'm right to argue that racism depends on being honor bound, then racism will decline as white people start to detach themselves from the imperatives of group honor. That process has already started to happen.

The first chapter argues that fear and honor helped compose a group called white people, who have used racial shaming and humiliation as well as violence to maintain their privileges. That dynamic remains latent, although sometimes it is blatant. For example, in a 2009 *Hardball* episode, two progressive white commentators restore their honor by mocking Eric Holder after he called Americans "cowards" for not talking more about race. The rest of the chapter takes a long view of how "white" came to mean honor while "black" came to mean shame.

The second chapter dips into many African American narratives to demonstrate how fundamental racial shaming has been in the United States. Recent studies of racial dynamics have emphasized their localized complications, or what one historian has called their "situational, adaptive, contingent" aspects.4 Situational racism might be true for people who think of themselves as white because the basis of their racism is intrinsically shaky and has to be continuously reconstructed. But until the civil rights movement, people defined as black experienced racism as an unchanging condition. From Lincoln's Emancipation Proclamation in 1863 through the 1960s, changes in white shaming practices consisted mostly of greater or lesser violence. Only in the 1960s, when the new technology of television made it possible for a nationwide audience to view racial shaming in the provinces, did defenses of racial honor start to look shameful themselves. At last "American" started to seem different from "white."

The second chapter also focuses on the miscegenation fears that prompted so many white humiliations of black men. Those fears seem nonsensical, since white men sought sex with black women so frequently. But conjuring up "the black beast" wasn't illogical to men who felt born to rule. Partly to counter the defeats and belittlements of ordinary living and partly to reassert their superiority, they declared themselves "honor bound" to protect "their women." By turning black men into animalistic rapists, white men could feel like medieval knights rescuing damsels from dragons. Not coincidentally, they could also restore their rule over the damsels.

Chapter 3 sketches several stages in honor-shame societies, from nomadic Bedouin tribes through other Mediterranean cultures and Renaissance city-states to the nation-building American elite and the plantation South. Ayaan Hirsi Ali's *Infidel* vividly describes the mixture of oppressiveness and protection in the traditional honor code. In all these instances, I argue, honor operates not just to embolden and constrain the behavior of individual men but also to define and protect a group. Then I take up Alexis de Tocqueville's observation that Americans changed honor from a local to a national dynamic. I add that national honor incorporated whiteness. The chapter concludes with an analysis of W.E.B. Du Bois's "The Souls of White Folk," which passionately indicts the racial "despising" that justifies white people's dominance.

The next two chapters explore the growing shakiness of the imperfect national union between honor and whiteness. After sketches of Stephen Crane's *The Monster* and Jonathan Franzen's *Freedom*, chapter 4 offers close readings of four canonized American novels. *The Scarlet Letter* uses race to undermine the honor code's patriarchal kinship relations. *Adventures of Huckleberry Finn*, *The Great Gatsby*, and *Lolita* show the further erosion of bonds between honor and whiteness, though they replicate the racism they seem to challenge. In *Adventures of Huckleberry Finn*, after Colonel Grangerford's passion for honor leads to the death of his son, Colonel Sherburn conflates honor with cruelty. In *The Great Gatsby*, Nick Carraway darkens the color of Jordan Baker's arms and Gatsby's car as he ages beyond the hope of honor. In *Lolita*, Humbert Humbert thinks of his trapped nymphet as "my little Creole."

Chapter 5 suggests that at least from Samuel Huntington's *The Clash of Civilizations* onward, many white Americans have redirected racial shaming at Muslims. On September 11, 2001, the Islamic terrorists' attacks made that targeting seem wholly legitimate. Almost a decade later, the House of Representatives held hearings in efforts to brand Muslims as terrorists. Hirsi Ali and Brigitte Gabriel have given many talks denouncing Islam's radical oppressiveness.[5] Surprisingly, even when their sailors were enslaved by North Africans, early Americans were often more tolerant. The chapter contrasts the intermittent war against the Barbary pirates from 1783 to 1815 with the second Iraq war from 2003 to the present. In the first, despite great anger at being humiliated by Barbary ransoms and white slavery, many Americans were fascinated with Arab culture. The second war sprang from vengeful contempt. As in the literary narratives, American fantasies of white honor reflect growing strains, though claims of collective humiliation continue to license aggression in the name of restoring honor. *The Clash of Civilizations* encapsulates the change. Five years before 9/11 and fresh from the culture wars of the 1980s, Huntington redirects othering from black people to Muslims and rests his case for the West's superiority on Anglo-European culture rather than light skin color.

With John McCain's *Faith of My Fathers* as a prelude, chapter 6 focuses on the 2008 presidential election. McCain's candidacy seemed to be white honor's last national stand. Though the Arizona senator may have a race-neutral sense of personal honor, his campaign encouraged voters to continue racializing national honor. His decisive loss temporarily raised hopes that such passions have less staying power than they used to.[6] Those hopes were premature. The final chapter probes the endless parade of implicitly racial shaming in 2009 and 2010, from the accusations of the "birthers" and Joe Wilson's "You lie!" to the Tea Party protests and the arrest of Henry Louis Gates Jr.

"Between me and the other world there is ever an unasked question. . . . How does it feel to be a problem?" So W.E.B. Du Bois begins *The Souls of Black Folk*. With a quiet irony, he makes white people the "other." Yet his tone is not at all playful. The cadenced formality of his opening sentence contains anger, sadness, and resignation, especially in the lingering residue of "ever." It is clear that the racial divide had been continuous in his life and that he believed it would pressure him throughout his foreseeable future. In fact it did, before he finally moved his capaciously embittered self to Ghana to end his days. Today many white people continue to not-ask, "How does it feel to be a problem?"

This book tries to provide some answers to a more historical version of Du Bois's question: How did "black" get to be a problem? Fear as well as contempt lurk in that question. Race has long since been exposed as a socially imposed category of perception—"a fiction of law and custom," as Mark Twain calls it in *Pudd'nhead Wilson*.[7] Nevertheless, that fiction continues to be felt as fact. It perpetuates a Them versus Us divide in millions of Americans, not least in me. Racial shaming helped secure that divide.

But clinging tight to whiteness is slowly becoming more desperate and dysfunctional. Here I disagree with writers such as George Lipsitz and Tim Wise, who sometimes despair about the intractability of white racism.[8] My focus on honor and shaming offers some long-term optimism. Racism counters threats to a group whose membership requires presumptions of racial superiority. Those presumptions are now questionable. The decline of white honor and white racial shaming has already started, and further decline is in the offing. Being honor bound to preserve racial privileges seems more self-constricting to more people than it used to. The group whose members call themselves white people has less cohesion, except as a fantasy of defensive nostalgia.

To the degree that whiteness continues to confer a sense of privilege, its appeal will persist. But it no longer has to be the default position for claiming rights and securing esteem. As the 2010 federal census revealed, the number of people who have abandoned a monoracial identity based on their skin color jumped almost 50 percent, and the number who identified themselves as both white and black more than doubled since 2000, to almost 2 million Americans.[9] For some, the choice of multiple ethnicities allows them to escape the continuing association of black identity with social shame. For many more, I think, honor no longer compels them to protect the racial group they grew up thinking they belonged to. In schools and in the workplace, the affiliations that confer respect are too diverse. The basis for bonding can no longer be reduced to light skin.

A century or so from now, dialogues about race will probably have dwindled into discussions of an absurdity that lasted for over four centuries. Future generations may play with other versions of the question that preoccupied medieval scholastics: how many angels could stand on the head of a pin? New bemusements may surface about these angels. Were they naked or clothed? Did they touch each other? What were the colors of their faces, and why did that come to matter so much?

CHAPTER 1

FEAR, HONOR, AND RACIAL SHAMING

Racial shaming affirms the coherence of a dominant racial group. When that fails, the next step is to terrorize. Then come brutality and murder, and finally ethnic "cleansing," a word that exposes the group's preoccupations with shared purity.[1] But such racial groups build their bonds on fictions. This chapter looks at the rise and decline of one of those fictions, white honor in America.

Overview

For several thousand years, small groups such as tribes, gangs, or city-states have developed codes of honor that inspire men to fight outsiders. The codes spur courage and loyalty, establish internal hierarchies, and punish cowards or transgressors, especially men who can't control their fears or women whose sexual activities challenge male controls. As an ideal, honor mixes mutual respect with presumptions of superiority and expectations of deference. Shaming deviant individuals keeps the code vital.

The targeted man can continue to belong, temporarily abashed, if he accepts the shame. A transgressive woman is more likely to face humiliation or be sacrificed to preserve male honor. Within the group, humiliating differs from shaming because it brings an abject and permanent loss of face. Insiders become ostracized outsiders. The message of shaming is "Honor is everything and you have to get it back." The message of humiliation is "You no longer belong because you've contaminated everything we stand for."

Sometimes groups include outsiders that the insiders have some use for. As captives and "barbarians" become servants, the danger of including them becomes more present and intimate. Shaming outsiders who seek to be insiders reaffirms hierarchies and boundaries. In larger groups with people from several ethnicities, the dominant ethnic group's fears of being challenged or tainted can racialize honor. Indentured apprentices who belong to the dominant race sometimes make their way in, at least by the servants' entrance. The door remains shut to servants or slaves from groups branded as shameful.

Faced with a mix of Native Americans and the forced immigrants they called slaves, European colonists invented white people as a kind of umbrella corporation to shelter acceptable diversities and minimize intragroup conflicts. Using racial shaming, humiliation, and much worse to make dark-skinned Americans feel like outsiders who were tolerated only for their labor, descendants of European immigrants reaffirmed the honor of their whiteness as well as the rightness of their mastery. Subordinating people they called black made them feel more white.

Here racial humiliation doesn't differ from shaming except in its intensity. Both imply scapegoating and both harbor violence, because disciplining an individual with darker skin aims at terrorizing his potentially threatening subgroup as well as himself. When racial shaming rebrands someone as inferior, he has no chance of regaining honor because he never had it. The message of shaming and humiliation is "You can belong as a servant, but you can't belong as a human being." The message of violence makes collective scapegoating more apparent: "You're everything we detest, in ourselves as well as your people."

Typically, shaming black people acts to reconsolidate white power rather than to make black targets feel ashamed. Some do, but many feel helpless anger. They've been shamed simply because they have a different skin color and yet refuse to remain abased. The shaming has reduced them to generic blackness. Bo Diddley's jump into the swimming pool presumed equality, so he had to be branded as contaminating. In white eyes, he was a lump of shit, like any other black man. Though the humiliation didn't threaten his job or his professional superiority, it rebranded him as a "nigger." Racial profiling does much the same thing. At some point in their lives, most African American men have experienced that mix of power, fear, and shaming. White police reduce them to one generic category: a suspected criminal, the black beast in modern form.[2]

In the last few decades, substantial numbers of African Americans have gained positions of economic or political power as well as eminence in sports and other forms of entertainment. At that point distinctions between outsiders and insiders in the larger group called Americans start to blur, and racial shaming can be countered. But as President Obama discovered in 2009, white people can still be vicious when they feel bossed by a black outsider.

Racial shaming resembles shaming of gays, lesbians, and transvestites but with some basic differences. Both forms of contempt reduce individuals to an allegedly inferior subgroup. But the idea of homosexuality makes traditional heterosexuals feel publicly disgusted and sometimes privately uneasy about themselves, whereas the proximity of black skin makes many white people feel fearful as well as superior. Shaming people for their same-sex desires or behavior says "We thought you were equal to us, but now you're yucky." Shaming dark-skinned people for acting like equals says "You'll never be like us, so get to the back of the bus." Gay people have been shamed for revealing that they're part of a despised but mostly invisible subgroup. Black people have been shamed for trying to rise above a despised group that's all too visible. Gays were deviant; blacks were subhuman, and therefore more contaminating.

For both groups, humiliation differs from shaming only in its intensity, which offers a greater license for violence as well as scapegoating. But racial shaming and humiliation enforce the obsequiousness of a subgroup, whereas homophobic shaming and humiliation punish displays of alternative sexuality. Though the prospect of having to accept gays and lesbians as their equals still deeply disturbs many heterosexuals, it seems less threatening to group cohesion because it doesn't undermine white supremacy. Queer theory's current celebrations of shame reflect the onset of gay people's access to mainstream respect. The few black celebrations of shame intimate self-hatred, not pride in being different.

Beginning in fear as well as contempt, racial shaming props up the wall between honored people with lighter skin and dishonored people with darker skin. Their fervor diminishes only as the dominant group disintegrates. For the last fifty years, Americans who have named themselves white people have been facing that unnerving experience.

From its beginnings, whiteness has been an imaginary unifier, since no one is purely white or purely black. Moreover, everyone on the planet belongs to multiple social groups. The communities we live in, the families we grew up in, the families we've chosen, the paths we've taken, masks we've put on, work, friends, quarrels, religion, pleasures, loyalties, gender, sexuality, and many other factors shape and reshape our sense of where we look for respect. These intersecting groups and roles often conflict. As they jostle for our allegiance, we discover uncertainties that complicate our attitudes about ourselves as well as others. To break the inward stranglehold of race consciousness, race-based groups have to become just one of many self-definitions. Their boundaries have to become porous, then silly.

That dream seems utopian now. But at least it's visible, on the far horizon.

Hardball versus Eric Holder

In the allegedly postracial United States, what happens to progressive white Americans when they're criticized by a new black boss?

Shortly after Eric Holder became the nation's first black attorney general, he called Americans "a nation of cowards" for not talking more about race. In speaking to Justice Department employees about African American History month, Holder lamented that even now, long after the civil rights movement, there's "almost no significant interaction" between black and white people outside the workplace.[3] "On Saturdays and Sundays America in the year 2009 does not, in some ways, differ significantly from the country that existed some fifty years ago." It's "truly sad" that the civil rights movement created "an America that is more prosperous, more positively race conscious and yet is voluntarily socially segregated." Americans "continue the polite, restrained mixing that now passes as meaningful interaction. . . . We still speak too much of 'them' and not 'us.'" Today, whites and blacks alike "retreat to our race protected cocoons" rather than talk with each other about race. True enough, I thought, as I read his remarks in my cocoon. Orlando Patterson had been saying it for years.[4]

I learned about Holder's address when I watched MSNBC's *Hardball*, where guest host Mike Barnicle and Matt Taibbi were trashing it. Barnicle said several times that Holder should have done what Bill Cosby did and talk about the breakup of black families and black students dropping out of schools: "That's why they're not living next to us." Taibbi, a raffish young *Rolling Stone* columnist, said Holder was "crazy" and suggested that the attorney general had taken some "bong hits" the night before. We have a black president now, Taibbi said, and we had the civil rights movement, and we have workplace integration, so what's the problem? Jonathan Capehart, a black editorial writer for the *Washington Post*, circumspectly suggested that Holder had a point, though calling Americans "cowards" might have been injudicious.[5]

This conversation exemplified the national impasse. It also made me think my own insulation from racial issues might be more typical than I'd supposed. Barnicle's mockery blatantly stereotyped black people as lower-class irresponsibles who make their own problems. That charge let him avoid the real issue, that middle-class black people tend to choose social segregation just as middle-class white people do. Barnicle's "us" is uniformly white, and his "them" should be trying to join "us." For Taibbi, white people have already done more than enough, so Holder must be hallucinating. Barnicle enthusiastically agreed. "Jonathan, do you think it's possible that Eric Holder is in the background there where Michael Phelps had the bong pipe?" Both white men relished the thought that a powerful black man might be taking drugs.

The attorney general's charge turned Mike Barnicle and Matt Taibbi into bulls trying to destroy a red flag. Though they didn't say so, their mockery intimated that their manhood and their honor were on the line. They also had to measure up to the name of Chris Matthews's show, *Hardball*. It was time for combat, not softball questions or sympathies.

For Barnicle, Holder's charge was the most compelling news item of the day. He raised the "cowards" issue twice, with different commentators. At the start of the first discussion, Barnicle showed a clip from Holder's speech. "Well, OK," he said, "I'll buy that. But the cowards thing?" Turning to a screen with a remote hookup to a prominent African American public intellectual, Michael Eric Dyson, he agreed that we might be "awkward" and "reluctant" in talking about race. "But cowards, no. What do you say?"

Dyson seconded Holder's charge. In race issues "we lag far behind" our successes in other areas. "We don't have the ability to step up to the plate and be honest" about it. "We shouldn't be post-racial." Instead, he urged Americans to address the racial issues that do persist. His baseball metaphor of stepping up to the plate implied that would be the manly thing to do.

Then Barnicle turned to a screen showing Pat Buchanan, a long-time conservative political figure and commentator. Barnicle asked, "What do you think happens with white guys like you and me when we talk about race in—honestly, at least from our perspective?" The subtext of anxiety about white manhood became more visible. Amid some laughter, Buchanan responded with a tough-guy pose: whenever he has "spoken honestly" about race, he said, "you really get fired upon."

As for Holder's assertion, Buchanan launched his sentences like missiles. "This is a remark of almost paralyzing stupidity." Yes, there's some "social self-segregation." But you "don't start it off by insulting the people you want to talk to. I mean, that was not an invitation to a discussion. It was an invitation to a fight, when you call us a nation of cowards." The United States has done more than any other country "to bring this people of color into full participation in American society. . . . To call us cowards, I think, it really not only chops off the conversation; it is a blatant lie."

To say "this people of color" shows Buchanan trying and failing, perhaps deliberately, to say something politically correct. His term "people of color" nods to the current fashion, but his use of "this" reduces African Americans to a single alien category, opposed to "us." For Buchanan the whole group remains unassimilated, even after white Americans have tried to bring them in.

More tellingly, "chops off" exposes the fear driving Buchanan's anger, and probably driving Barnicle's preoccupation with the issue as well. Fears of symbolic castration—by a black man who has just gained power over whites—spur Buchanan's enraged disrespect. Perhaps Holder offered an easier target than his boss in the first giddy weeks after the inauguration. In any case, faced with the "insulting" charge of cowardice, the pugnacious conservative rejected any imputation of shameful fear. He was defending his manliness and white honor.

Dyson and Buchanan started interrupting each other and the web transcript shows lots of "CROSSTALK" as they shouted. While Buchanan kept saying "insult," Dyson doggedly repeated his call for "honesty" and "truth." "OK," Buchanan said, "let me tell some truths. Let me tell some truths. Let me tell some truths." Black people have a "70 percent illegitimacy rate" and "commit crimes at seven times the rate of white Americans." "We are not responsible for the fact that many more children in the African American community, 75 percent, are born out of wedlock, as I said. All of these things are the responsibility of the African American community." Even worse, "in the statistics on group crime against individuals, gang rape and gang assaults, the numbers are almost 100–1. . . . You should look to your own responsibilities, instead of our faults." As Buchanan inflated his statistics, the subtext of fear kept bubbling into his anger. They're beating us up! They're a bunch of bastards! How dare they say it's our fault!

Dyson responded that Buchanan was "trying to scapegoat" blacks for issues that "the dominant American culture" has caused. "You don't want to be responsible. . . . It's time that we share the burden and redistribute the pain." "Stop blaming everybody else," Buchanan rejoined. "In 1948, the African American community was far more responsible, far less criminal than it is today." Trent Lott couldn't have said it better: African Americans were much more civilized before the civil rights protests. While Dyson kept repeating "E Pluribus Unum," Buchanan declared that there's "no better country on earth for African people than America." Now the "American" in his "African American" disappeared, and "this people" became "African people." His "we–they" divide was absolute.

As Barnicle tried to bring their screen-to-screen conversation to a close, the two men inched toward an agreement that disintegrated on the spot. "We still have work to be done," Dyson said. Buchanan instantly segregated that "we." "I think you do have work to be done and we have work to be done. I agree with that."

Throughout, Jonathan Capehart tried for a more temperate tone. At first he defended Holder's "provocative language," which might start a discussion that the country "needs to have." But Holder probably shouldn't have used the phrase "nation of cowards" because it deflects attention from the issue. The Buchanan-Dyson argument "is not the kind of conversation . . . he wanted Americans to have." After Taibbi talked about bong hits, Capehart deftly supported Holder by punning on Taibbi's critique: "The attorney general is hitting on something" that concerns a lot of Americans. America isn't as integrated as it could be. On the other hand, Holder's speech "was a little too pessimistic for my taste." It's "fantastic" that Holder said Americans "have never been more racially conscious," but his "very dour, pessimistic view of where the country is" blunts his "positive and uplifting" message.

Nudged by Capehart's complexity, both white men tried to be a little nicer to Holder. Barnicle responded, "I appreciate where he's coming from." Then he reiterated that Holder should have talked about "the collapse of the black family, teenage parenting, babies having babies," and the African American dropout rate. Taibbi backed off a little too. He said Holder was right to raise the issue, but his "hyperbole . . . probably turned some people off" from realizing the need for such discussions. At that point the hour was over.

Unlike the Dyson-Buchanan brawl, the Barnicle-Taibbi-Capehart discussion seemed amiable. Even Taibbi's crack about bong hits may have been a gesture toward hip brotherhood. The two white commentators' fears were not nearly as evident as their intermittently respectful disdain. Yet the symbiotic relation between what historian Edmund Morgan has called "American Slavery, American Freedom" has persisted in a new guise. With upbeat affirmations of racial progress, Barnicle and Taibbi felt free to shame ungrateful and irresponsible African Americans as well as Eric Holder. If some black people are still poor and needy, if some black families are feckless and dysfunctional, we white people have done more than enough, so black people have to solve those problems, they said. Besides, black men should be much nicer if they want to stay powerful. The two men were closer to Pat Buchanan than they probably imagined.

This TV show displayed progressive as well as conservative white men who resolved or disowned their racial tensions through public shaming. A new black attorney general had called them cowards. Their use of shaming got them off the hook of talking about voluntary residential segregation. At the onset of a supposedly postracial society, racial scapegoating came back with a vengeance, the moment a powerful black man said something uncomfortable.

Eric Holder said that during the last fifty years, there had been little change in social interaction between blacks and whites. The episode shows that Holder's time frame should be doubled. The commentators aren't that different from the whites who looked at W.E.B. Du Bois and said, "I know an excellent colored man in my town." Over 110 years later, Jonathan Capehart—a Pulitzer Prize winner—performed excellence by walking a tight line between asserting and accommodating. "We wear the mask," Paul Laurence Dunbar's 1896 poem declares. In 2009 Capehart put it halfway on and kept his credibility. Holder let it slip, and progressive white men humiliated him.[6] A day later, on February 19, business reporter Rick Santelli's rant on CNBC started the Tea Party.

Fear, Honor, and Fictions of Race

America's racial divide began with European immigrants' mix of desire and anxiety. European colonists developed slavery in its most inescapably race-based form. They invented their fictions of racial hierarchy not only to rationalize making darker-skinned people do degrading physical labor but also to alleviate some mutually reinforcing fears. They feared that natives and servants might claim equality. Less consciously, they feared their inequality with people back home, and they feared that because of splintering and conflict, their "we" might not be a group. Most basically, they feared being stranded in a strange, alien world, where everything felt out of control.

Racism relieved all four fears. Moreover, racism licensed the provincial pleasure of lording it over other human beings. When light-skinned people declared themselves white, their obscure feelings of shame and insecurity could be transformed into presumptions of rightful mastery.

Using black people for service and profit also helped assuage a mostly disowned anxiety about provincial status. White racism became a fallback comfort zone. People could say to themselves, "I may not have much, but at least I'm white." As another benefit, racial hierarchy provided a simplifying narrative with a bogeyman. Any white man could play the role of chivalric protector.

On the other side, black men's bodies became the main target for shaming and fear. Slavery and subservience enforced shameful unmanliness. To assert daily supremacy, whites complacently called any black man "boy." Yet they feared any imagined evidence of black men's resistance or independence.[7] Black folklore tells of the "laugh barrel," a place where a black person could laugh uproariously at the outrageous or ridiculous behavior of white people, then look up from the barrel with a sober, deferential face.

Intellectual justifications for white supremacy didn't proliferate until the late nineteenth century, after African Americans had become full citizens who could claim equality. Nell Irvin Painter's *The History of White People* deftly sketches the profusion of self-contradictory theories that invented and exalted the race variously named Caucasian, Aryan, Saxon, Anglo-Saxon, Nordic, or Teutonic. But practical racism thrived from the 1650s onward. As Morgan's *American Slavery, American Freedom* concludes, colonial white Virginians' racism "absorbed . . . the fear and contempt" that Englishmen "felt for the inarticulate lower classes." The racial divide enabled a "devotion" to liberty and equality—for whites only. By "lumping Indians, mulattoes, and Negroes in a single pariah class," whites could lump "small and large planters in a single master class."[8] Proudly disdaining European aristocracy, Americans substituted a pseudo-aristocracy based on race.

Being pseudo requires constant vigilance. For over 300 years, racial shaming not only instilled fear among black people but also reflected white people's fears of losing mastery. Most people defined as nonwhite internalized their own churning mix of fear and shame. They accepted or resisted their subjugation or found ways of maneuvering within their postures of submission.[9]

Both words in the term "white supremacy" suggest anxious grandiosity. "Supremacy" comes from the Latin *supremus*, the superlative of *superus*, which means "above, over." So supremacy means the state of being supreme: superior to all others, highest in rank, or dominant. How can millions of white people each lay claim to being supreme? If all the members of an exclusive country club proclaimed themselves its president, then walked and talked in unison, it would look ridiculous. But white people justified their collective supremacy by believing an equivalent absurdity, that all light-skinned people look alike. Though white supremacy contradicts two other American values, democracy and individual enterprise, its illogic wasn't seriously threatened until the civil rights movement.

"White" is even more problematic. Racialized pseudo-lordliness requires two pseudo-colors, "white" and "black." When I look at my flesh, its color looks pinkish tan, with a touch of yellow. "Black" people's skin colors range from fair to beige to dark brown. But "tan" and "brown" don't carry enough contrast. The darker skin hasn't been blackened enough. A long European tradition had linked black to evil, and colonists seized on the association to justify race-based slavery, in part because black servitude confirmed their whiteness. Annette Gordon-Reed pithily summarizes decades of revisionary scholarship: "The black 'race' . . . was an invention of whites." Of all the continents, "Africa is the most linguistically, culturally, and genetically diverse." Yet from early colonial times onward, the settlers associated whiteness with "power and privilege," while blackness meant "relative powerlessness and second-class status," or animalistic inferiority.[10]

To put it another way, no one is black or white. Instead, some people have been made to feel black so that others can feel more white. As Scott Malcomson puts it, "When a light person is truly white, he is dead." In ordinary usage, Malcomson notes, white implies a double negative. "Just as being free meant not being a slave, being white meant . . . not being black."[11] Blackness brings shame and stigma, while whiteness confers honor and high status. Millions of Americans have become modern versions of Hester Prynne. Whether their skin is dark or brown, they have a big black B on their face. Racial shaming has legitimized white supremacy so intimately and comprehensively that many light-skinned Americans don't see the honor-shame dynamics that make it seem so natural.

At the onset of English colonialism, Macbeth does that transformation to himself. Shortly before fighting Macduff, he tries to talk himself out of being afraid.

> I cannot taint with fear. . . .
> The mind I sway by and the heart I bear
> Shall never sag with doubt nor shake with fear. (V, viii, 3, 9–10)

"Sway by" already makes his resolve seem shaky. Then, when a servant enters, Macbeth shouts, "The devil damn thee black, thou cream-faced loon!" His curse is a scapegoating so that he can avoid acknowledging his own "cream-faced" fear. More subtly, he implodes the dichotomy he clings to. White becomes a state of fear, while black becomes damnation, the ultimate shaming. That little sequence anticipates the next four centuries of making white and black.

The origin of whiteness as a group obsession began with European colonists' fears of the natives. In *Our Savage Neighbors*, Peter Silver shows that between 1734 and 1783, "midcentury spikes in newspaper talk of people's being 'white' were driven almost wholly by Indian matters," especially during Indian wars. The concept of white people helped differentiate northern European immigrants from Native Americans and to a lesser extent from Africans while also expanding "English" to include German and Irish settlers. By the early nineteenth century, as threatening Indians were pushed west, "white" and "black" became the primary dichotomy, while "white" remained a battleground for inclusion and exclusion as huge numbers of European immigrants expanded the U.S. population.[12]

Scientists continue to debate whether the 1 percent of genetic differences among any two humans and the much smaller percentage of
that difference attributable to racial characteristics constitute a valid
basis for defining race. But there's no doubt that genetic variations
within ethnic groups are far more significant. As Zora Neale Hurston
has Janie say to a black snob in *Their Eyes Were Watching God,* "We'se
uh mingled people."[13]

Less than three decades ago, in 1986, Henry Louis Gates Jr. startled
me and many others by arguing that "black" should be placed in quotation marks, since it's an unreal construction that has had profoundly
real effects.[14] In 1998 the American Anthropological Association issued
a statement declaring that "physical variations in the human species
have no meaning except the social ones that humans put on them."
That basic change of perception has affected even the U.S. census,
which now asks for self-identifications among many categories of race
and ethnicity. Since the late 1950s, there has been considerable pressure
on the census to eliminate the category of race entirely. Ironically, the
counterpressure now comes from those who want data to protect the
civil rights and political power of various minorities.

Changes in census questionnaires encapsulate the history of arbi-
trary racial constructions in America. In 1790 census interviewers
defined citizens as either "Free" or "Slave," since the Constitution
declared that a slave counted as three-fifths of a white person. In 1850
the categories expanded to three: Black, White, and Mulatto. By 1890,
as white racism approached its greatest national intensity, the categories had proliferated further, to White, Black, Mulatto, Quadroon,
Octoroon, Chinese, Japanese, and Indian. In 1970, near the end of
the civil rights movement, the census abandoned enumerators and
allowed self-identification. In 1977 the Office of Management and
Budget issued a directive establishing four racial categories: American
Indian or Alaskan Native, Asian or Pacific Islander, Black, or White,
with "Hispanic Origin" ambiguously added. In 1980 the question
asked for "ancestry," implying ethnic origin more than race, and in
2000 respondents could select multiple races or "multiracial" for
the first time, along with "some other race." Since many Hispanics
checked that last category, the 2010 census asked for "Hispanic or

Latino origin" along with five basic racial categories. Only "white" didn't have multiple possibilities, and only "some other race" allowed an unvoiced multiracial option. "White" still came first, and "Black, African Am., or Negro" reflected the still-shifting labels attached to Americans with African ancestry.[15]

As that sequence implies, making racial categories means making "white" as well as "black," long before many other ethnic groups began to jostle that imposed dichotomy. For centuries "black" has been the negative defining "white." The "one-drop rule" expanded that negative from skin color to genealogy. Using "black" to label all descendants of mixed-race coupling has been a uniquely American practice. It's a scapegoating that unified white people locally, regionally, and nationally. The label branded the four successive waves of immigration that center Ira Berlin's recent history, *The Making of African America*.[16] As whiteness put on the mask of honor, personal competition for quasi-aristocratic status in the provinces turned into national claims for the white race as a natural aristocracy.

When I watch President Obama on TV and I see the color of his skin before I see his big ears or his enviably wide smile, I think of his color as "black," a translation he has encouraged. In doing so, I'm reducing his complexity to a visual category that I can disown. When I meet a white person, I instantly differentiate individual aspects. When I meet an African American or Latino or Asian American, I often see the category first, with the person trailing far behind. My perceptions aren't yet an example of racial shaming because I don't make them public. But they're an unvoiced mode of othering, affirming my distance.

Wherever there's shaming, honor is at stake. As with "white" and "free," a man's honor negates a negation: I'm not a coward. Honor springs into life as a defense against the danger of being branded as weak or afraid. That charge threatens a man's sense of his own worth as well as his social standing.[17]

In arguing that honor's imperative to gain dignity and respect ultimately functions to protect a group, not just to secure recognition from peers, I differ from Alexander Welsh and Kwame Anthony Appiah. Welsh's *What Is Honor?* (2008) equates the concept with personal dignity gained by the respect of one's peers in a group, whereas Appiah's

The Honor Code (2010) argues that honor can spur progressive change because of nations' need for respect. Welsh and Appiah admirably counter many others who have argued that honor has been replaced by ideals of dignity and human rights. But both writers miss honor's basic function for group defense.[18] In many premodern societies from Afghanistan to Somalia, individual prowess and young men's lives matter much less than self-sacrifice to ensure collective survival. Protection of male lineage matters more than the lives of sexually transgressive wives or daughters. In the latter case, what looks barbarous and evil to modern Americans preserves small groups accustomed to scarcity and siege.

Welsh writes that "identity always faces two ways, toward oneself and toward the comparison group." For Appiah, the "honor world" is "a group of people who acknowledge the same codes, and whose respect is sought."[19] Both writers minimize the negative effects of honor in nation-sized groups, and neither writer situates individual identities in plural groups. The dichotomy they see between group and self misses the most important long-term threat to honor—the fact that everyone on the planet belongs to conflicting groups. When people think of themselves as part of a homogeneous group or of groups that reinforce each other, they're much more likely to rely on honor and shame to frame their perceptions of themselves and others.[20]

I emphasize honor rather than masculinity because honor has been the basis for traditional ideals of manliness. "Masculinity" emerged as a central term only after the Civil War, when corporate workplaces partially supplanted communities as sources for middle-class men's self-respect.[21] In the new world of bureaucrats and professionals, the word carried a compensatory push. Today masculinity seems modern and honor seems dated. Masculinity requires proving a man's dignity but minimizes his bonds with a group. A man's preoccupation with his individual body can become nearly all-consuming, for example. Yet honor persists as concerns about dignity and moral reputation, whether personal or national.

Historians of honor in the Mediterranean region emphasize that the code's various rituals manage small-group conflicts and establish rank. In 1982, Bertram Wyatt-Brown's *Southern Honor* led the way in applying those perspectives to the American South. The "threat of shame" and "contempt" intensified young southern men's preoccupation with honor. It functions as "a mask . . . to escape the implications of weakness and inferiority."[22] That threat helped consolidate white people within the mask of what I'm calling a pseudo-aristocracy. As Walter Johnson emphasizes in *Soul by Soul*, possessing slaves enabled whites to "buy their way into the master class." Southern whites were much more preoccupied with the slave trade than with duels.[23]

In the North, a mixture of democratic, workplace, and religious values partially undermined social competitions for honor. But after the Civil War, when many northerners balked at the costs of Reconstruction and its threat of black equality, agreement about white superiority reconstructed honor as shared racial mastery. The postwar chaos of feelings—anger, humiliation, vengeance, vindictiveness, and mourning—could be subsumed in the equivalent of a national men's group so long as black men didn't challenge white privileges.

As one result, honor became less class-based, less localized, more inclusive, and more gender neutral. Any white American could join as long as they accepted racism in thought and practice. White faces signified collective honor, honor brought personal liberty, and black people longed for access to the freedom that white people fetishized.[24]

Racial Shaming

In relatively homogeneous groups, shame differs from humiliation. Humiliation is a soul-crusher. It derives from the Latin *humus* (earth) and is linked to the Latin *humilis* (low). As Evelin Lindner formulates it, "Humiliation is about *putting down* and *holding down*."[25] It enforces abjection; it makes you feel dirty and degraded and terrorized. You're afraid of asserting anything.

Though Silvan Tomkins and others consider humiliation a variant of shame, shame carries more contradictory feelings. Paradoxically, feeling ashamed harbors a vestigial strength of self, if only to acknowledge that the shaming may be deserved. Self-contempt comes from a self that has turned malevolent against its own inadequacy. Such malevolence mirrors the contempt of others. Shame also carries a vestige of mourning for one's self-worth. Finally, shame requires a keen sense of valuing one's place in a group. Shamed people experience the group's scorn as if it were their own.

But racial shaming converges with humiliation. It imposes unmerited shame as it corrals black people within a group already marked as contemptible. As early as 1837, Hosea Easton, an African American minister, railed against the ubiquitous use of the word "nigger" to teach white children what to fear and what not to be. In 1944, *The Negro Digest* ran a monthly column on "My Most Humiliating Jim Crow Experience." For whites, such humiliations of African Americans affirm the dominance of the white race. For blacks, humiliations bring rage. As Evelin Lindner writes, "Humiliation seems to be the catalyst that turns grievances into nuclear bombs of emotions."[26]

Racism isn't racial shaming, but it's the enabling precondition. Racists use shaming as one of many tools to enforce fearful submission and to ward off their own fears that difference might not mean inequality. Except at the top of the hierarchy, race is a double imprisonment. It locks an individual into a category, then locks the category into a dungeon. For people so doubly branded, deference, secrecy, and group bonding become basic survival strategies. On every rung of the hierarchy and in every time period of the U.S. nation, from the Revolution through the civil rights movement, the fear of slavishness has birthed a peculiarly American passion for freedom, especially among men.[27]

Shaming comes easily to members of a dominant group. It's a weapon that is used to display power. Yet its performance of anger or disgust masks several kinds of anxiety. White racism has always been riddled with contradictions and internal conflicts, and varieties of racism proliferated as the intensity of need for it increased. Most American white people felt threatened by any prospect of equality with someone who looked different and seemed lower in status. Worse, whiteness might disintegrate as the basis for entitlement if it wasn't resolutely protected. For over three hundred years, shaming after shaming firmed up the pretense that dichotomized skin colors justified white control.[28]

A willed lack of self-knowledge helps support racial dominance.

The interviews with California residents in Bob Blauner's *Black Lives, White Lives* constitute a course in Practical Hegel: not the philosopher of abstract dialectics, but the Hegel who wrote that the Bondsman gains greater knowledge of the Lord than the Lord has of himself. In Hegel's abstracted parable, two people meet and vie for mastery. Because of fear, one consents to be the slave of the other. But that consent brings greater self-consciousness and more awareness of the other, since the master depends on the slave for recognition of his mastery.[29]

In 1968, pressed by the civil rights and Black Power movements, Blauner's white interviewees felt their superiority threatened for the first time. Until then they "had been able to confine their 'whiteness' to remote corners of their consciousness" without much knowledge of the black people they encountered. In sharp contrast, black interviewees knew a great deal about their white employers. One of them, the pseudonymous "Florence Grier," had worked for many white women as a domestic. "I call the upper crust 'Mrs. Roosevelt.'" They're indifferent about you, so long as you get the job done, she said. The middle-class woman "stands and watches every move you make" to make sure "the windows and everything" are "shined like brass. She wants everything just up to par. . . . Her *whole life* is bound up in this need to show off to the neighbors. . . . The *poor* white . . . is the one who keep his foot on your head all the time. He needs to be better than you."[30]

For her, race and class intersect. The more anxious white people are about their status, the more they need to flaunt their superiority. That intersection gets further complicated in several interviews with white people, whose urgent assertions of racial hierarchy betray anxiety about being disrespected by white peers as well as fears of black equality. They often talk about their fears of Black Power politics or violence or affirmative action, though that policy brings expressions of rueful comprehension as well as anger. In 1980 a black interviewee muses that a white man isn't really afraid of "what you could do physically to him. It's not that kind of afraid. It's afraid of what your ability is, the possibility that I may go beyond him. . . . If everybody get these opportunities, it may knock him back. Or his youngster." Shaming and humiliating became first-level strategies to "keep me back."[31]

Remarkably, most black interviewees understand white people's racial anxieties while remaining angry about the effects. They understand what Hegel's bondsman knows and what Deborah Eisenberg observes of anti-Semitism: "that the great and malignant hazard of privilege is obtuseness." As Roger Wilkins muses in *Jefferson's Pillow*, "Privilege is addictive. The most natural thing in the world is for each human being to view the privilege he enjoys as, well, the most natural thing in the world."[32]

Slavery Still Matters

Shaming doesn't have to be racialized. It can secure class, gender, regional, ethnic, national, or sectarian boundaries. Rita Felski's "Nothing to Declare" describes the intense shame she felt as a lower-middle-class Australian child.[33] In the 1970s, second-wave feminism featured the "click" experience: the moment a woman realized that her belittlement by men was a social problem deserving anger, not a personal problem deserving shame. In the 1990s, people used "ethnic cleansings" to "purify" dominant groups in central Europe and Africa. As with racial shaming, these modes of group humiliation reflect what I'll call the Schadenfreude Syndrome: the sense that "at least those people are more worthless than I feel."

Racism is just one way of establishing "us" and "them." Men have presumed their generic right to rule women and aristocrats have justified their entitlements by elevating themselves over inferior "others." Such formations also use honor and shaming to enforce social hierarchies. Until the advent of white-collar work in bureaucracies and the professions, those groups had a material basis for their claims of privilege. Men's physical strength mattered on farms and in the trades, and elites used money and education to legitimize their power. Yet throughout the history of these group entitlements, the problem of fluid boundaries has been intermittently acute, especially in democracies faced with defeat or economic distress. Nazi Germany's systematic branding and destruction of the Jews remains an extreme example.[34] In contrast to Germans who turned fears into ferocious intolerance, most white Americans tolerated black people who accepted their inferiority, though literal branding sometimes reduced them to the status of cattle.

Economically, subordinating black skin color had material value only while slavery provided cheap African labor. Nonetheless, white Americans gave race a special intensity of group differentiation. Unlike men versus women, or upper class versus lower class, a blackened Them signified humiliation, while a whitened Us signified self-evident honor and liberty. What class meant in England, race came to mean in the United States.

Slavery made the difference. Only in the New World did slavery become driven by commodity production and defined by color.[35] Only in the American colonies did slavery gain such entrenched scale and scope. Only in America did white people sustain the one-drop rule for two centuries. In *The Relentless Revolution*, Joyce Appleby argues that early capitalism's "Janus-like" culture of audacious innovation depended on race-based colonial slavery.[36] After the Revolution, the success of capitalism in the United States depended partly on southern slavery, not only because it supplied raw materials for northern manufacturers, as the colonies had done for Europe, but also because it became a contemptuous metaphor that goaded white men toward pluck and enterprise. The black man's body became a symbol of shame and a stimulus for fear. Only in America did lynching terrorize black people, particularly men, for almost a century.

Slavery made racism its almost inescapable corollary, and racial hierarchy soon became an abiding frame for self-perception. After the emancipations of 1863 and 1865, white people developed a great variety of ways to perpetuate race-based servitude. In 1928 Ulrich Phillips, the most eminent historian of the South, defined the South's "central theme" and distinctiveness as the superiority of "the white folk" because they are "a people with a common resolve indomitably maintained–that it shall be and remain a white man's country." "Indomitably" and "country" resurrect southern honor in two contrary ways. The bravado of "indomitably" pretends that the Civil War never happened. The grandiosity of "country" presumes that the region's white supremacy is now the nation's.[37]

Phillips was right, at least about his second claim. After the end of Reconstruction, most white northerners accepted or embraced cross-regional bonding under the banner of white supremacy. The cost seemed to be a benefit for all white people, since the bonding invited forgetting that slavery had anything to do with the Civil War.[38] Since the 1950s, the counterpressures of the ideals of American equality have made that structure of semi-slavery crumble, except in many urban areas. But the perceptions linger.

In 1906 Werner Sombart asked, "Why is there no socialism in the United States?" One answer has been that many Americans equate socialism with slavish dependence, or with taxing the competent to support incompetent Others. The racial divide looms just below the surface of those definitions. The racial divide also helps explain most Americans' relative lack of class consciousness, even at the extremes of rich and poor. As so many historians have said, seeing black people as inferior established whiteness as a cross-class unifier. The legacy of slavery still shapes conservative fears of American "serfdom."[39]

Ironically, the word slave comes from "Slav." Despite Western Europe's long history of enslaving Eastern Europeans, "Caucasian" later became the imagined standard for white beauty. Nell Irvin Painter highlights the ridiculousness of the word's formulation. In 1795 Johann Friedrich Blumenbach invented it on the basis of one skull from Georgia in the Caucasus mountains. He may have avoided the term "Georgian" because he knew about Georgia in the American colonies. He rested his arguments for the supreme beauty of whiteness on the skull of a woman who had probably been a sex slave and died of venereal disease.[40]

The transformation of racialized fears into honor and shaming has been crucial in the American production of "white" and "black." From Harriet Jacobs to W.E.B. Du Bois and Zora Neale Hurston, black writers recount that when they were children, they didn't know they were "black" until white people made them feel ashamed of their skin color. What Charles Chesnutt wrote in his 1901 novel *The Marrow of Tradition* could apply in 1680 or 1980: black people have been "branded and tagged" with racial "stigma."[41]

Some have tried to transform shame into celebration. In recent decades, as Michelle Alexander suggests, gangsta rap has embraced the stigma of criminality as "a powerful coping strategy." Gays and lesbians have embraced queer theory for similar reasons. Unlike sexual orientation, however, criminality remains "self-defeating and destructive." While many black families and communities try to contain the shame in a cone of silence, young white audiences treat much of gangsta rap as a kind of radical chic, or what Alexander calls "a modern-day minstrel show."[42] For persons or groups on the march toward cultural entitlement, the paradoxical transformation of shame into a badge of honor may liberate transgressive daring. Ascriptions of shame that keep groups or individuals unempowered give no public benefits except to the empowered.

Among the array of what critical race theorists call micro-aggressions, shaming kept black people, especially black men, in their place. As Mark Twain says of Roxy in *Pudd'nhead Wilson*, every black person became "heir of two centuries of unatoned insult and outrage." In *The Souls of Black Folk*, W.E.B. Du Bois muses that his late young son is better off dead than having to face "the studied humiliations" that Du Bois faces every day.[43] Barack Obama's March 2008 speech on race highlights "the memories of humiliation and doubt and fear" that still prompt deep anger and bitterness in older generations of black people, including his minister and spiritual mentor, whose angry audacity he would soon have to disown.

Much more than with hate speech, which betrays desperation, seeing "black" as more basic than "person" remains one of the most effective modes of racial shaming. That's how I spent my childhood, and I still catch myself doing it. The arrogance of racial categorizing fends off the ultimate fear—of losing the illusion that pale skin enhances individuality. Most "white" Americans remain torn between keeping and relinquishing the imagined honor of their imagined skin color.

CHAPTER 2

HOW DOES IT FEEL
TO BE A PROBLEM?

A year after Bo Diddley jumped into the Las Vegas swimming pool and faced a sign declaring "Contaminated Water" and days after the 1960 presidential election, John Lewis and two black companions went into a Nashville fast-food restaurant to order ten-cent hamburgers. As Taylor Branch recounts, "A visibly distressed waitress poured cleansing powder down their backs and water over their food, while the three Negroes steadfastly ate what they could of their meal." When Lewis and James Bevel returned to complain, the manager said that the place was closed for "emergency fumigation." He then locked the front door, turned on the fumigating machine, and exited at the back, leaving Lewis and Bevel trapped inside. Only after a preacher, a news photographer, firemen, and a crowd gathered outside did the manager return to let them out. The crowd may have gathered because amid the fumes, Rev. Bevel was preaching an impromptu sermon "about the deliverance of Shadrach, Meshach, and Abednego from King Nebuchadnezzar's fiery furnace."[1]

In 1972 or 1973, when Barack Obama was in an elite Hawaiian school, he was pointing to names on a tennis tournament list. Long afterward, a white friend recalled what happened. "Tom M. came over and told him not to touch the draw sheet because he would get it dirty. . . . The message was that his darker skin would somehow soil the draw. Those of us standing there were agape, horrified, disbelieving." Eleven or twelve years old, Obama simply looked at him and said, "'What do you mean by that?'" After some floundering, the student said he was joking. "But we all knew it had been no joke, and it wasn't even remotely funny. Some of our innocence was gone."[2]

By the early 1970s, then, some elite white students in Hawaii felt the shame of such shaming. In Nevada and Tennessee only a decade earlier, similar incidents seemed normal, even mandated, at least to the white people involved. Why? And why do such stories now seem bizarre?

For Branch, the Nashville fumigation incident showed the manager's "association of Negroes with insects and other vermin." That association seems too tame to explain such instantaneous white fear and disgust, except as a rationalization. If a dog instead of Bo Diddley had jumped into that Las Vegas swimming pool, the white swimmers probably would have laughed. More was at stake here than a fear of bugs and dirt, even in the last of the decades when many white middle-class Americans still wrongly associated polio with dirt and the alien poor.[3] The presence of Diddley's band in shared waters, or the attempt of three black men to eat a hamburger, contaminated a racial group's sense of its boundaries and its superiority.

After 1920, when many city and town swimming pools began to let men and women swim together, American whites wouldn't allow black people to swim with them in pools or on beaches. Whether in the Chicago race riot of 1919 or the Mississippi riots about beach integration in the 1950s, white fears of proximity to partially clothed black bodies often prompted lethal violence as well as humiliations. White fears of other kinds of bodily race mixing have also been well documented. At least through the 1940s, Red Cross blood supplies were segregated. On a Savannah minor league baseball team during the late 1950s, when Curt Flood threw his dirty uniform in with his white teammates' dirty uniforms, the trainer removed it with a stick.[4]

Racial shaming characterizes all societies that enforce race-based exclusions. In 1993 a white American novelist, Jill Ciment, stepped into a Japanese public bath, and all the Japanese women climbed out. In 1901, fearing competition from Chinese and Japanese immigrants, Australia passed a "White Australia" policy that restricted the immigration of "nonwhites"; it lasted until the 1970s. Racism legitimates an ethnic group's dominance, and racism intensifies when that group feels entitled but threatened. Racial shaming is at the gentle end of the weapons available to remove the threat.

How White Shaming Worked

Consider again how strange that posting of the "Contaminated Water" sign seems now, and how natural it seemed then, even in 1959 in Las Vegas, far from the South. Was it meant literally, metaphorically, or both? The key lies in Bo Diddley's memory, after half a century, that the experience remained "the most humiliating moment of his life." The white people weren't consciously trying to humiliate him. They leaped out of the pool in a state of not-quite-terror, ostensibly in fear of the threat of physical contamination, but more latently in reaction to the threat of cross-racial intimacy. Yet the African American band leader felt humiliated in the extreme. As William Ian Miller's *Humiliation* points out, humiliation is "richly gendered as feminine" and is linked with the bottom, filth, or women who are "brought low, done dirt, subjected to a host of metaphors" that demean and dehumanize them.[5] If white racism thrives on making black men feel unmanly and feminized, it also thrives on making black people feel dirty.

White humiliations were by no means exclusively directed at men. In *Dreams from My Father*, Obama tells a story of how segregation affected his mother when she was a young white girl. After World War II her family moved to Texas, and one afternoon she invited a black girl to play with her in her yard. A crowd of white children gathered to jeer, shout racist epithets, even throw a stone. When her father called the children's parents to complain, every adult responded, "White girls don't play with coloreds in this town."

Obama's memoir returns several times to the issue of shame. As he first listened to the Rev. Jeremiah Wright preach, he felt the stories of "ordinary black people" merging with biblical stories "of survival, and freedom, and hope" as well as with his own story. These stories "gave us a means to reclaim memories that we didn't need to feel shamed about."[6] The problem, Obama emphasizes in his March 2008 speech about race, isn't black anger about the long history of white humiliations. Yes, "the anger is real; it is powerful," but it has to be understood, not wished away or condemned. Again and again, black men have experienced "the shame and frustration that came from not being able to provide for one's family," and that assault on their manhood has "contributed to the erosion of black families." But the anger of Obama's former minister and many other older-generation black people lacks what Rev. Wright called "the audacity of hope." This tension between anger and hope remains an intractable divide in many, perhaps most, older black people who grew up in white America, and it's quietly present in Obama's writings. Though his speech sounds an upbeat note of potential progress, Obama's memoir concludes with his realization of the personal and racial "shame" that burdened his Kenyan father and grandfather.

In the spring of 2007, Senator Joe Biden infamously praised Senator Obama for being "clean" and "mainstream" as well as "articulate." Most of the publicized anger focused on the demeaning aspects of "articulate." But the word "clean" evokes a longer history of white nervousness about being contaminated by black people's shameful dirtiness, along with lingering white expectations of being "clean cut." A short line runs from Biden's remark to the moment young Booker T. Washington was first washed in the mainstream. As Washington recalls in *Up from Slavery*, only after he had cleaned a room four times did Miss Mary Mackie say, "I guess you will do to enter this institution."[7] Those two instances may seem faintly comic. But they expose an unconscious translation: white shaming becomes white fears of black dirtiness. At best, a few well-washed individuals can alleviate the fears. At worst, the fears invite ethnic cleansing.

Today most Americans associate ethnic cleansing with less modern and more flagrantly racist cultures. Yet its impulse has been sporadically present in American history, from widespread antebellum hopes of recolonizing black people in Liberia to postbellum hopes of sending black people to Haiti or the Philippines to the 1923 massacre and eradication of Rosewood, a black Florida town.[8] Nor was the impulse specifically focused on black people. Native Americans experienced ethnic cleansing when tribe after tribe was removed to less valuable land and contained in reservations. In the first volume of Alexis de Tocqueville's *Democracy in America*, he predicted race war in the South, not because slavery brought economic benefits—even white southerners saw slavery as "prejudicial to their interests"—but because its abolition would "increase the repugnance of the white population for the blacks." Tocqueville was also startled at the disjunction between Americans' passionate beliefs in equality and their ruthless treatment of Indians.[9]

In the early 1870s, there was a double ethnic cleansing in north-western Louisiana. First, on Easter Sunday of 1873, a white militia numbering as many as 165 white men massacred somewhere between 62 and 81 black people in Colfax, and perhaps more. Three white men died. Many white gunmen talked of the necessity for honor killings of black people whose local political and economic power humiliated them. They called their black targets "beeves," or beef cows. Hours after the massacre, they executed forty-eight more black victims. National magazines briefly featured the Colfax killings, until the Panic of 1873 swallowed up the story.[10] The federal government captured the killers, who went free because a U.S. Supreme Court decision affirmed states' rights instead of punishing racial terrorism.

Later that year some of the white gunmen went up the Red River to Coushatta, fifty miles away, where they killed six Republican white men, perhaps aided by the men's guards. The Knights of the Camellia, as many called themselves, were loosely allied with another group calling themselves the Old Time Ku Klux Klan. One Yankee, who survived a later assassination attempt, sardonically emphasized the southern whites' sense of honor. In his memoir he calls them "the chivalry." White residents of both towns still feel great satisfaction about these events. In 1951, the town of Colfax put up a plaque commemorating the white victory in what they called a black "riot." The plaque still stands by the side of U.S. Highway 84. It states that this event was "the end of carpetbag misrule."[11]

Many localized American massacres of black people by white people differ only in scale from national versions of ethnic cleansing in other countries. They were equally real and equally horrific. In Mississippi, after about thirty blacks were killed, a white man explained that black men's parading had been an "'impudence to the white people. . . . 'We are going to kill all the negroes. The negro men shall not live.'" Sometimes white terrorists flogged or killed white Republicans, too. These floggings tried to enforce "acts of contrition, meant to shame anyone, white or black, who had been led into wayward alliance with the Republicans." Philip Dray's *Capitol Men* recounts story after story of postbellum southern whites who flogged or killed black men. Not a few raped black women, too. "Such acts dehumanized black women, humiliated their male kinfolk, and reinforced the idea that white men controlled the region's sexual dynamics."[12]

Terrorizing worked, at least regionally.[13] As South Carolina senator Ben Tillman gloated to the northern press, "We stuffed ballot boxes. We shot them. We are not ashamed of it." By 1890, when Tillman took office as governor of South Carolina, he announced that "the triumph of Democracy and white supremacy over mongrelism and anarchy is most complete."[14] Fears of losing group dominance have impelled all these attempts to restore group purity. In 1944 Gunnar Myrdal's *An American Dilemma* emphasized that "one deep idea behind segregation is that of quarantining what is evil, shameful, and feared in society." That was a way of "rationalizing and defending the caste system."[15]

Debates about the Supreme Court's 1954 decision in *Brown v. Board of Education* have returned again and again to the "stigma" associated with the Jim Crow laws. As the Fifth Circuit Court said in its 1996 *Hopwood v. Texas* decision overturning race-based criteria for admission to law school, the *Brown* decision "recognized that government's use of racial classifications serves to stigmatize."[16] In the 1857 Dred Scott decision, the Supreme Court did that itself, by approvingly declaring that the states had "deemed it just and necessary thus to stigmatize" people of African descent with "deep and enduring marks of inferiority and degradation."[17] In 1967, the Supreme Court's *Loving v. Virginia* decision overturning laws against interracial marriage noted that such "racial classifications" are "measures designed to maintain White Supremacy."[18]

Among historians, too, presumptions of black inferiority went almost unquestioned until the mid-1950s. David Brion Davis recalls that at Dartmouth and Harvard, Ulrich B. Phillips's racist account of *American Negro Slavery* (1918) remained the standard account until Kenneth Stampp's *The Peculiar Institution* (1956), which shifted the whole field. As Davis sums up his instruction from eminent white historians, "in terms of ideology regarding race, the South won the Civil War." Slaves were happy Sambos, the Civil War shouldn't have happened, and the Ku Klux Klan humorously restored Negroes to their appropriate place.[19]

Long before Lincoln's 1863 Emancipation Proclamation, Alexis de Tocqueville saw the problem clearly: "The Negro makes a thousand fruitless efforts to insinuate himself among men who repulse him; he conforms to the tastes of his oppressors, adopts their opinions, and hopes by imitating them to form a part of their community. Having been told from infancy that his race is naturally inferior to that of the whites, he assents to the proposition and is ashamed of his own nature. In each of his features he discovers a trace of slavery, and if it were in his power, he would willingly rid himself of everything that makes him what he is."[20] That description in the first volume of *Democracy in America* anticipates Booker T. Washington's masks or Toni Morrison's characterization of Pecola Breedlove in *The Bluest Eye* or Michael Jackson's attempts to whiten his face once he gained crossover popularity.

It's clear from many African American narratives that white shaming worked. In "Letter from Birmingham Jail," Martin Luther King Jr. writes about its relentlessness "when you are humiliated day in and day out . . . when you are forever fighting a degenerating sense of 'nobodiness.'" In a powerful speech to a black audience in Orangeburg, South Carolina, during the primary campaign, Michelle Obama spoke of her struggle to overcome "that gnawing sense of self-doubt that is common within all of us."[21]

African Americans' consciousness of their race as a badge of shame appears in texts with increasing intensity after the Civil War, though David Walker and Hosea Easton had railed against it decades earlier.[22] Tellingly, "black" as a self-definition through skin color rarely appears in the antebellum narratives by Frederick Douglass and Harriet Jacobs. Instead, when Douglass invokes the color in *My Bondage and My Freedom*, he ascribes it to the "blacker cloud" of his religious doubts or to his oscillations between "the blackest atheism" and faith. Elsewhere in *Bondage* the term only occasionally refers to skin color.[23]

By 1903, when Du Bois's *The Souls of Black Folk* appeared, "black" had become a central signifier of group identity. Yet his opening chapter blames white ascriptions for giving the label such power. Black "double-consciousness" begins with the effort "to escape white contempt." It perpetually struggles with "that deadweight of social degradation partially masked behind a half-named Negro problem . . . that personal disrespect and mockery, the ridicule and systematic humiliation . . . the all-pervading desire to inculcate disdain for everything black, from Toussaint to the devil." Such pervasive white desire creates in black people "a sickening despair."[24]

Much later, Du Bois recounted his shock when the anthropologist Franz Boas came to Atlanta University, where Du Bois was teaching. In

1906, Boas "said to a graduating class, 'You need not be ashamed of your African past'; and then he recounted the history of the black kingdoms south of the Sahara for a thousand years. I was too astonished to speak."[25] Shame also bedeviled Pauli Murray. When she applied for admission to the University of North Carolina in 1939, the attempt led to a protracted and very public battle. When she "confronted my fear . . . the accumulated shame began to dissolve in a new sense of self-respect."[26]

With more bravado, in "How It Feels to Be Colored Me" (1928), Zora Neale Hurston writes of moving to Jacksonville, where she lived for the first time with white people. Only then, at the age of 13, did she discover that "I was not Zora of Orange County any more, I was now a little colored girl." Even as an adult, "I feel most colored when I am thrown against a sharp white background."[27]

The climax of James Weldon Johnson's anonymous *The Auto-biography of an Ex-Colored Man* (1912) occurs when the narrator witnesses a Georgia lynching. "A great wave of humiliation and shame swept over me. Shame that I belonged to a race that could be so dealt with; and shame for my country." Bitterly he decides to "change my name, raise a moustache, and let the world take me for what it would; that it was not necessary for me to go about with a label of inferiority pasted across my forehead." What "was driving me out of the Negro race . . . was shame, unbearable shame. Shame at being identified with a people that could with impunity be treated worse than animals."[28]

Richard Wright's *Native Son* (1940) exposes that issue more complexly. The narrative keeps returning to what Bigger Thomas feels when he looks at himself through Jan's eyes and sees "the badge of shame which he knew was attached to a black skin." Jan's attempt to shake hands gives Bigger "a dumb, cold, and inarticulate hate." Later Bigger feels his family's "naked shame under the eyes of white folks." His family should be "contented" with him, he thinks, because he had done what white people "dreaded," so his family's "shame was washed away." But it isn't washed away in himself. Still later, remembering Jan's handshake "made him live again in that hard and sharp consciousness of his color and feel the shame and fear that went with it, and at the same time it made him hate himself for feeling it." In "How 'Bigger' Was Born," Wright records that he wrote this novel "'to free *myself* of this sense of shame and fear."[29] Though the quiet retreat of Johnson's protagonist into invisible passing differs sharply from Bigger Thomas's pride in his violence, the stigmatization that generates such opposite solutions remains the same.

James Baldwin's *The Fire Next Time* (1963) jolted white readers with his cry of pain and anger. His grandfather was "defeated" because he "really believed what white people said about him." As a teenager harassed repeatedly by New York police, Baldwin temporarily "fled into the church" to counter "the incessant and gratuitous humiliation and danger one encountered every working day, all day long." All Negroes "are taught really to despise themselves from the moment their eyes open on the world." That situation won't change, he says, until white people realize that "*whoever debases others is debasing himself.*"[30]

These familiar passages reflect a central strangeness. Despite their infinite variety, African Americans have been conscripted into a tainted group. Until very recently, their common experiences of being shamed by whites constructed what their diverse personal experiences couldn't undo. White people's shaming of blacks created an internalized frame within which blacks' encounters with themselves and others always had to maneuver.

A few black writers and characters revel in their ascribed dirtiness. In Zora Neale Hurston's *Their Eyes Were Watching God* (1937), Janie feels most at home on the "muck." Earlier she had fallen in love with Joe Starks, a "seal-brown" man who presented himself with a white man's authority and who had worked "for white folks all his life." After her new husband arrives in an all-black town with his "big voice," he promptly paints his two-story house "a gloaty, sparkly white" and lords it over everyone, including Janie. Only after she goes with Tea Cake to the Everglades muck can Janie fend off Mrs. Turner's similarly "color-struck" wishes to rise above their darker neighbors. Mrs. Turner says to Janie, "Us oughta class off." Janie responds with a sentence I've already quoted, "We'se uh mingled people."[31]

In Toni Morrison's *Sula* (1973), when Sula makes love with Ajax, she cherishes the "free fall" beyond herself, through black to gold to alabaster to "*loam, fertile, free.*" As their bodies mix, she mixes soil and water in her mind, wondering "*when do the two make mud?*" Nel can't allow herself Sula's freedom. Her meditation on "mud" freezes her in a "gray ball" of hate for her best friend, who has also bedded her husband. Only at the end, when Nel realizes that she misses Sula, not Jude, and she cries without "bottom" or "top," does her gray ball break and scatter "like dandelion spores in the breeze." "Leaves stirred; mud shifted; there was the smell of overripe green things." It's as if Nel's mind at last embraces what Sula had realized with Ajax: "*It is the loam that is giving you that smell.*"[32]

In Morrison's next novel, *Song of Solomon* (1977), a former midwife uses her pleasure in dirt to express her rage. Now living in a dead white woman's house and caring for the woman's Weimaraners, Circe has a split self. Her "dainty habits . . . matched her torn and filthy clothes." She tells Milkman Dead that she'll never clean her room again: "Everything in this world they lived for will crumble and rot."[33]

Through these very different modes, black people absorbed, refracted, and resisted white attempts to define their blackness as contamination. The distillation of all these states of mind comes in Morrison's *Beloved* (1987), with a passage that African American reviewers highlighted. Toward the end of the narrative Denver muses "that anybody white could take your whole self for anything that came to mind. Not just work, kill, or maim you, but dirty you. Dirty you so bad you couldn't like yourself anymore. Dirty you so bad you forgot who you were and couldn't think it up."[34] The dirtying feels worse than being murdered or brutalized.

So white people were the problem and black people really knew what it felt like to be shamed. Why did white people do it?

Two Explanations

Of the many explanations that have emerged to make sense of what I'm calling racial shaming, at least two have become widely accepted. The first combines motives derived from economics and status. Many white people wanted to preserve their jobs and their sense that at least some group was below them. Especially in the antebellum and postbellum South, upper-class white gentlemen and ladies wanted slaves or servants to do the physical labor that would undermine their claims to aristocratic leisure. Many poorer whites feared competition.[35] In 1865, African Americans owned 20,000 farms in the South; by 1922, they owned 1 million farms. To undermine that progress, racism and segregation became what Ivan Evans sardonically calls "a major

Southern accomplishment—employing racial violence to dilute class distinctions amongst whites." Not coincidentally, Evans argues, racism restored and preserved the dominance of an agrarian elite during times of falling cotton prices and a prolonged depression at the end of the nineteenth century.[36]

Mary Douglas's anthropological classic, *Purity and Danger*, exposes the fears of group and personal pollution that have led to such widespread policing. Focusing on the Hindu caste system and other preindustrial cultures, she argues that body orifices symbolize the vulnerabilities at group margins. "Primitives are not trying to cure or prevent personal neuroses by their public rituals." Instead, each ritual is "an attempt to maintain a particular culture, a particular set of assumptions by which experience is controlled." Ultimately, "anxiety about bodily margins expresses danger to group survival."[37]

In *How Race Is Made*, Mark Smith argues that whites used smell as one of their "authenticators" for racial divisions. White sensory responses became "most vicious" when certainty about race was evaporating. When I asked some senior white southern colleagues why pools and beaches were segregated during their childhoods, three said their parents told them that black people smelled bad.[38]

Only in the last two decades, since Alexander Saxton and David Roediger opened the door for whiteness studies, have light-skinned academics begun to unlearn what Toni Morrison has called "the habit of ignoring race" if it happens to be their own. As a belated consequence of the civil rights movement, whiteness studies emerged in the 1980s because some white people were gaining distance from the traditions of universalizing whiteness while romanticizing and vilifying aspects of blackness.[39]

A second explanation focuses on white fears of amalgamation, called miscegenation after 1863, when David Croly invented the term as part of a political dirty trick to defeat Lincoln. The trick failed, but the term stuck.[40] Such rhetoric had widespread appeal, especially from the 1880s to the 1970s. The fears even spilled over into white recoils against rock music in the 1950s and 1960s.[41]

To anyone with egalitarian values, those fears seem flagrantly illogical. Despite the vehement public outcries against white-black mixing, there was little or no fear that black women would contaminate white men. From Thomas Jefferson to Strom Thurmond, the white iceberg frequently displayed a hot tip. Part of the impetus behind the one-drop rule in Virginia during the 1920s was the desire to avoid the problem of mixed-race children.[42] White people had a specific fear that has been widely analyzed in histories of American racism: they were afraid of the proximity of black men to young white women. Miscegenation became a charged synecdoche for the prospect of any interracial intimacy or equality, especially with black men.[43]

What looks illogical now seemed quite natural to slaveholders whose code of honor shaped their perceptions of themselves and others. Justifications for a slavery-based freedom presume social hierarchy. Some men are born to rule, while others are born to serve.[44] By 1860 the sectional divide on that issue had become acute, and divisions grew within the South as well. As President Lincoln said in 1864, "With some, the word liberty may mean for each man to do as he pleases with himself and the product of his labor; while with others the same word may mean for some men to do as they please with other men and the product of other men's labor. Here are two, not only different, but incompatible things, called by the same name—liberty." For many white men, liberty meant the freedom to do as they pleased with darker-skinned women as well.[45]

As Alabama congressman J. Thomas Heflin declared during his campaign in 1901, "God almighty intended the negro to be the servant of the white man." For many men north and south, sexual mastery was simply another perquisite of their liberty to command. According to one historian, "Informal interracial sex constituted a white male privilege."[46] White men's presumptions of hypersexuality among black men and black women become habitual, and they used those presumptions as a license for their own hypersexuality.[47] The courageous black hero of Melissa Fay Greene's *Praying for Sheetrock* recounts that in the 1930s on the southeast coast of Georgia, his mother and other young black women walking to work had to hide in the woods whenever they sensed that "white guys be coming along" looking for them. A century earlier, Alexis de Tocqueville noted that "to debauch a Negro girl hardly injures an American's reputation; to marry her dishonors him." In Jean Toomer's *Cane* (1923), as a white man "sauntered" toward his rendezvous with his black lover, "his mind became consciously a white man's." In that spirit Bob Stone yearns for the way it used to be: "He went in as a master should and took her. Direct, honest, bold. None of this sneaking that he had to go through now." Soon afterward, a black man gets lynched for killing this white rival.[48]

Occasionally a white southern man did get shamed for having sexual relations with a black woman. Col. Richard Johnson, a Kentucky Democrat and the alleged killer of Tecumseh, was the only vice-president whose election had to be ratified by the Senate. During his 1836 campaign with Martin Van Buren, people discovered that one of Johnson's slaves was his common-law wife and the mother of his child, and some of his pledged southern electors refused to vote for him. The shaming passed, and he took office. Rumors that President John Tyler had fathered a daughter with a black woman and later sold the daughter into slavery surfaced only after his death. Tyler's predecessor, William Henry Harrison, fathered six slave children. When he ran for president, his brother sold four to get them out of Virginia.[49]

The most harrowing story in Du Bois's *The Souls of Black Folk* tells of "black" John and "white" John, two boyhood friends who grow into black anger and white privilege. Home from Princeton, white John, "not a bad fellow,—just a little spoiled and self-indulgent, and as headstrong as his proud father"—impulsively demands a kiss from the other John's "tall, willowy" sister, whom he knows as just "'Jennie, the little brown kitchen-maid!'" Scared, she runs into the woods as he chases her. There the protagonist finds "his dark sister struggling in the arms" of white John and kills him with a tree limb. The story ends with John humming a German song and thinking of rope coils as he is about to be lynched.[50]

In *American Dilemma*, Gunnar Myrdal reprints an astonishing 1933 memoir by Rollin Chambliss, who grew up in Georgia. As he recalls his boyhood days, he realizes that racial presumption was everywhere. "I don't know if it ever occurred to any of us that a Negro girl was capable of virtue." When one of his friends verbally accosted a black girl walking by, an African American man came to protest. The boy got his shotgun, and the man went away. "'You have to know how to handle Negroes,'" the boy said. Chambliss reflects that the white boy would have shot the black man without a qualm.[51]

While many white men took advantage of black women's subordination, pervasive white hostility to racial equality focused on protecting white women from black men. At the start of a decade-long struggle to integrate a Mississippi beach, a 1959 editorial in the *Gulfport Pictorial Review* noted in passing that "it would be very dangerous to try mixing races on this beach" due to "the difference in family and sex training between most white women and negro men." For Edward Ayers, the "racial discomfiture" of late nineteenth-century white southerners at the prospect of integrated railroad cars reflected their fears of the "sexual charge . . . among strangers temporarily placed in intimate surroundings" on the train.[52] Ironically, the trumpeted fear of the black beast reversed antebellum abolitionist stereotypes of white men as sexual predators preying upon black women. Before the Civil War, images of the black beast were scarce. Now the stereotype evoked primal threat and panic.[53]

In *Cultures of Violence*, a comparison of racist violence in the American South and South Africa, Ivan Evans astutely analyzes southern uses of the black beast image. The specter instantly triggered cross-class rage and sparked a passion to defend "communal honor." In "welding together the white folk," the image transformed white men into "guardians" of white women's virtue. It helped to depoliticize "internal fault lines" and deepen the racial divide. "Asserting or restoring the *patriarchal powers* of the white-male-as protector" animated "rape panics," in part because "the image of the white-woman-as victim" complemented the image of white men as chivalric rescuers.[54]

In South Africa, Evans argues, lynching wasn't necessary because a strong state enforced white supremacy with massacres and greater race separation. In the American South, black and white people lived in close proximity. Since boundaries were hard to establish, lynching and segregation ensured "the regulation of contact, particularly sexual contact with white women." Faced with a hostile or indifferent national government and weak local states, white southerners invoked honor to legitimize lynch culture, a type of racialized violence unique among industrializing Western countries. The code reestablished a simple antebellum hierarchy: "Women were subordinate to men; men were honor-bound to defend their women and children; the rich were rich because God blessed them; and blacks, who were both inferior and evil, deserved both the 'social death' of segregation and the measures that preserved it."[55]

That mixture of hierarchy and fear in white people's strategic uses of the black beast image extended to the North. As early as the 1830s,

Alexis de Tocqueville found American race prejudice more intense in the North than in the South. In the late 1960s, several black people interviewed for Bob Blauner's *Black Lives, White Lives* said they preferred the direct racism of white southerners to the belittling they had experienced in the North. From California to New York, white people used the specter of a black man with a white woman to legitimize their racism. The image also helped resolve the tension between their presumption of white superiority and their acknowledgment of racial injustice. Thomas Sugrue's study of Detroit after World War II shows that white working-class people who raged at the prospect of neighborhood integration equated protecting their daughters with protecting their homes. Yet few whites were uncomfortable about having their children held by black women. Whites' instantaneous rage, fear, and disgust surfaced at any evidence or thoughts of white women's proximity to black male sexuality or even black men's sweat.[56]

Sweet Land of Liberty, Sugrue's 2008 book about civil rights struggles in the North, highlights northern white people's "fears of sex" from "promiscuous mixing" at pools, parks, and beaches. Recoiling from interracial contact, they established intractable patterns of residential segregation. Ostensibly whites were more concerned with property values. But fears of miscegenation provided the subtext. The all-white National Association of Real Estate Boards relentlessly enforced the racial divide. From the 1930s through the 1960s, its "ethical guidelines" stated that no realtor should show a house to anyone who would hurt property values. A supplementary brochure specified: no bootlegger, madam, gangster, or, even worse, "a colored man of means who was giving his children a college education and thought they were entitled to live among whites." That intense effort at boundary-making demonstrates visceral fears of mixing.[57]

Jeff Wiltse's *Contested Waters* vividly details the shift from class-based segregation to race-based segregation of U.S. swimming pools after towns and cities accepted gender mixing. Racial tensions swirling about a new St. Louis pool in 1913 foreshadowed decades of white resistance and violence at the thought that black men might be swimming with white women. As Wiltse notes, several other factors exacerbated these tensions, especially the black migration north and the greater curbs on immigration as well as white fears of disease. The two most basic factors "remained mostly unspoken" and "mostly unacknowledged": the fear that black men could "interact with white women at such intimate and erotic public spaces" and the fear that black men's strong bodies would undercut "assertions of white men's superior manliness."[58]

Almost all these issues converged to spark the Tulsa race riots— probably the worst in U.S. history. On May 30, 1921, a nineteen-year-old black shoe shiner tripped as he entered an elevator and grabbed the seventeen-year-old white female operator to keep from falling. She screamed, and a white clerk thought she had been assaulted. Tulsa police arrested the young man but then tried to downplay the incident. An editorial in the sensationalist local newspaper announced, wrongly, that whites would lynch him. Misinformation became prophecy, and 1,500 whites assembled, faced by armed black men defending the accused. During the next sixteen hours, as many as 300 people were killed, most of them black. Eight hundred African Americans were injured, and 10,000 were left homeless as fires razed the Greenwood district. Most tellingly, that district was called "the Negro Wall Street" because of all the prosperous black people who lived there. Later the newspaper's editorial disappeared from its archives.[59]

In Hawaii, the celebrated Massie trials of 1931–32 began when a young white wife from Alabama, Thalia Massie, said she had been raped by four or five Hawaiian men. Police quickly picked up some Hawaiian youths and accused them, despite testimony that earlier in the evening the woman had slapped an officer at a party and then walked home drunk without her husband, "closely followed by a white man." In 1927 she and her naval cadet husband had been indicted for trying to kidnap a baby. Later, after she lost a baby of her own, a psychologist reported that she needed psychiatric help. When that report was handed to her on the stand at the second trial, she ripped it up, to widespread sympathy.[60]

Those complications got lost in the nationwide outcry about the necessity for white honor to protect "our women" against those dark-skinned rapists. Both of the major Hawaiian newspapers vigorously campaigned for conviction. In media reports from Hawaii to the East Coast, the accused men's color kept oscillating between brown and black. Yet the jury split six to six, so the men went free. The *New York American* was outraged that "this crime against pure womanhood" by "five natives" could end with their "freedom on bail after a disagreement of a jury of their kind." The *American* also mentioned "the other forty outrages on virtuous white women." No such assaults have ever been documented.[61]

At that point several whites, including the wife's mother and husband, kidnapped one of the youths and shot him to death. The young man's funeral drew the largest turnout since the death of the last queen fifteen years earlier. Later in 1932 a mixed-race grand jury dominated by whites said there wasn't enough evidence for a trial, though the accused whites had been found driving a car with the youth's body in the back seat. They were on their way to a throw the corpse into a blow hole. After the judge twice told the grand jury to reconsider, they voted twelve to eight to indict the accused whites. Following the judge's strict instructions, the defendants were convicted. Then, at President Herbert Hoover's urging, the governor commuted their ten-year sentences to one hour, after which they had to leave Hawaii. Two years later Thalia Massie divorced her husband in Reno, and in 1963 she died in Palm Beach of an overdose of barbiturates, after two previous attempts.[62]

Among many ironies here, the defense attorney for Massie and his co-defendants was Clarence Darrow, who emerged from five years of retirement to take his last case. He needed the money, and apparently he hoped that somehow he would better Hawaiian race relations. In 1926 Darrow had roused himself from an earlier retirement to defend Dr. Ossian Sweet and several other black people who had shot into a mob of whites stoning Sweet's house after his family had integrated a white Detroit neighborhood. Darrow's eight-hour closing statement vividly made jurors think about their own race prejudices, and he won.[63] Now Darrow argued that Thalia Massie's husband had killed Joe Kahahawai because of "temporary insanity" when he heard the young man confess, "Yeah, we done it." The Hearst newspapers labeled the second trial "the Honor Slaying." Many years afterward, one of the other defendants, Deacon Jones, not only confessed to having shot the man but also admitted that he had said so to Darrow during the trial.[64]

In *Faith of My Fathers*, Senator John McCain briefly recounts that story, which had occurred just before his father arrived in Hawaii. For McCain, Lieut. Massie "had committed an unpardonable breach of the code"—not by making a false accusation, but by involving enlisted men in the crime! "Many of his fellow officers felt shamed by Massie's conduct," and they thought he should have killed himself.[65]

From the South after 1863 to Hawaii in the 1930s to northern suburbs and cities in the 1970s, the threat of interracial sex between black men and white women simplified white people's fears of racial equality. Postures of manly protectiveness for white women justified perse-cuting black people and persisted beyond the civil rights revolution. Americans today are horrified at stories of brutality toward dissidents in Iran, Zimbabwe, and a host of other countries. Until the 1950s, similar attacks and murders happened in the United States on a daily basis, without much stir.

The tension implied in the seemingly illogical fear of sex between black men and white women exposes a third explanation. Racial shaming thrived because it resuscitated patriarchal honor, with a collective twist.

Fear and Honor

Highlighting the honor-shame dynamics in white fears of miscegena-tion and dark-skinned beasts invites another perspective. These fears focused on black men and white daughters in an attempt to restore a chivalric kinship frame that featured patriarchal honor in social contexts that threatened to undermine the code.[66]

In 1892, Ida B. Wells wrote about why three of her black friends had just been lynched in Memphis: "not rape but competing with a white-owned business." Her article led to the destruction of her newspaper and her exile from Memphis. As she put it, "Nobody in this section of the country believes the old threadbare lie that negro men rape white women. If Southern white men are not careful . . . a conclusion will then be reached which will be very damaging to the reputation of their women." To acknowledge that a white woman might choose consensual interracial sex would not only damage the woman's reputation, it would also deflate white men's honor, a balloon already punctured by the war and hard times. Lynching black men who threatened white men's sexual or economic dominance assuaged feelings of inadequacy.[67]

Chivalric ideals of honor sought to control white women as well as humiliate black men.[68] Such ideals intensified in hard economic times. To quote Rollin Chambliss again, the unquestioned belief that "a Negro who touches a white woman must die" was "born of pride in our own culture, and possibly of an unrecognized fear that it might not persist. It was intensified by the chivalric ideal of womanhood which has been traditional in the South." Tellingly, Chambliss's claim to "our own culture" is the base of that belief, and "the chivalric ideal of womanhood" is only the metonymic superstructure. Sometimes, as Glenda Gilmore argues, the black beast stereotype aimed to keep black men from political power more than to prevent sexual intimacies with white women.[69]

To explain these dynamics, Mary Douglas suggests a key analytic turn: analyzing race-based group psychology rather than the individual psychologies that Joel Williamson and many others focus on. I suggest another shift: reconceptualizing honor as a primary defense against the fear of being shamed by real or imagined peers. Daily shaming defined black people as "colored," a group designation that required humility and submission.[70] As George Fredrickson emphasizes in *Racism*, "Scapegoating the available and vulnerable Other" helped manage feelings of "humiliation" in the dominant group.[71] Racial shaming warded off fears of being shamed by peers.

Racial scapegoating also brought white people together with the promise and practice of group dominance. In *The Strange Career of Jim Crow*, C. Vann Woodward concludes that the Negro became a "national scapegoat" to unify white people in the North and South after the Civil War. Then the Negro became "a sectional scapegoat" to unite the "Solid South." Ida B. Wells went further. In the words of her biographer, Wells came to think that the terrifying image of the black beast was "largely constructed for the consumption of the North." Northern tolerance or indifference gave southern whites the freedom to preserve the Old South with "inauthentic" rituals of violent chivalry.[72]

Becoming honor bound required some self-deformations. Black writers from Douglass and Jacobs to Du Bois observed that white people were warped by their presumptions of paternalistic power over black people. As Du Bois puts it in *Black Reconstruction*, mastery of slaves tended to make planters "arrogant, strutting, quarrelsome kinglets. . . . Their 'honor' became a vast and awful thing, requiring wide and insistent deference" from black people.[73] Du Bois's mordant term exposes the provincial insecurities in those "kinglets" who were so far from being kings.

Almost three decades later, Langston Hughes's *The Ways of White*

Folks (1934) recounts stories about failed white paternalists and their black servants or children. In the most powerful story, "Father and Son," a white colonel has fathered a mixed-race son "by his Negro mistress . . . who kept his house and had borne him all his children." Returning from college, the son repeatedly vows "not to be a white folks' nigger" and demands that his father acknowledge him. After the young man strangles his father and kills himself, the narrator repeats the son's conclusion that his father was like every other white man, looking to kill any black man who won't submit.[74]

In 1935, Hughes's Broadway play on the same theme ran for 373 performances. *Mulatto: A Play of the Deep South* dramatizes the conflict between a Georgia plantation owner and his mulatto son. Seeing something special in two of his mixed-race children, Col. Thomas Norwood sends Robert and Sally north to be educated. After their return, a white overseer seduces Sally and Robert demands to be treated as a white man instead of being forced to work in the fields. When Norwood threatens to shoot him, Robert strangles his father and kills himself before the lynch mob arrives. The father-son relationships in both the story and the play had autobiographical elements, though Hughes's father was black.[75] Both the story and the play feature an imperious plantation aristocrat who can't bear to recognize his own son's potential equality.

What prompted the paternalists' kingly strutting? White people's relish for lording it over black people illustrates their pleasure in displaying their mastery but also their anxiety about preserving their privileges. Their shaming of African Americans deflects fears of being shamed by their peers or, worse, by those they regard as their inferiors. In small social units, a man of superior status can't be dishonored by a man of inferior status. If he's insulted, he will beat or kill the offender, whereas if he's insulted by a peer, various rites of honor to manage the conflict come into play.[76] Between large groups, especially in a racialized hierarchy, shaming members of the allegedly inferior group restores the comfort of membership as well as dominance. Obsessions with "dirt" indirectly express white people's fear of not being all that white if they too get reduced to inferior status.[77]

As Du Bois observes in *The Souls of Black Folk*, "The Negro dimly personifies in the white man all his ills and misfortunes." Elsewhere Du Bois observes that behind lynch mobs "is a knot, large or small, of normal human beings and these human beings at heart are desperately afraid of something."[78] In *The Fire Next Time*, Baldwin muses that "the white man's unadmitted—and apparently, to him, unspeakable—private fears and longings are projected onto the Negro." In *Dreams from My Father*, Barack Obama suggests to a friend that white people "'learn to hate'" because their "'demons'" make them "'so afraid.'" Perhaps slavery itself, he muses, had been set in motion by white men's "fears of inconsequence."[79]

Benedict Anderson's *Imagined Communities* takes Obama's insight further. Anderson asserts that racism didn't exist before the establishment of colonial empires, which "permitted sizeable numbers of bourgeois and petty bourgeois to play aristocrat off centre court: i.e., anywhere in the empire except at home." Ensconced in his "tropical Gothic," a man could become Molière's "bourgeois gentilhomme," with a large native supporting class of houseboys, grooms, washerwomen, maids, "and, above all, horses."[80]

Feelings of being shamefully inadequate to a metropolitan aristocratic norm magnified white colonists' preoccupations with honor as well as their racism. Earlier forms of slavery didn't use racism to legitimate mastery. As the authors of a 2003 article on "Race and Genomics" put it, "The modern concept of race grew out of the experience of Europeans in naming and organizing the populations encountered in the rapid expansion of their empires."[81] Frantz Fanon puts it more pithily in *The Wretched of the Earth*. "The colonist is an exhibitionist . . . to remind the colonized out loud: 'Here I am the master.'" In his earlier book, *Black Skin, White Masks*, Fanon argues that white colonists and colonized blacks are reciprocally "enslaved" by their sense of superiority and inferiority.[82]

In *Racism: A Short History* (2002), George Fredrickson takes a different approach. He argues that racism originated "in the idioms of religion" during the fourteenth and fifteenth centuries. Fredrickson doesn't make much of the simultaneous onset of colonialism. He argues that not until the eighteenth century, during the Enlightenment, did many Anglo-Europeans justify their dominance by claiming white superiority. Only at the end does his analysis converge with Anderson's formulation: "What characterizes many of the perpetrators of violence against the Other (whether identified racially or religiously) is social marginality. The greatest danger of direct violence comes from those descended from privileged or at least securely settled groups who find themselves on the outside."[83]

Defining racism as a conscious ideology of inherent racial superiority, Fredrickson argues that full-fledged theories promoting American racism emerged only in the 1830s as a response to abolitionism. That claim seems to me at least a century wide of the mark. In 1661 Maryland's "Shamefull Matches" act prohibited marriages between white women and black slaves. All such wives and all children of such unions would be slaves. Then some planters arranged marriages between white women servants and slaves to produce offspring, who would be property. At Lord Baltimore's request, the law was repealed twenty years later, although throughout the next century, several descendants of such interracial marriages were considered slaves. In 1665, faced with interracial children who claimed to be white because they had white fathers, Virginia reversed centuries of British precedent to declare that such children inherit status from their mother, not their father. In doing so, the state declared that such children are black.[84]

In *Notes on the State of Virginia* (1784), despite his long affair with the light-skinned Sally Hemings, Thomas Jefferson expressed revulsion at black people's physical appearance while denigrating their intellectual capacities.[85]

The idea of a "pure" Aryan race took hold in the mid-nineteenth century as a reaction to the increasing threat of interracial mixing, much as "blood" became a ubiquitous though challengeable metaphor for racialized identities.[86] Yet the presumption of white dominance goes back to the first settlers' enslavements. Eric Love argues too simply that "the United States was originally conceived as a white nation" and grew "for the exclusive benefit of white citizens." Dutch New York was a brief pocket of multiethnic heterogeneities, and immigrants were relatively welcome if they would assimilate. Before Bacon's Rebellion in 1676, Virginia also had multiracial possibilities.[87] Nevertheless, presumptions of white superiority have been central to America's founding and development.

Anderson's suggestive argument takes us furthest. It locates the onset of white racism in European immigrants who were bent on colonizing and capitalizing yet felt inferior to those at the metropolitan center of power.[88] Honor-shame dynamics animated the colonizers' claims to be provincial aristocrats. The claims shaped their perceptions of themselves and their others. They could become lords over people of darker colors by taking Native Americans' property or turning black people into property. Under the strutting and the expropriation, fears of being shamed by provincial or cosmopolitan peers intensified the racializing of honor.

George Orwell's 1936 essay "Shooting an Elephant" provides a more dramatic colonial narrative of these issues. Orwell exposes the fears of being shamed that impel race-based dichotomies. Stationed in lower Burma in the early 1930s, during the only time "I was hated by large numbers of people," Orwell "first grasped the hollowness, the futility of the white man's dominion in the East" when he had to shoot an aggressive elephant in front of 2,000 Burmese. As he does so, against his will, he realizes that "when the white man turns tyrant . . . he becomes a sort of hollow, posing dummy, the conventionalized figure of a sahib" who has to impress "the 'natives'" by doing what they expect. "He wears a mask, and his face grows to fit it. . . . And my whole life, every white man's life in the east, was one long struggle not to be laughed at." He concludes, "I had done it solely to avoid looking a fool."[89]

Though Orwell's biographer suspects that he may have fictionalized this incident, his narrative illustrates a compelling truth. In a social structure dominated by one racial group, ideals of honor become a goad, especially when boundaries seem threatened by another group previously defined as lower, or not quite human. Then members of the dominant group feel on display, to themselves and their Others. Threats of intermixture and equality can prompt shaming words and violent behavior, whether against elephants or people of other colors. Orwell had beaten his servants in Burma. When honor becomes a way of holding a group together against threats from below, fears of being shamed by peers or inferiors also impel people "to avoid looking a fool." So the mask of honor gets put on, and its bearers strive to keep it there.[90]

Long after Hawaii's 1931–32 Massie trials, Deacon Jones's confession in the 1960s vividly illustrates Orwell's sense that honor can be a false posture of racialized bravado. Jones was a lower-class thug by his own account, "ready for a brawl" on the evening he killed Joe Kahahawai for allegedly raping Thalia Massie. Repeatedly he told his interviewer that Thomas Massie was from a much higher class, "a brilliantly educated boy." That's why Darrow decided to have Massie take the rap, he said, to make the honor killing aspect seem compelling. Several times Jones contemptuously calls the victim a "kanaka," or Hawaiian, a term he alternates with "nigger."

More surprisingly, Jones candidly talks about the need to fake bravery. "You don't tangle with a big bastard like that. You need a bit of false courage." When the interviewer asked him whether he felt any "animosity" toward the victim, Jones replied, "I don't hate anybody. Hate is another expression of fear and I didn't fear this black bastard, although I had no use for him. To me it was a challenge." With almost sexualized satisfaction, he says that "I shot him. . . . That was the climax, right there. When I shot that son-of-a-bitch, I knew what I was doing." Much as Orwell does when he shoots the elephant, Jones postures himself into violence to deny any fear. Faced with the shock he sees in the face of upper-class Thomas Massie, he pretends to have killed others already. "I was going to be something I wasn't."[91]

What happens to white people when faking honor doesn't quite work? They have to admit to some fear under the lordliness. Here, to apply Orwell's conclusion, I speculate that many if not most American white people developed an inverse Du Boisian veil. On the outside, there was a mix of indifference, superiority, and loathing, with instantaneous disgust and shaming when provoked. That's why whites leaped out of the pool when Bo Diddley jumped in. A strategy of collective shaming had long since been internalized. Inside the veil loomed several fears—of facing black equality, of losing the self-respect and peer bonds secured by whiteness, of being scorned if white people admitted interracial empathies.[92]

When shaming links blackness to pollution, fears of self-blackening pollute white consciousness.[93] Throughout the twentieth century, white racists had to fend off the growing evidence that race had little biological validity, that many if not most white people had "mixed blood," and that perceptions of race were socially imposed.[94] Nevertheless, through the 1960s and beyond, white people justified the racial shaming they did with the language of contamination.

Shaming and Civil Rights

Why did the centuries-long intensity of racial shaming by whites diminish so sharply in just the last fifty years? I suggest three reasons.

First, after its victory in World War II, the United States reached what Benedict Anderson calls "centre court." As an imagined community as well as a world-class power, America became a primary Cold War contender, then the undisputed champion after the USSR imploded in 1989. White racism no longer had to compensate for feelings of provincial inferiority.

Second, the double movement of expansion and consolidation that has characterized racism as well as capitalism and colonialism took a turn toward tolerance. Global capitalism threatened the provincial insularities that had justified quasi-colonial rule. People of darker colors were possible consumers as well as cheap labor. As Alexander Saxton points out, racism became dysfunctional—at least for international consumption—because the United States was competing for the allegiance of nonwhites.[95]

Third, the civil rights movement succeeded because in the 1950s and especially the 1960s, racists looked shameful on TV. The new technology of television forced white racism onto the national stage as an array of local bigotries that deserved national shaming. As Glenda Gilmore emphasizes, southern racism depended on local political control to construct the South as an imagined white community. Now the conflict between the land of opportunity and the land of segregation became visible daily, in the headlines and especially on TV news reports. No longer could seemingly honorable white viewers ignore the blatantly dishonorable white representatives of the law, and not just in the South. The pervasive acts of white violence to keep black people in their place began to lose legitimacy. A growing white awareness of the shamefulness of racial shaming signaled a decreasing need to define whiteness through honor and a decreasing need to define honor as collective racial purity.[96]

The advent of the word "racism" as an American pejorative in the 1960s reflected the onset of a widespread rethinking about race. The term was first used in the late 1930s, but only to apply to Nazi Germany. In France from the late nineteenth century to the 1930s, *racisme* was used as a positive term for French superiority, much as "prejudice of color" was in the United States. Amazingly, only after the national impact of the civil rights movement did the word become a readily available American label for the negative effects of white supremacy.[97]

Such rethinking had been a long time coming. From the 1850s to the 1960s, the imperfect American union between honor and whiteness held firm. White supremacy was simply a given, with a presumptive universality that seemed nonracial. What Wayne Flynt has said of the South today characterized most white northerners before the 1960s: "Southerners generally don't personalize race. The more abstract race becomes, the more racist it becomes." Race had long since become a shameful brand for nonwhites. In the late 1940s, without any consciousness of the irony, *Billboard* listed all the black popular music releases under the title "Race Records," as if only black people fit the category.[98]

In 1955 came a seismic change. Rosa Parks refused to move to the back of a bus in Montgomery, Alabama, and Emmett Till's mother demanded an open casket for her son's wake in Chicago. Haunting photographs forced his Mississippi lynching into white people's awareness. *Jet* and *Look* featured pictures of Till's mutilated body. The fourteen-year-old boy from Chicago had been visiting family members in Money, Mississippi. Allegedly he whistled at a young white female clerk or said something flirtatious. The clerk told her husband, who went with his brother to kidnap Till, shoot him, deface him, and throw the body in the river tied to a 70-pound weight. It was the normal reaction of men who felt honor-bound to protect their women. In only 67 minutes, the all-male, all-white jury acquitted them. Four months later, safe from double jeopardy, they proudly confessed to William Bradford Huie, a *Look* reporter who had paid them to talk, that they had done it to make an example of Till, since he bragged about having sexual relations with white women in Chicago. Years later both men died with no remorse, though with considerable resentment that they hadn't made more money from Till's death. Although white residents of Money had acquitted them and paid for their defense, black residents had shunned their stores.[99]

Lynching was an old southern story: shaming turned violent. In what is now called the long civil rights movement, there had been protests against lynching since 1919, usually led by blacks and communists and usually without much white response, except perhaps to the attempted lynching of the Scottsboro Boys in 1931. But in 1955 the impasse between the nation's sense of shock and the seeming lack of shame or guilt among white people in Mississippi kept bringing reporters back to

Money. Till was just a boy, not a threatening black man. The impasse accelerated a national transformation. Northerners had to pay attention. For the first time, they saw members of their own group as black people had often seen white Americans for over 300 years, through shocked, amused, or contemptuous eyes. In 1919, W.E.B. Du Bois had called America "a shameful land"; now northern whites thought that might be true.[100]

Here the nonviolent strategy of Martin Luther King Jr. played a crucial role in getting media attention. Day after day, white viewers saw black protesters as more civilized than racist southern governors and sheriffs or the raging Chicago crowds in the 1966 riots. Many Americans admired the demonstrators' principled bravery.[101] Years after John Lewis was nearly beaten to death in Selma, Alabama, John McCain wrote an admiring chapter about Lewis in his 2004 book, *Why Courage Matters*. As McCain put it, Lewis made many Americans "ashamed that they had not loved their country as much as the marchers; that they had not the courage to march into such injustice."[102]

In effect, King's strategy enacted a chiasmus by reversing white stereotypes about who was honorable and who was shameful. The reversal undermined presumptions of whites' superiority and group cohesion by sharply contrasting the brutality of white law officers with the resolute nonviolence of black protesters. National shaming slowly trumped local shaming and forced progressive change.[103]

International shaming may also have had some influence. In 1963, musing on the *Brown v. Board of Education* decision, James Baldwin wrote, "Most of the Negroes I know do not believe that this immense concession would ever have been made if it had not been for the competition of the Cold War." African decolonization played a role too, he declared. "Africa was clearly liberating herself and therefore had, for political reasons, to be wooed by the descendants of her former masters." Baldwin's second assertion strikes me as wishful thinking. But he's right to connect "this immense concession" to a new self-consciousness about America's international status. In *The Honor Code*, Kwame Anthony Appiah argues that a nation's need for international respect can prompt moral progress. More cynically, as Baldwin implies, the Supreme Court's affirmation of racial equality presented U.S. democracy as superior to Soviet repression. That stance didn't have much immediate effect on white Americans' attitude toward black people, but it did improve the nation's image.[104]

The civil rights movement exposed the dishonor that had always been inherent in white supremacy. The movement partially succeeded because presumptions of white group honor were already on shaky ground. During the civil rights years, white activists and black protesters gained national respect that overrode local anger. To many Americans, at least temporarily, it seemed more important to affirm liberty and equality than white supremacy as basic national values.

Not that giving up chivalry came easily. Before the Supreme Court's *Brown v. Board of Education* decision in 1954, President Dwight D. Eisenhower told Chief Justice Earl Warren that all the white southerners wanted was to protect their daughters from being "required to sit in school alongside some big overgrown Negroes." Almost twenty years later another president not from the South, Richard Nixon, was taped talking to an aide about the Supreme Court's *Roe v. Wade* decision, which made abortion legal. Nixon was ambivalent. "There are times when an abortion is necessary. I know that. When you have a black and a white. Or a rape."[105]

Unlike personal honor, racialized group honor is hollow, as many white southerners fearfully sensed during the 1960s. Orwell had discovered that three decades earlier. To many light-skinned Americans, the long, strained fusion between honor and whiteness had begun to look shameful or even foolish. At last "American" didn't have to mean "white."

CHAPTER 3

HONOR BOUND

"Every Democrat must feel honor bound to control the vote of at least one Negro, by intimidation, purchase, keeping him away, or as each individual may determine." That declaration was Point Twelve of a 33-point agenda drafted by Martin W. Gary for the Democratic Party in South Carolina that was designed to intimidate black and Republican voters in the 1876 election. Eighty years later, on the day before his reelection in 1946, Mississippi senator Theodore Bilbo called on "every red-blooded American who believes in the superiority and integrity of the white race to get out and see that no nigger votes." Honor had turned to "red-blooded," "control the vote" had turned to "no votes," and "Negro" had turned to "nigger." The same appeal had become desperately dishonorable, though not to Bilbo.[1]

What does it mean to be honor bound? The phrase connotes constraint as well as determination. It could mean a bounding leap, or a direction to be bound for. Here it declares a vow that binds you to a code of honor more dear than your life. As Edmund Morgan points out, the word remains unchanged from the Latin *honor*, derived from the Latin *onus*, which means "burden."[2] It binds men to twin imperatives: seek reputation and prestige and take care of family and kin. The more honor a man has, the more dependents he gets, and the more dependents he has, the more honor he gets. Similarly, southern gentry gained honor proportionate to the number of slaves they owned. In many developing countries, what Americans interpret as corruption is seen by the corrupt individual as a display of honor because he is funding his kin and friends first and foremost, albeit at the expense of his nation. In honor cultures, above all, a man must avenge any insult or challenge, whether to himself or to his group.

Why has that vow held men around the world in thrall? For white men in America, how did a race-based version of that code bring them together, inwardly as well as in an imagined national community, after a shattering civil war?

Honor-Shame Societies

When I encounter lives preoccupied with honor, I'm likely to be attending a nineteenth-century opera or reading a book by John McCain. To most Americans the word seems more suitable for Muslims or for *Gone with the Wind*. Even in the South, the intensity of honor isn't what it used to be, despite some flare-ups. Malcolm Gladwell's recent bestseller *Outliers* engagingly popularizes the idea that the concept of honor applies to a retrograde Scotch-Irish Appalachian subculture filled with feuds and violence. It's not modern, it's not urban, it's not us. It's restricted to southern white men, for whom insults spark vengeance. Gladwell concludes that the southerners' culture of honor reflects the values of their herder ancestors, who needed aggressive responses to protect themselves and their reputations from any taint of weakness.[3]

Gladwell misses honor's role in defending groups as well as individuals. He also misses honor's continuing presence and power. For over 2,000 years, honor has been one of the most basic transhemispheric imperatives to prompt and regulate men's competition for status while securing kinship and tribal bonds. Groups benefit from the competitions, since rivalries strengthen every man's skills. The concept began as a warrior code to protect a small embattled tribe or kinship group from its enemies. From the start it was more defensive than imperial. Eventually the groups extended to villages, towns, city states, armies, nations, and races. The code often governs behavior in modern organizations such as the Mafia, street gangs, or sports teams.

The warrior code requires friends, neighbors, and even family members to shame cowardly men or women who transgress male controls.[4] Honor can also inspirit women to fight for a group, though the codes often separate men's honor from women's virtue. That dichotomy enhances a man's honor as patriarchal protector. Honor can be ascribed through lineage and patronage or acquired through social contests. Especially in what anthropologists call "agonistic cultures," the more a man enacts a warrior ideal, the more honor he gains.

Honor can't be separated from the social uses of shaming. J. G. Peristiany sums up the premodern codes and their Mediterranean context: "Honour and shame are the constant preoccupation of individuals in small scale, exclusive societies where face-to-face personal, as opposed to anonymous, relations are of paramount importance." He highlights "the insecurity and instability of the honour-shame ranking." A man is "constantly 'on show'" to prove himself to his peers. These codes give courage to warriors. The codes regulate and inspirit small patriarchal societies that need defending.[5]

A dutiful daughter can serve as a gift to augment her father's honor, while a sexually active daughter becomes a prime signifier of her father's and therefore her family's shame. A father or other male relative may kill an unchaste daughter, with little community disapproval. In *Nomad* (2010), Ayaan Hirsi Ali sums up the code: "An honor killing happens when a girl shames her family's reputation to the point that the only hope for them to restore that honor is to kill her. Her offense almost always relates to sex."[6] The reciprocal expectations that flagrantly constrain the autonomy and agency of young women help secure alliances in conditions of danger and scarcity.

Much less frequently, Muslim fathers kill homosexual sons to exorcise the shame they bring to their family's honor. Other honor-shame societies in ancient Greece or Renaissance Florence tolerated or even celebrated sexual relations between men. According to a Turkish sociologist, tribal Kurdish families publicize the murders of sexually active daughters "to help cleanse their shame." But gay honor killings remain hidden because a homosexual "taint[s] the concept of male identity upon which the community's social structure depend[s]." Conversely, in a more cosmopolitan city-state, one of the highest magistrates in fifteenth-century Florence responded to Savonarola's death, "Thank God, now we can return to our sodomy."[7]

Karen Armstrong's two biographies of Muhammad succinctly evoke the nomadic Bedouins'"chivalric code," which mandated *muruwah*, a word that loses its force when translated as "manliness." In *Muhammad: Prophet for Our Time* (2006), Armstrong argues that the term was as crucial as camels for survival on the desert. *Muruwah* implies not only courage in battle but also patience, endurance, and a determination to "avenge any wrong done to the group." The "honor of the tribe" superseded competing for individual honor, and stronger men had to protect the tribe's weaker members. "Above all, a tribesman had to be generous and share his livestock and food."[8]

Armstrong's earlier biography, *Muhammad: A Biography of the Prophet* (1991), notes the "deep fatalism" inherent in *muruwah*'s "fierce and absolute loyalty" to the tribe. On the desert only the tribe was real, and men would willingly die for the tribe's survival, which was always "desperately precarious." The Bedouins' widespread practice of polygamy had less to do with men's sexual desires than with political advancement and care for vulnerable women who lacked male protectors. Within and against this seventh-century code, Muhammad established Islam, which dramatically expanded the idea of the group from tribe to true believers. Now each man's "chivalrous duties" to care for the poor and vulnerable extended "to include all Muslims" instead of just the tribe.[9]

Ayaan Hirsi Ali's *Infidel* (2007) vividly recounts her experiences moving from an imperiled honor-bound family in tribal Africa to cosmopolitan mobility. The code that kept her family alive when she was a child suffocated her spirit before she gained freedom in the Netherlands and the United States. Like Azar Nafisi's *Reading Lolita in Tehran* (2003), *Infidel* gained a wide American audience in part by stimulating sympathies for strong-minded modern heroines oppressed by alien, retrograde, patriarchal cultures. Differences among Islamic faiths and practices in Iran, Pakistan, Afghanistan, Iraq, Syria, Saudi Arabia, and Egypt—or Somalia or Indonesia for that matter—could easily be erased in the appeal of that grand narrative. As several critics have said, Americans delight in saving brown women from brown men.

Yet *Infidel* portrays a more complex concept of honor than Hirsi Ali's later polemics imply. The memoir portrays her family as a crucible of patriarchal stresses. Intermittently, so is she. As the narrative begins, her grandmother praises her when she's five for reciting 300 years of her patriarchal lineage and beats her when she's eight until she learns 800 years of that lineage. Yet the honor of her father and all his fathers before him secured as well as constrained her identity. Clan honor and loyalty ensured family survival. Graphically Hirsi Ali describes the family's desperation during times of exile, when her father is in political danger far away and they have no resources. Only their extended kinship network keeps them alive.

The clan also provides a stable basis for identity. "It felt good to belong. This is what the bloodline was: this self-evident feeling of not having to justify your existence or explain anything." A little later she muses, "I didn't fit in. There was a sense of belonging in Somalia: I could take for granted who I was, and enjoyed the easy acceptance of my family and clan." But there's a "price I had to pay for that sense of belonging. Everyone was involved in everyone else's business. The complete lack of privacy, of individual space, and the social control were suffocating."[10]

Her mother exemplifies that price. Initially intrepid, she became profoundly depressed, while her commanding but absent husband balanced his political activism with other wives, all befitting his honor. Long after Hirsi Ali chooses self-reliant activism rather than submission to family and Islam, her guilt about enraging her father persists. When she plunges back into her family cauldron in her next book, *Nomad*, her father continues to preoccupy her. Though most of *Nomad* is a reductive screed against Islam, unresolvable tensions with her father leave her "living a life of ambiguity—with an outward presentation of modernity and self-reliance and an inward clinging to tradition and dependence on the clan." Such a life "stunts the process of becoming one's own person." Yet her love for her father persists.[11]

These intimate tensions oppressed and empowered her. Why do Islamic cultures so stifling to women produce forceful political and cultural figures such as Hirsi Ali, Azar Nafisi, or Marjane Satrapi? For one thing, all three young Islamic women had both a strong sense of high social status and patriarchal oppression in their backgrounds. Each developed a sometimes presumptuous self-confidence, and all three were able to seize cosmopolitan options unavailable to most women in their cultures.

Across many honor-shame cultures, men's control of women's sexual activity secures patrilineal lineage, since an unsanctioned baby threatens not only the family's reputation but also the transfer of property from father to son. In war, raping a woman linked to the enemy aims less at satiating sexual desire than at shaming the woman's male protectors. The threat of shaming stabilizes male hierarchies, especially in small groups beset by internal instabilities and external dangers. Such codes, which first took hold in Mediterranean cultures and Japan, function most intensely in tribes, villages, and kinship units.[12]

Honor involves more than an individual man's patriarchal standing. His whole sense of self reverberates with his male lineage, his ancestors and kin. Gift exchanges foster those bonds, which dictate violent revenge for any insult. An offense to one member disrespects everyone bound to him. Emboldened or entrapped as we are by expectations of individual achievement, many Americans may not know what it feels like for a man to feel grounded in a group rather than in independence, work, and ambition. As Bertram Wyatt-Brown has put it, drawing on the anthropologist Julian Pitt-Rivers, "the honor-shame ethos is deeply conservative and defensive." Every man "identifies with his lineage and his posterity. Kinlessness and solitude are the twin dangers to be avoided at all costs."[13]

In ancient Greece, Pericles' Funeral Oration remains the most eloquent statement of the warrior code. According to Thucydides, Pericles defines honor as having "the respect of one's fellow men." To die valorously "shows us the meaning of manliness in its first revelation and in its final proof." Such honor rewards "men who were ashamed to fall below a certain standard." Dying for Athens made them "worthy of their city." Several times Pericles grounds honor in the fear of being shamed. Those who chose to die in battle "fled from the reproaches of men," and found the "culmination of glory, not of fear," in their heroic ends.[14]

George Orwell's fear of being shamed in Burma mixes a personal sense of inadequacy with a consciousness that he represented the

British ruling class. Pericles' passion for honor is resolutely social. He affirms that men's fear of "humiliation" ultimately benefits the survival and triumph of their democracy. Tellingly, his oration concludes with "a short word of advice" to women, who have their own standard of reputation to measure up to. It's very simple: "the greatest glory of a woman is to be least talked about by men."[15]

Elsewhere in *History of the Peloponnesian War*, Thucydides approvingly recounts the speech of an Athenian who argues that fear, honor, and interest motivate men to go to war. They fear dangers to the "security" of their state, but they fear more the loss of honor that comes with displays of weakness or cowardice. These two speeches distill the appeal and requirements of honor in the ancient Mediterranean world.

Two other factors loom in Thucydides' version of this code. First, personal honor depends on a man's duty to his city-state. The first words of his history are, "Thucydides the Athenian wrote the history." Shame lurks in that self-identification and perhaps motivates his wish to write history, since he was exiled from Athens for twenty years. As a general in the first battle of Amphipolis, he was widely blamed for losing the city because of his lack of aggressiveness. Second, he starts his history by proudly declaring that Attica "has always been inhabited by the same race of people." Ascriptions of honor or shame presume homogeneous racial identifications and fierce group loyalty.[16]

Often wary of the law, inhabitants of more rural or dispersed honor-shame societies relied on their elders to settle disputes, from the Mediterranean to the American southwest. In nineteenth-century Greece, passions for honor diminished as respect for the rule of law increased.[17] As late as 1894, Mark Twain's *Pudd'nhead Wilson* satirized the antebellum southern gentry's preference for resolving conflicts through duels instead of the courts. When one of the Italian twins challenges Tom Driscoll to a duel after Tom publicly insults him, Tom shirks the fight by turning to the law. His white lawyer, David Wilson, and his faintly black mother, Roxy, are both appalled that he has dishonored his family's name. More tellingly, Wilson's reaction helps remove the shaming label of "Pudd'nhead" that had been affixed to him by his

Missouri townspeople twenty years earlier, when he first arrived. Soon he is elected mayor.

Larger Mediterranean groups that depended on trade as well as warfare made law part of their honor-shame dynamics. In northern Italy during the Renaissance, the leaders of various city-states commissioned prominent artists to paint pictures of elite men who had fled after being charged with a crime. Those paintings would be hung upside down on the city's walls as spectacles of public shaming. Many of the accused men voluntarily returned, because the humiliation to their families overrode their desire to escape punishment. Men who were exiled beyond their city walls felt banished from everything that defined them.[18]

If exile unmanned them, *virtù* ennobled them. That word has dwindled into "virtue." From Dante to Benvenuto Cellini to Benito Mussolini and Silvio Berlusconi, it connotes a man's ability to impose himself on his environment with impetuous force and devious calculation. In Jacob Burckhardt's version of a Renaissance sound bite, "a man in Italy was forced to be either hammer or anvil." One of the most disturbing passages in Machiavelli's *The Prince* opposes *virtù* to "Fortuna." "Fortune is a woman," he writes, "and the man who wants to hold her down must beat and bully her" to display mastery over his fate. In modern psychological terms, beating Fortune helps a man beat down the weak, feminine part of himself. Try to be feared, not liked, Machiavelli counsels. As Robert M. Adams summarizes the Tuscan ethic, it was much better to be a monster than a dupe.[19]

In what became the United States, the idea of the group expanded beyond the confines of the city-state. At various times, in various places, honor presumed loyalty to region, class, nation, or race. Before the white South came to exemplify sectional honor, the Revolution succeeded because a national elite confirmed each other's gentility through rituals of conflict and conflict resolution, including duels. Alexander Hamilton was a principal in ten "affairs of honor" before he was killed by Aaron Burr in his last duel. When James Monroe was John Adams's vice-president, he almost challenged the president to a duel because he thought Adams had dishonored him. In the new republic, a man of honor who wanted to maintain his position among the ruling elite had to defend his reputation at all costs. One historian suggests that the Civil War was the South's "final and disastrous duel for survival."[20]

Three examples can represent the countless instances joining personal honor to nation-building during the revolutionary era. The most well known remains the stirring pledge at the end of the Declaration of Independence: "our lives, our fortunes, and our sacred honor." Jefferson's words make honor the "sacred" culmination of that ascending sequence. *Virtù* looms in his call to overthrow British authority, though his display of reasoning mutes the audacity. Those complementary modes of self-presentation suited an eighteenth-century gentleman. Honor meant more than personal dignity; it displayed a man's ability to lead. A lesser aspect of honor looms in one of the principle causes of the colonists' rebellion. Taxation and honor are incompatible, because taxation implies unmanly dependence.[21]

Jefferson's pride in being an "author" preserved *virtù* with more explicit intimations of paternity. To be an author meant making a public impact, whether with words or action. Samuel Johnson's 1755 dictionary defined the word as "the first beginner or mover of anything."[22] Two years after Jefferson's death in 1826, Noah Webster's *An American Dictionary of the English Language* held to the traditional definition. "The Latin word [*auctor*] is from the root of *augeo*, to increase or cause to enlarge. The primary sense is one who brings or causes to come forth." The inscription on Jefferson's tombstone features "Thomas Jefferson, Author," and lists three public acts: writing the 1786 Virginia Statute for Religious Freedom, founding the University of Virginia, and writing the Declaration of Independence. For Jefferson these achievements were interchangeable forms of civic paternity. Carving "author" on his tombstone meant not that he had published a book—one that had been used against him in the 1800 election—but that he had a place in history as a "Founding Father."[23]

A second example illustrates how ideals of honor and fame had little to do with what we might call celebrity. Alexander Hamilton waxed rhapsodic about "that love of fame which is the ruling passion of the noblest minds." The original Latin word for fame was *fama*, or being talked about by strangers. By Hamilton's time, at least among the American gentry, fame had become equivalent to reputation among one's peers and "strangers" were important only when they were educated white men of property and privilege.[24]

Though Hamilton's choice of the word "fame" rather than "reputation" implies some yearning for wider respect in a new democracy, most Federalist leaders were more strictly honor bound. For the elite in the new republic, honor meant what Joseph Addison called *"the esteem of wise and good men."* Addison believed that public men of distinction should crave that approbation above anything else. They should be ruled "by the law of *honour* or *outward esteem*," he declared. Such honor is "a more obvious, and, generally, more binding law, to men so employed, than that of *virtue* or *self-esteem*." Whereas Machiavelli urged his prince not to bother with virtue, Addison ruefully mused that honor and virtue rarely coexist in the same person. The absence of virtue doesn't matter, he concluded, since honor "prompts to the same conduct which virtue prescribes."[25]

That class-linked sense of honor brought a cruel contradiction. Even as it spurred men to rebel against British rule, it made slavery a scornful synonym for dishonorable dependence. Edmund Morgan's *American Slavery, American Freedom* develops the contradiction's social consequences. What looks like inhumanity today made perfect sense to many white citizens of the new country. In *The Shaping of Southern Culture*, Wyatt-Brown argues that the seeming paradox of liberty and slavery disappears in the ethic of honor, which defined slavery as "a proper division of labor." Liberty meant "a hegemonic right to rule rather than a universal principle," and equality meant that "claims to honor are open to all members of the white fraternity on an equal footing," so long as the white men had "some minimal social standing." Humiliating black men often enhanced their standing, at least to themselves, as did their sexual exploitation of black women. As a necessary converse, slavery prevented black men from gaining honor through protecting their women or through affirming their lineage.[26]

In white rituals of honor, dueling was appropriate between equals, while caning was reserved for inferiors. Joanne Freeman argues that

68

HONOR BOUNDHONOR BOUND

the codes of regional honor diverged in the early nineteenth century as aristocratic presumptions were challenged by more democratic dynamics in the North, and as many in the northern elite became dubious about duels. When South Carolina representative Preston Brooks caned Massachusetts senator Charles Sumner on the Senate floor in 1856, the cane signified contempt, while the nearly lethal violence implied desperation. Sumner couldn't return to the Senate for over three years. Brooks's caning of Sumner shows that "the nationalization of politics led to a backlash of defensive regionalism, played out most dramatically in honor disputes on the floor of Congress."[27]

Another example shows Benjamin Franklin being shamed. As one result, he redefined his peer group. In January 1774, Franklin was vilified by many members of Parliament for having leaked some letters from Massachusetts governor Thomas Hutchinson to an English friend, Thomas Whately. It was a major spectacle of humiliation. The solicitor general, Andrew Wedderburn, denounced him before the Privy Council in an address that took nearly an hour. "I hope, my Lords, you will mark and brand this man for the honour of this country, of Europe, and of mankind. . . . He will henceforth esteem it a libel to be called a man of letters." Other blasts by Wedderburn were so coarse that newspapers didn't print them. Franklin later called the tirade a "Bull-baiting."[28]

Franklin was in the audience. When Wedderburn's attack began, he immediately rose from his seat and stood silently during the entire excoriation. As a friend described him, "The Doctor was dressed in a full suit of spotted Manchester velvet, and stood conspicuously erect, without the smallest movement of any part of his body. The muscles of his face had been previously composed as to afford a placid tranquil expression of countenance, and he did not suffer the slightest alteration of it to appear."[29]

Within two days, Franklin was fired as deputy postmaster general for the American colonies. More important, after another year of fruitless effort, he gave up his hope of reconciliation with Britain and returned to America. When Parliament voted to declare Americans "rebels," this Anglophilic member of the Royal Society cast his lot with the revolutionaries. The English had blamed the messenger, he concluded, and they refused to hear the message. As he wrote to Thomas Cushing, "where complaining is a crime, hope becomes despair." Edmund Morgan pithily sums up the dilemma: "The American Revolution was a civil war, and for no one more than Franklin."[30]

The American Englishman's mute erectness was an astonishing display of bravado, since he had clearly violated the honor of the men who had welcomed him into their cosmopolitan club. No gentleman should read another gentleman's private mail. Franklin not only read Hutchinson's letters, he sent them to friends who publicized them. Moreover, he betrayed a man considered his social superior. Why would the son of a Boston candlemaker destroy his new class standing? The answer, to me at least, is that he was standing up for his country. In fact, he was building that country.

Various biographies detail the complicated circumstances. While living in England, Franklin had received an anonymous packet containing private letters from Hutchinson and his brother-in-law, Lieutenant Governor Andrew Oliver, to Thomas Whately, an English defender of the Stamp Act. Whately had just died, and someone still unknown had sent the letters to Franklin, who sent them to Cushing, a friend in Boston. Though Franklin suggested that they be circulated only among friends and "a few such other Gentlemen," Cushing read them aloud to the Massachusetts Assembly. Soon they were in print, and by a vote of eighty to eleven, the Assembly petitioned to recall Hutchinson and Oliver. Ostensibly the Privy Council was meeting to consider that petition.

The contents enraged colonists, because Hutchinson contemptuously asserted that the people's liberties and their right to popular government should be abridged. Eventually Hutchinson had to return to England. At first no one knew Franklin was involved. Gossip focused on a friend of Whately, John Temple, whom Whately's brother challenged to a duel in Hyde Park. After that inconclusive encounter, the brother threatened a second challenge. To avoid bloodshed, Franklin placed a notice in the *London Chronicle* that "I alone am the person who obtained and transmitted to Boston the letters in question." The notice appeared on December 25, 1773. It was his Christmas present to England.[31]

The Privy Council first summoned Franklin in early January, but when he saw that the solicitor general was there, he realized that he needed a lawyer. He was granted three more weeks to prepare. During the interim, news of the Boston Tea Party reached London, further inflaming the situation, to Franklin's private dismay. Nevertheless, at the end of Wedderburn's public humiliation, Franklin's counsel said his client refused to be examined. Throughout, Franklin maintained his silence. For a few days afterward he hid, afraid that he would be arrested or his papers confiscated.

Franklin had released the letters in the hope that rational English minds would be more favorably disposed toward the colonists' sense of injustice. A few were, notably Edmund Burke and William Pitt the Elder, both good friends of Franklin. But most members of Parliament were outraged, especially in the House of Lords. In mid-March of 1775, just after Franklin had embarked for what would soon become the United States, Burke gave one of his most impassioned speeches, "On Conciliation with America," to no effect.

Over a year before he left, Franklin's release of the letters signaled what his proud silence during the shaming confirmed, that he now defined himself more as an American patriot than as a member of the English gentry. From that point of view, Hutchinson was an oppressor, not a gentleman. Where another gentleman might have covered his face, Franklin faced down legitimate charges of dishonor by displaying honor's most basic element, a refusal to show any fear, vulnerability, or submission. He was like Uncas at the stake near the end of James Fenimore Cooper's *The Last of the Mohicans*. His impassive cool made him look impervious to the scorching contempt of British leaders. The colonial had turned the tables.[32]

Franklin's act expanded what it meant to be an aristocrat. Here Benedict Anderson's idea that race enables emigrants to "play aristocrat off centre court" can be qualified. Racial hierarchy was only one way that elite Americans affirmed each other's gentility and faced down British scorn. In the South, slaves displayed a man's gentry status. Franklin turned to a different kind of colonial aristocracy, based more on merit than on inherited wealth or divisions between mental and physical labor. Bedouins believed that *muruwah* was transmitted through the blood. Italian men during the Renaissance believed that *virtù* required physical and mental dominance. But Jefferson and Franklin believed that honor required displays of reasoning as well as the courage to rebel against unjust authority. They sought the esteem of a new group, the national elite they helped create, and they sought to free that group from subservience to the metropolitan center overseas.

I'm advancing these broad-brush sketches of honor's various cultural manifestations to reach a simple point. Today honor seems to be a retrograde affair. Alexander Welsh reduces it to "dignity," though he does ground dignity in a peer group's respect, and Gordon Wood associates it with an individual's aristocratic reputation in tension with democratic values that undermine the code.[33] Anthropologists talk about the change from cultures of honor to cultures of dignity, especially after World War II.[34] But a personal drive to enhance respect constitutes only the outer shell of the code's enabling energies. Under all the personal striving the code inspires, honor defines a group and protects the group's survival.

Honor continues to matter most to men who define themselves primarily as members of an intimate, knowable group in stressful conditions. From Samurai warriors to American gangs and army units, the honor code protects the embattled group in conditions of threat and conflict. To the degree that people live in multiple groups or become mobile beyond knowable communities, honor matters less or not at all, except as personal dignity. Shaming matters less too, because shaming helps consolidate a group.[35]

Contradictory aspects of honor become valued differently as the definition of group expands from tribe to city and then beyond knowable communities to class, race, and nation.[36] In America, defining oneself as "white" has sometimes stabilized a sense of belonging where local and immediate bonds are hard to come by. At least white skin seems instantly recognizable. Honor functions to protect that imagined group's stabilization, especially when the dominance of whiteness is threatened. Honor attenuates only when such belonging starts to feel unreal, when membership becomes a matter of choice rather than necessity, or when people start to define themselves through multiple associations. Then the survival of one's group doesn't seem so crucial.

In the last fifty years, all three of those changes have threatened the group called white Americans.

From Bedouin tribesmen to Florentine aristocrats, from elite leaders of the American Revolution to plantation owners in the antebellum South, honor was sparked by its contradictions. As a warrior code, it demands valor, displays of virility, and aggressive responses to any insult. Yet honor demands prudence, calm, and the wisdom to adjudicate conflicts. Honor requires ambition, contentiousness, and success in combat; honor requires self-sacrifice, duty, and modesty. Amid the welter of shifting imperatives, honor-shame societies have shared at least three basic values. Maintaining or enhancing a man's reputation among his peers animates his behavior. Preserving the group supersedes individual ambition. Above all, a man of honor must never show any weakness or fear. Then he would instantly lose face. How his peers see him matters much more than his inward state of mind because the group matters more than the individual.[37]

Ultimately honor helps men define insiders and outsiders and see outsiders as threats. That's a fundamental survival strategy for small groups, and it may even be hard-wired in the brain.[38] In the nation of immigrants that became the United States, that code often functioned as a life raft for social survival. It preserved a sense of local identity and sometimes a sense of superiority. Though the code directly challenges the American valuing of pluralism and equal opportunity for everyone, defending shared honor secures respect as well as membership in a beleaguered community.

For Americans of nearly every ethnic persuasion, the pursuit of collective honor through spectacles of controlled violence has long since been outsourced to wars and sports, particularly football and basketball. Agonistic sports give many fans a chance to imaginatively exercise their vicarious masculinity. On the field, an athlete's trash talk claims honor by shaming a rival. In many urban areas, young men's insecurities about belonging lead to agonistic displays. To be "dissed" often requires assault to avenge the shaming. Honor is alive and well in these small groups, sometimes racialized but more often not.

Concerns about masculinity differ from concerns about honor. Masculinity emphasizes the individual, not the group. The word didn't come into widespread use until the late nineteenth century, when corporations reoriented a great many men from the goal of gaining status in their communities toward the goal of advancing or at least surviving in a more national workplace. Gail Bederman finds the noun's first use in 1854.[39] Subsequent preoccupations with masculinity diminish honor to displays of independence. After the New Orleans Saints' Super Bowl victory in January of 2010, a running back talked about how Sean Payton, the coach, had built their confidence. "He doesn't care what anybody thinks. He's all man."[40] That statement would be inconceivable in a culture that emphasizes reputation. It's the end point of the transformation from village patriarchy to democratic diversity and mobility in a nation-state.

From a different angle, Jonathan Haidt's influential 2008 Internet article analyzed an implicitly honor-based moral framework among American conservatives who value hierarchical families, not equal individuals, as the fundamental units of social being. "What Makes People Vote Republican?" doesn't use the word "honor." Nevertheless, Haidt applies Emile Durkheim's honor-related values that progressives tend to minimize: tribal "ingroup/loyalty," "authority/respect," and "purity/sanctity," accompanied by "disgust" for carnality. Whereas liberals emphasize rights, the root meaning and function of the word "moral" is to bind groups together and regulate selfishness. Haidt notes that a visit to India opened his blinkered liberal mind to the values and virtues of interdependent families and tribes.[41]

Honor has a long and often admirable history. Its problematic qualities proliferate when large, expansive groups demand that its members be "honor bound" to preserve the group's superiority rather than protect its survival.

Tocqueville on American Honor

In 1840, the second volume of Alexis de Tocqueville's *Democracy in America* argued that the pressures of ambition, mobility, and workplace advancement augmented the dangers of "individualism." The word had been invented in the 1820s by conservative French Jesuits who were appalled at its threat to community and social hierarchy.[42]

For Tocqueville, individualism was one of democracy's two greatest dangers, along with the "tyranny of the majority" that his first volume warned against in 1835. Americans reading the translation of his second volume promptly turned the term into a badge of national identity. His chapter on honor shows how American individualism had already relocated the concept. In traditional societies, honor defines reciprocal obligations in a localized hierarchy. Except in the South, Americans applied it to mobile individuals in the nation-state. These individuals were free because they were white.

A passage from Frances Fitzgerald's *Fire in the Lake* (1972) illuminates the change. In the Vietnamese language, she writes, no word matches the West's personal pronoun "I." "When a man speaks of himself, he calls himself 'your brother,' 'your nephew,' your teacher,' depending upon his relationship to the person he addresses." Even in the "new impersonal world" of cities, the word used originally meant "subject of the king." In that language, the self was "a system of relationships," unlike the American perceptions of self and nation-state that governed the long failed war in Vietnam.[43]

Tocqueville exposes that transformation in the making. As race and nation became the primary large-group affiliations by which white Americans defined themselves, their affiliations with family, kin, and community sometimes contracted to a majority of one. In Tocqueville's eyes, democracy tends to throw every man "back forever upon himself alone and . . . confine him entirely within the solitude of his own heart."[44] When ambitious, foraging selves reduced honor to personal dignity, the defense of self, race, and country became all in all.

In *What Is Honor?*, Alexander Welsh celebrates Tocqueville's "brilliant" perception "that nationhood could well be absorbing individual honor" by supplanting feudal hierarchy as the legitimating basis of honor. Rejecting Tocqueville's insistence that honor requires social stratification, Welsh resuscitates honor by equating it with dignity and respect, which he sees as "the active principle of honor both ancient and modern."[45] It's easy to extend that concept to women and black people or anyone else who gains social respect and preserves self-respect. Welsh's translation of honor into terms suitable for contemporary egalitarian individualism marks the end point of the transformation that Tocqueville witnessed at its creation.

Tocqueville's argument is a little more complex than Welsh's brief consideration of it allows, though as Welsh says, the French observer always "keeps thinking around the subject and coming up with more insights."[46] In chapter 18 of book three, Tocqueville asserts that "honor is simply that peculiar rule" by which "a people or a class allot praise or blame." Medieval definitions of honor as "fidelity to the person of the lord" rather than "patriotism" have been replaced in America by "commercial" definitions, except in the South. The "quiet virtues" of business have replaced the "turbulent virtues" of military valor, which has only "a subordinate rank" in people's respect, far below the passion for wealth. "Boldness of enterprise" receives the highest approval, along with male chastity, a highly debatable assumption.[47] One wonders about Tocqueville's database.

Unlike Europeans, who see idleness as a mark of aristocratic status, white Americans who are not from the South see idleness as shameful. Even men of wealth are "compelled to embrace a profession." Unlike all other commercial nations, America shows a "strange indulgence" for bankrupts; "their honor does not suffer by such an accident."[48] It is business courage, not success, that matters. At least in the nineteenth century, wealth became an American signifier of hard work, not a display of inherited family status. (As late as the 1930s, in his prison diaries, Antonio Gramsci expressed baffled admiration that American millionaires didn't retire to live a life of leisure, as any rich European man would do.)[49]

As Tocqueville muses about why honor seems more entrenched in the American South, he comes up with a new idea. There has to be "a close and necessary relation between the inequality of social conditions and what has here been styled honor," an observation that "had not before been clearly pointed out." Besides, in every other part of the United States, "all men are in constant motion" amid constantly transforming social situations. Such men gain only "glimpses of the rules of honor" and did not have much time for the rules of the code. Tocqueville's speculation that honor requires inequality anticipates

Benedict Anderson's speculation that colonials played aristocrat by
making race.[50]

Tocqueville's other new idea has even more far-reaching implications. The more equal the ranks, he argues, the more honor "denotes
the individual character of that nation to the world." Personifying
the nation as an "individual" aids the quest for international recognition and respect. But equality has a price. Unlike Welsh, Tocqueville
concludes that if there were no inequalities and dissimilarities, honor
"would disappear."[51]

Tocqueville's key insight, that democracy joins "individual character"
to national honor, percolates through the rest of this book. Yet his
observations carry a paradox. In the antebellum United States, passion
for the union was a sectional affair. The nation mattered far more in
the North than in the South. In the North, Bertram Wyatt-Brown
argues, honor "was less connected to family and community. Instead
it was tied to institution and abstract symbol—nationhood, the flag,
the perpetual Union." For Daniel Webster and for many others, "Union
was synonymous with liberty." After the Civil War, race helped put
South and North together again. As Tocqueville noted in 1835, "the
white citizen of the United States is proud of his race and proud of
himself." Such citizens had combined to produce "the most grasping
nation on the globe."[52]

National honor presumed the expansion of one race's dominance. In
The History of White People, Nell Irvin Painter finds four "enlargements
of American whiteness": the elimination of property requirements
for white male voters, the grudging inclusion of German and Irish
immigrants and then southern European immigrants after the Civil
War, the inclusion of Mexican Americans and working-class ethnics
into the middle class after World War II, and the inclusion of Asians
and Latinos after 1965. I think the last two enlargements also challenged
white supremacy.[53] Robert Levine similarly traces the complex inter-
weaving of nationalism and race in American constructions of white
supremacy throughout the nineteenth century. Eventually a grudging
inclusiveness developed—first elite white men, then white men, then
white men and women, then other European immigrants. In *The Honor
Code*, Kwame Anthony Appiah argues that national honor has been a

progressive force that worked to eradicate dueling and the slave trade as well as Chinese foot-binding. But when light-skinned Americans appropriated the honor of being white, that collective self-definition mandated flagrant racism as well as racial shamings.[54]

To the degree that honor was for white people only, white people looked to their peers for recognition. Like honor, racism became what Deborah Eisenberg calls an "adjunct of nationalism." She marvels at "how efficient and universal an instrument" racism and anti-Semitism can be "in establishing and maintaining self-respect."[55] In the American version of racism, whites assiduously practiced shaming nonwhite people to preserve the privileged group. Like honor, racism feels intensely individual. But it's a collective code manifested through individuals. It is extraordinarily difficult to withstand the pressure of a group to which you really want to belong, especially when that group claims lordly status.

When Honor Turned White

This section's heading bows to Noel Ignatiev's fine book, *How the Irish Became White*. It also plays with "turning white" as an implicit state of fear. I've been arguing that fear as well as rationalizations for race-based power impel all proclamations of white superiority. By emphasizing the fear, I also imply that honor took a cowardly turn. The paradox of using race-based shaming to secure personal and national honor exposes the dishonor in crushing the aspirations of people who are assigned to another group.

When whiteness joins with honor, as it did in the United States after the Civil War, shaming becomes more generic than personal. Among a very large group defined by the superiority of white skin color, threats or insults from people with despised colors have to be instantly countered and contained. Defending equality or sympathizing with an accused black person may mean you're not white enough.

In the United States, the relentless shaming that made race consciousness so vivid on every side transformed honor from its traditional status as a personal state of self-respect in small groups to an identification with a race-based aristocracy on a national scale.[56] To preserve their racial honor, whites singled out black men who ventured to transgress real or imagined public/private boundaries, master/servant boundaries, or intimacy boundaries. In the South, as Edward Ayers notes, "the cult of honor became less formalized (and probably more dangerous in the process)" after the 1860s.[57] The cult of honor licensed white revenge for any imagined disrespect, especially by black men. After the North accommodated the white South by ending Reconstruction in 1876, these southern responses became national reflexes.

Before the Civil War, the antebellum South's code of honor already opposed the impersonal commercial relations that had taken hold in the North. As Ayers summarizes the code, honor "thrives in a rural society of face-to-face contact" and shared values. Depending on "a hierarchical society" and a "weak" state for settling disputes, it is "a system of beliefs in which a person has exactly as much worth as others confer upon him." "Women . . . could have no honor—only virtue"; black people could not have honor either, in white eyes. Men grounded personal feelings of worth in the regard of their male peers. Combative hot-headedness and readiness for duels counted for almost as much as ownership of land and slaves.[58]

Especially in Virginia, many thoughtful white men understood that slavery was intrinsically dishonorable. It's well known that Jefferson struggled in vain to extricate himself and his new country from the intractable contradiction slavery posed to his belief that "all men are created equal." When he died, he (perhaps discreetly) didn't free Sally Hemings, though he did free their children, leaving over a hundred other black people enslaved. As Annette Gordon-Reed recounts, Sally Hemings was freed within two years of Jefferson's death, and an 1830 census taker declared that she and two of their children were white. Jefferson, a flagrant racist, may have considered all four of their surviving children white. He let some other white-looking slaves run away, and he freed several other Hemingses, including Sally's brothers.[59]

Patrick Henry's candid response to an antislavery book got to the heart of the matter. Less familiar than his famous cry "give me liberty, or give me death!" is Henry's letter to Anthony Benezet, thanking him for his book opposing slavery. "Every thinking honest man rejects [slavery] in Speculation, how few in practice? Would anyone believe that I am Master of slaves of my own purchase? I am drawn along by ye general Inconvenience of livving without them; I will not, I cannot justify it." For Henry, convenience trumped honor.[60]

How did the nation-state transform that frame of mind by joining racism to white honor? Most studies of race in America after the Civil War, even in the postbellum South, don't have honor or shame in the index. On the surface, the absence seems reasonable, since the consolidation of the country undermined the basis for personal honor in small, stable, mutually monitoring communities. Ideals of Christian virtue also put the code on the defensive after the war.[61] Yet many whites felt honor bound to block African Americans who wanted political power and social equality. As W.E.B. Du Bois wrote in the passage that gave David Roediger the title for *The Wages of Whiteness*, northern white laborers were "compensated in part by a sort of public and psychological wage. They were given public deference and titles of courtesy because they were white." After the Civil War a great variety of court decisions at state and national levels created the legal fiction of white collectivity, despite remarkable shifts and ambiguities in defining what constituted "black blood." As Eva Saks has shown in detail, the postwar language of "blood" preserved whites' prewar status before political and economic threats to their group dominance emerged. Implicitly it preserved the long-running legal definition of black people as property. Most of these laws criminalized sexual intercourse between black men and white women.[62]

In the antebellum South, as in other honor-bound cultures, male honor often featured fathers' ability to control their chaste and dutiful daughters. As chapter one emphasizes, after the Civil War that metonym expanded to the large-scale chivalry exemplified by white men's ability to protect the virtue of white women without regard to kinship. Fresh from their humiliating defeat, southern white men made chivalry their fallback position.[63] Women continued to function as signifiers for mutual self-respect among white men, but now in an arena beyond the family. When economic adversity exacerbated the loss of the war, men found a new source of self-respect in their war against the "black beasts." Now any white woman needed an honorable man's protection.

In threatening times, monsters can be invigorating as well as clarifying. The specter of black men ravishing white women became a compelling shorthand for white men's fears of losing economic and political privilege. Kenneth Warren suggests that in the post-Reconstruction United States, whites represented claims for justice and equality "as vulgar demands for social intimacy" and used "a reconstruction of social distance between black and white persons in American society" to restore ideals of order. That hierarchic "decorum" depended on reducing victims of injustice to "objects of disgust." Disgust, fear, and claims to honor converged in outrage at the thought of black rape, which became the most useful intensifier for anxieties about interracial intimacy and economic competition.[64]

American laws against "amalgamation" were on the books from 1661 to 1967. The first state law criminalizing marriage between black men and white women was passed in Maryland in 1661. The United States was unique among all nations throughout world history for the length of time its states enforced laws prohibiting interracial sexual relations and marriage. Some of them were in force for over three centuries, until the Supreme Court struck them down in *Loving v. Virginia* (1967). Similar laws in South Africa held sway only from 1948 to 1984. In the 1856 Dred Scott decision, the Supreme Court made the United States unique in another way. Historian Don Fehrenbacher writes that as a consequence, "*American Negroes, free and slave, were the only people on the face of the earth who (saving a constitutional amendment) were forever ineligible for American citizenship.*"[65]

Such prejudice wasn't unique to white Americans. Winthrop Jordan's *White over Black* shows that European colonizers perceived Africans as inferior because they saw Africans as black, a color associated with evil and baseness. Europeans also linked Africans to apes and other bestial creatures. By the 1750s, when David Hume declared Africans "naturally inferior to the whites," explicit arguments for white racism had begun to cohere, though it would be another century before the ideology was widely accepted. By 1900, "Caucasian" had become interchangeable with "Aryan," "Anglo-Saxon," and "Teuton" as self-evident justifications for white supremacy.[66] Long before then, white Americans' paranoia about black men's sexual involvement with white women had gone far beyond European norms.

Even before the failure of Reconstruction, a shared passion for white honor helped rejoin South and North, in part by turning to nativism. John Higham's *Strangers in the Land* shows how white New England patricians reacted to the flood of immigrants from southern Europe. In sometimes conflicting ways, they joined racism and nativism with regional defenses of their upper-class status. By 1916, Madison Grant's *The Passing of the Great Race* argued that racism was more crucial for preserving the white elite than Christianity, democracy, or national consciousness.[67] Woodrow Wilson, a Virginian, made racism a keystone of his domestic policies, and the effects lasted for decades.

"The Souls of White Folk"

By World War I, American national identity presumed whiteness as the country's leaders sought international honor and prestige. W.E.B. Du Bois's "The Souls of White Folk" (1920) exposes the shaming effects of that presumption. His essay also illuminates a basic paradox. When honor protects whiteness, whiteness becomes dishonorable.

"The Souls of White Folk" tries to return white people's humiliations. Du Bois angrily calls World War I a colonial war in which white people's nations competed to exploit people of darker colors. World War I seemed "horrible" only because "white men are fighting white men" for a change. At bottom the war was simply for "colonial aggrandizement" and expansion. For Du Bois, "this seeming Terrible is the real soul of white culture." Modern Europe has discovered "the eternal world-wide mark of meanness—color!"[68]

Du Bois's revision of the story of the world war appeared five years after Lenin had published his critique of capitalist imperialism, and his argument has a Leninist tinge. Few historians give much credit to Du Bois's claim that "this competition for the labor of yellow, brown, and black folks . . . was the cause of the World War."[69] Most of Du Bois's essay sounds imperiously reductive, even as he indicts "the heaven-defying audacity" of imperialism. In his account, World War I is like the many other imperial wars he lists: it helped white people avoid class war by using "the exploitation of darker peoples" to keep poor whites half content. But the "subjection of the white working classes cannot much longer be maintained." A global utopian apocalypse may be at hand because people of darker colors so outnumber white people, Du Bois contends. Much as Tocqueville predicted for the United States in 1840, Du Bois predicts race war, now on a worldwide scale. Besides, white people will lose because "the day of the very rich is drawing to a close, so far as individual white nations are concerned." In all of his writings, no other sentence that I've encountered seems quite so dated.[70]

Du Bois's rage against racial shaming, not his Marxist conclusion about the war, gives the essay its scathing energy. Again and again he repeats the word "despising." As the most prominent black intellectual in the United States, he couldn't believe that white racism still branded himself and other black people, just as it stigmatized undifferentiated darker people worldwide. Whites aren't just out for exploitation, he says; they also want to humiliate. "When the black man begins to dispute the white man's title . . . when his attitude toward charity is sullen anger rather than humble jollity; when he insists on his human right to swagger and swear and waste," then "the philanthropist is ready to believe that Negroes are impudent, that the South is right." The faces of white men show "a deep and passionate hatred, vast by the very vagueness of its expressions."[71]

He addresses white readers directly. "Ask your own soul what it would say if the next census were to report that half of black America was dead and the other half dying." Readers who are pleased at this thought are complicit with race-based hatred and despising, equivalent concepts that keep circling back in Du Bois's essay. He rails against "the despising and robbing of darker peoples" and "the human hatred, the despising of men." If you say to a people, "'The one virtue is to be white,'" don't be surprised that "the people rush to the inevitable conclusion, 'Kill the "nigger!"'"[72]

For Du Bois, racist shaming enforced the colonial expansion that triggered World War I. Relentlessly he hammers at his theme. "We whose shame, humiliation, and deep insult his aggrandizement so often involved were never deceived." The war was "not for assimilation and uplift, but for commerce and degradation." That sequence rests on "degradation." The current white "gospel" preaches "the necessary despisings and hatreds of these savage half-men, this unclean *canaille* of the world—these dogs of men. . . . above all, it pays!" The labor of colored peoples "is kept cheap and helpless because the white world despises 'darkies.'"[73]

Over and over, Du Bois returns to the "hatred and despising of human beings" whom Europe wishes to exploit. Will Europe continue "the despising and robbing of darker peoples? If Europe hugs this delusion, then this is not the end of world war—it is but the beginning!" This "shameful war . . . *is nothing to compare with that fight for freedom which black and brown and yellow men must and will make unless their oppression and humiliation and insult at the hands of the White World cease.*" What is coming is "the armed and indignant protest of these despised and raped peoples."[74]

Du Bois can't let go of that word "despising." "Europe's greatest sin" is "human hatred, the despising of men." America "trains her immigrants to this despising of 'niggers' from the day of their landing," and the immigrants train their compatriots. His conclusion tries to transcend his rage by imagining "this Soul of White Folk" hanging like Prometheus, "bound by his own binding" and crying, "'I am white!'" Very well then, he concludes. "Why, then, devour your own vitals if I answer even as proudly, 'I am black!'"[75]

According to his biographer, David Levering Lewis, Du Bois revised this essay for a decade. His final version "belched fire" and "seemed almost to scream."[76] The rage anticipates Du Bois's final years, when he joined the Communist Party and moved to Ghana in despair at the hopelessness of overcoming U.S. racism. The most cogent aspect of this essay, Lewis concludes, remains its emphasis on how white leaders used racism to sell imperial expansion to white working classes.[77] I see it differently. Rage at the daily, hourly, minute-by-minute humiliation of being a black man sparks Du Bois's fire. His desperate anger bespeaks an equally desperate pride in black manhood. Critics have rightly faulted Du Bois for his lifelong patriarchal presumptions. But his impelling passion to reclaim black manhood resists pervasive white perceptions that any black man is a problem, a threat, a beast, or a boy.[78]

"The Souls of White Folk" gives new bite to Emerson's dismissal of New England philanthropists in his essay "Self-Reliance": "Thy charity abroad is spite at home." Whether in charities or wars, the recurrent drive to uplift less modernized peoples has propped up national fantasies linking whiteness to honor. These crusades have helped minimize white citizens' nervousness about not living up to democratic and egalitarian ideals at home. The unspoken illogic carries the implication that "if we're so generous and self-sacrificing in fighting for other countries, then black people should be Americans like us and help themselves. Otherwise they deserve to be despised and degraded."

For Du Bois, white souls are terrified of the black people they humiliate. As he argues in "The Negro Mind Reaches Out," "Back of all these attitudes is Fear. . . . the fear of the colored world."[79] Such fears also consolidated a group called whites. As a white person in the early twenty-first century, I can say that with ease. As a black person in the early twentieth century, Du Bois felt reduced to a degraded and exploited group. America could fight its wars with advanced technologies. Du Bois's only weapons were words.

CHAPTER 4

FOUR NOVELS

In the last chapter, I sketched the expansion of the honor code from protecting a small group's survival to protecting a very large group's racial supremacy. Racial shaming not only separated insiders from outsiders but also helped light-skinned Americans feel more white. Using novels and wars, the next two chapters explore the growing sense of desperation in those attempts to secure racialized honor.

The first section briefly considers Stephen Crane's *The Monster* (1899) and Jonathan Franzen's *Freedom* (2010), with a nod to William Faulkner's *Light in August* (1932). These narratives present racial shaming with a shifting mix of empathy and satire. Then I trace the increasing shamefulness of whiteness through close readings of *The Scarlet Letter* (1850), *Adventures of Huckleberry Finn* (1885), *The Great Gatsby* (1925), and *Lolita* (1955). I've chosen these four novels because I think they're representative and canonical, because they were published thirty to forty years apart, and because I love them. Each narrative replicates and undermines its culture's racial shaming practices. Other novels might be used to reinforce or complicate my analyses, and using movies could expand this chapter to a book. Giving detailed attention to just one sequence of narratives carries a risk but also a reward. Racial tensions come alive without being resolved into sound bites and stereotypes.

Close reading has often been dismissed as a form of apolitical aesthetics. Especially when the critical practice took hold, it gave many privileged sensibilities a glimpse of drug-free transcendence. But the method doesn't have to be so detached from social conflicts. For the last sixty years, awareness of racial hierarchy as an oppressive fiction has come to many white people as well as to every African American. The experience has thoroughly reoriented how critics attend to literary texts and what texts get attended to. Yet close reading remains the basis for everything literary critics do, because it can illuminate the complex tensions muffled in both ideologies and fictions. Attention to the uses of language doesn't have to serve any kind of supremacy, aesthetic or otherwise.

Toward *Freedom?*

Except for the levels of violence, racial shaming must have looked changeless to African Americans for centuries. On the white side, the ground was shifting. From the 1820s on, race became a primary category for establishing the superiority of whites and the inferiority of nonwhites.[1] In a second shift, at the turn of the twentieth century, immigrants from Europe and Asia and African Americans moving north brought greater fears of racial mixture and more strenuous allegiance to an abstract white America. From Cuba and the Philippines to Iraq, the government's attempts at overseas expansion ambivalently sought to extend the reign of civilizing whiteness.[2] In 1902 and 1903, many white Americans pushed to solve the "Negro problem" by recolonizing black Americans in the Philippines, where blacks would allegedly be more comfortable.[3]

At the same time, those intensifications of white supremacy betrayed its fragility. Slowly the United States' rise to cosmopolitan status as a world power undermined the whitened honor that justified racial shaming, especially after World War II, though the attacks on September 11, 2001, sparked a renewed surge directed at Muslims.

The four novels I focus on dramatize and challenge conventions that defined what was shameful. What Chillingworth does to revenge himself against Dimmesdale, what Tom and Huck do to enslave Jim, what Gatsby does to repossess his dream of Daisy's whiteness, what Humbert does to bed Lolita are all obviously shameful. More surprisingly, honor becomes a marginal concern. These novels reflect complex ambivalences about race and sometimes a simplifying racism. In each narrative, claims to white honor fail to contain the threat of racial mixture and equality.

Other texts could serve to advance these claims. Just to mention three: in *Light in August*, Faulkner's Joe Christmas mixes honor and shame with white and black. As Bill Hardwig puts it, he is "trying to straddle both sides of a crumbling fence." Over three decades earlier, Stephen Crane's novella *The Monster* dramatizes what it feels like to lose face over race in a small northern community. Dr. Trescott's black servant, Henry Johnson, is physically defaced by a fire as he saves Trescott's son. Then the doctor is professionally defaced for trying to take care of this "monster." One of his friends-turned-shamer, Judge Hagenthorpe, has a cane with an ivory head, as if whiteness has become a prop for crippled authority. By the end, Trescott's resolute adherence to honor seems as hollow as his wife's fifteen empty teacups. She set them out for a party, but nobody came.[4]

Over a century later, Jonathan Franzen's *Freedom* presents a hyper-segregated America where every white character wants to feel extraordinary. Like their Minnesota neighbors, Walter and Patty Berglund are barely aware that their town has been built by the practice of dispossessing black people. They're preoccupied with freeing themselves by becoming ruthlessly competitive. "Nice" and "good" quickly become four-letter words. No one wants to love and be loved. Instead, Walter and his much more successful son Joey want women who are adoring fans, while Patty becomes an adoring fan, though not of her husband. She wants to be raped, first by ineffectual Walter, and then by Richard, an "anti-rock star" who enters with black hair, a black T-shirt, and a black room. Richard's dark appeal centers her all-white universe, especially when he "banged her into ecstasy" against the wallpaper in the house of Walter's dead mother. To compete with Richard, Walter sets up a huge bird sanctuary that provides environmentalist cover for a rapacious Texas billionaire.

All that, Franzen implies, is what happens when white people fetishize freedom. The drive to be extraordinary hides an inward void as well as the erasure of black people. But black keeps returning, not only as Richard but also as Walter's fan and lover Lalitha, a young Indian American woman whom someone calls "that nigger girl."[5] In a hauntingly ambiguous ending, Patty nestles like a little wounded bird into Walter's arms, and they subside into the masquerades and compromises of ordinary living. Throughout, in a post-Hawthornian mode, the novel updates Crane's strategy of blending empathy with sometimes-formulaic satire. Franzen makes *Freedom* a public shaming of "nice" white liberals. The novel exposes how dreams of freedom invite dishonor.

As in so many other American fictions, these stories explore what they resist: that white may not mean superior and black may not mean inferior.

The Scarlet Letter

One story of public shaming in Ayaan Hirsi Ali's *Infidel* (2007) can illustrate the traditional honor code that Hawthorne ambiguously challenges. Fawzia, an unmarried distant relative, arrives at the family doorstep in Kenya with a three-year-old boy. Though Hirsi Ali's mother wants to reject Fawzia as "the living face of shame," she and her sister persuade their mother to let her in. Soon Somalis "shunned" and "molested" Fawzia on the street for being a "harlot." Worse, she has "no clan protector. She was prey." She even thinks she deserves the abuse. Fawzia stays with them for a few months, then disappears from their lives and the narrative. If they had been in Somalia rather than non-Islamic Kenya, Fawzia probably would have been flogged or killed. As Hirsi Ali tells her readers, "Most unmarried Somali girls who got pregnant committed suicide."[6]

Four centuries earlier, in Puritan Massachusetts during the 1640s, Hester Prynne's community tries to bring a sexually active woman under patriarchal control, though without flogging or killing. *The Scarlet Letter* begins with the most famous instance of public shaming in American literature. Yet Hester transforms her public shaming before she steps outside the prison door. Using gold thread, she makes the scarlet letter's branding beautiful, "greatly beyond what was allowed by the sumptuary regulations of the colony." As one of the angry women says, she has made "'a pride'" out of her punishment.[7]

Unlike Hirsi Ali, who barely mentions racial prejudice, Hawthorne uses race to undermine male honor and stimulate sympathy for a transgressive woman.[8] In *The Scarlet Letter*, blackness augments the indeterminacy of what's honorable or shameful. Surprisingly, well before Rev. John Wilson condemns the "'blackness of your sin,'" the "black shadow" of the town beadle represents "the whole dismal severity" of Puritan law. More subtly, Hester mixes white, black, and red, as if she were a living embodiment of a multiethnic country in the making. She has "deep black eyes" and her "dark and abundant hair" has a "glossy" luster as it reflects the light.[9] The red letter brands her for her sexual experience in the forest that Indians pass through.

Though blackness evokes several nonracial conventions here, Hawthorne's heroine can't quite be constrained within gender or Puritan stereotypes. Hester—no reader ever wants to call her Mrs. Prynne—resembles a nineteenth-century "dark woman" such as Rebecca in Sir Walter Scott's *Ivanhoe* or Cora in Cooper's *The Last of the Mohicans* or Poe's Ligeia or Melville's Isabel in *Pierre*. But in chapter 13, the narrator shows surprising sympathy with Hester's challenges to such gender conventions. In addition, Hester's black eyes and hair do not reduce her to a cautionary tale of an adulterous woman consorting with the Devil. As good Puritans, Hester and her daughter share the associations of blackness with evil. But Hawthorne uses blackness mostly to mark the Puritans' vindictive use of it. That ambiguously racialized chiasmus, or reversal, undermines the Puritans' rhetoric of shaming, though it's unlikely that anyone except modern readers would agree with Hester that "what we did had a consecration of its own."[10]

The narrator also complicates dichotomies that make white honorable and black shameful. Arthur Dimmesdale's most "striking" aspect is "a white, lofty, and impending brow." Already there's an ambiguity: what's impending? Despite his white brow, the minister's "large, brown, melancholy eyes" and "tremulous" mouth suggest a deer-in-the-headlights demeanor. His "apprehensive" forehead hides and displays his fear of being apprehended.[11] He seems unmanly from the start. He resembles the young wife by the scaffold, not his Puritan elders. As David Greven has noted, Hester is a better man than her lover.[12]

More pointedly, Roger Chillingworth is introduced as "a white man," though "clad in a strange disarray of civilized and savage costume." Here as always when white people are dominant, whiteness comes to consciousness mostly when it's threatened. Chillingworth looks like "a person who had so cultivated his mental part that it could not fail to mould the physical to itself," and his "heterogeneous" garb can't quite conceal that "one of this man's shoulders rose higher than the other." That "slight deformity" betrays him to Hester as her husband. More melodramatically, his face "darkened" as if a "snake" were gliding over it.[13] Already Puritan links between blackness and the Devil are converging with nineteenth-century fears of a black beast who passes as white.

What about the clothes? Chillingworth wears that "disarray" because for at least a year, as he tells a bystander, he "was long held in bonds among the heathen-folk, to the southward." He has learned their medicinal lore.[14] Now he seeks ransom in Boston—we never learn who paid it—and he finds his wife on the scaffold with a scarlet letter and a child.

One might expect narrative sympathy for the cuckold's plight, or at least for someone who has endured captivity. Instead, Chillingworth's New World knowledge and clothes contaminate his Old World standards of wronged honor. By the end of chapter 4 Hester asks him, "Art thou like the Black Man that haunts the forest round about us?"[15] Her husband avoids the question. The image of the Black Man intensifies the mix of hauntings: Puritan fears of the Devil, contemporary fears about black people, and Hester's more intimate fear of what her husband's whiteness hides. It's her first attempt at executing a private shaming.

Surprisingly, Chillingworth shows no anger at his wife for her betrayal. "We have wronged each other," he tells Hester in their prison interview. He knew that she never loved him, and he now realizes that he was much too old for her. Nor does he seem interested in acquiring land or controlling his wife, traditional signifiers of honor. Only at the end do readers learn of his "very considerable amount of property, both here and in England," when Pearl inherits it. Instead, he focuses on the unknown lover "who has wronged us both!" He acknowledges conventions of honor only when he answers why he will conceal his real name. "It may be . . . because I will not encounter the dishonor that besmirches the husband of a faithless woman. It may be for other reasons." To him honor conceals the real man. As he says a little later, though Hester's lover "hide himself in outward honor . . . he shall be mine!"[16] For Chillingworth, honor is just a mask put on by himself or his prey.

Similarly, Hirsi Ali reduces her father's honor to reputation. Musing about the curses in the letter he sends after she announces her divorce, she realizes "how deeply I had damaged his reputation. And I felt real fear: if he came to Holland, my father could beat me, perhaps kill me. I had shamed him."[17] Yet Hirsi Ali's father forgives his daughter because she takes such good care of her increasingly unstable sister in the Netherlands. In stark contrast, Chillingworth becomes Dimmesdale's Iago. As many critics have observed, his rage for vengeance becomes an erotic desire to penetrate another man's secret.[18]

With a complementary weirdness, Dimmesdale also evokes the "Black Man," not only to Pearl but also to himself, despite "the holy whiteness of the clergyman's good fame." When he returns from the forest after Hester tells him who Roger Chillingworth really is, he feels transformed. "In truth, nothing short of a total change of dynasty and moral code, in that interior kingdom" can explain his giddy impulses to sin and transgress. The narrator hastily attributes Dimmesdale's transformation to "the infectious poison" of his sexual sin with a married woman. That explanation doesn't sufficiently account for the minister's exuberant impulses to shock his parishioners, the blackening that he now shares with Chillingworth, and the rush of creativity that inspires his greatest sermon. Stripped of his dynastic whiteness, he becomes a great writer, whose voice resonates with "anguish" and "pain" while his words prophesy "a high and glorious destiny for the newly gathered people of the Lord."[19] As with Hester, art begins after his honor yields to mixture and contamination.

When Dimmesdale escapes Hester's husband by dying on the scaffold, Chillingworth ineffectually invokes conventions of honor, shame, and blackness: "Do not blacken your fame, and perish in dishonor!" He also appeals to Dimmesdale's work status: "Would you bring infamy on your sacred profession?" Dimmesdale replies, "Thy power is not what it was!"[20] To the last, Chillingworth is the narrator's garbage can where he discards the rhetoric of honor by linking it to blackness and self-masking.

In an honor-shame society, Roger Prynne would be the hero. Here he becomes ludicrously preoccupied with his rival's honor rather than his own. He loves to hate the minister, not his wife. After Dimmesdale's death, the avenger "withered up, shrivelled away . . . like an uprooted weed that lies wilting in the sun." Very weirdly, the narrator then muses about "whether hatred and love be not the same thing at bottom." The odd resonance of "bottom" invites homoerotic variations on the narrator's fantasy that in heaven Chillingworth and Dimmesdale will find their "hatred and antipathy transmuted into golden love." Until that farewell fantasy of their spiritual union, Chillingworth remains melodramatically demonized. Yet the two men had converged long before, since both men are honored but dishonorable and both men's minds have deformed their bodies. As "those best able to appreciate the minister's peculiar sensibility" whisper, the scarlet A that seems etched on his bare chest came from "the ever active tooth of remorse, gnawing from the inmost heart outwardly."[21]

To simplify Hawthorne's haze of ambiguities, *The Scarlet Letter* discredits patriarchy, honor, kinship, and to a lesser extent whiteness as secure grounds for self-respect. Ancient devilishness and modern racism destabilize male decorum, until Hawthorne reduces Hester to muted submission. Up to the moment that Dimmesdale dies rejecting Hester in order to claim salvation, the narrative gingerly locates self-respect in Hester's challenges to orthodoxy, not in the minister's attempts to conceal and conform. In chapter 13 Hester privately questions the social structure that fashions men and women to make "the whole race of womanhood" so unhappy. That's astonishingly radical, and Hawthorne's observation is no doubt indebted to his friend Margaret Fuller, the most daring and adventurous intellectual woman of her era. But the narrative skittishly backs away from the possibility that women are an oppressed race.[22] By the end, Hester has dwindled into an unpaid therapist for other women with private sorrows.

Perhaps Boston gives Hester a sense of belonging. Perhaps she feels loyal to the women who confide in her or relishes her role as counselor. Perhaps her nineteenth-century narrator enjoys the spectacle of a strong-minded woman brought under his own moral control. Or perhaps Hawthorne is giving American readers what they want. He understands that Americans will read about a transgressive woman only if she remains satisfactorily miserable, as several contemporary reviewers approvingly noted.[23] In any case, like Hester's daughter, Hawthorne soon seized his own cosmopolitan options and spent most of the decade in Europe.

Hester's unhappiness suffuses her whole life, as the narrator takes care to emphasize. Unlike Pearl, she fails at trying to resettle herself abroad. After many years spent vaguely overseas, she returns to her little cabin and reattaches herself to the Puritan culture that shamed her. Worse, Hester accepts that her "dusky grief" blocks her from either experiencing "sacred love" or becoming a "prophetess" for new relations between men and women. In his attempt to bring closure to the tale, the narrator blackens his now "dusky" heroine while whitening Chillingworth, who may now be joining Dimmesdale in "the ethereal medium of joy."[24]

At the margins of her adopted home, Hester becomes an inward exile. She has no family except for her daughter, who leaves her. No network of kinship interdependencies helps her survive. Amazingly, Hester doesn't even have any friends. She's more self-reliant than Emerson or Thoreau. No one protested when she was shamed in public or when the chief minister and governor tried to take away her daughter. Not even the women whom she privately counsels at the end of the novel take public risks on her behalf. As Dimmesdale dies, her former lover rejects her ultimate dream of reunion in hell. For him she would embrace an eternity of shame, but he retreats to the spiritual pale.[25]

Hester's inward exile can illuminate the pain buried in the far more flamboyant life of a recent feminist, Ayaan Hirsi Ali. As *Infidel* recounts, she experiences a double exile, first from Somalia, then from her more beloved Netherlands. In *Nomad* she states what the book's title belies, that "America is now my home."[26] As a public activist, Hirsi Ali has gone much further than Hester even dreamed of, though many intellectuals have dismissed her pro-West, anti-Islam arguments.[27] More privately, she shares with Hester a sad acquiescence to a home that's not really her home. The modern ideology of individual rights can't quite simplify their mix of pride and shame.

To return for a moment to the previous chapter's theme, why does a mid-nineteenth-century novel present honor on the rocks, whereas a recent memoir presents the code as alive and oppressively well? The answer lies in the size of the group honor protects. The embattled conditions that make male-dominated kinship groups essential to survival persist in modern Somalia. In large groups, the pressures of patriarchal honor can be challenged, and *The Scarlet Letter* does just that. Hawthorne ostensibly situates his romance in a small beleaguered New England town on the colonial edge of nowhere. But the novel's tensions between men's honor and a woman's self-reliance reflect strains between patriarchy and individualism in an expanding nation-state. *The Scarlet Letter* exposes the shaky underpinnings of white honor at the moment of its consolidation in American culture. In its use of blackness for negative self-definitions, the narrative makes honor almost disappear, except as a mask. More paradoxically, honor becomes shameful in white men who aren't quite white, and shame seems half-honorable in a scarlet woman who proudly displays her body's mixture of white and black.

It would take another hundred years or so to see the shamefulness of using blackness to signify shame, and many Americans still don't see it. Today the new Puritans invoke honor to "take our country back," implicitly for white rule. Though *The Scarlet Letter* uses blackness as a conventional stabilizer, Hawthorne unsettles the presumptions that make such racial branding possible.

Honor and Shaming from Huck to Humbert

Three later novels make skin color more central to honor-shaming dynamics. With increasing irony, *Adventures of Huckleberry Finn*,

The Great Gatsby, and *Lolita*—published between thirty and forty years apart—dramatize the racialization of honor. By *Lolita*, racial shaming has become flagrantly shameful. These narratives replicate the white racism they sometimes seem to undermine. Twain mocks the stereotypical racism of "Pap," Huck's father, much as Fitzgerald mocks Tom Buchanan's racism. Those characters serve as introductory foils to give the narrators good liberal credentials, despite the more subtle forms of prejudice that steal into the stories later on. More complexly, all three novels illuminate the shaming inherent in white ideals of group honor.

Tensions between personal empathy and group honor pervade Mark Twain's *Adventures of Huckleberry Finn* (1885). Honor and shame hold their traditional sway on land, but not on the river. There Huck and Jim even swim together naked, with no sense of transgression and no fears of contamination or cross-racial intimacy. Similarly, in *Tom Sawyer Abroad* (1894), Huck, Jim, and Tom swim naked together in an African oasis. Middle-class Tom, the town delinquent, and the person critics later called "Nigger Jim" cavort and splash with no narrative self-consciousness.[28] That social dynamic had not yet galvanized white recoils, as long as men and women weren't swimming together. At least in the first half of the story, Huck bests his conventionally racist conscience by learning to honor Jim's dignity. Many critics have rightly celebrated Twain's succinct description of the story in his 1895 journal: "a book of mine in which a sound heart & a deformed conscience come into collision, and conscience suffers defeat."[29]

Yet shame shapes Huck's moral development. Huck is what later southerners would call "white trash." Inhabiting that degraded social category liberates Huck's voice from his "deformed conscience," particularly conventions of honor and morality. A now-famous moment of reciprocal shaming brings Huck toward accepting his equality with Jim as well as his need for Jim's friendship. After getting separated from the escaped slave and drifting along the Mississippi through what Huck twice calls the "solid white" fog, he sees "a black speck on the water" and rejoins Jim, who is sleeping on the raft. He tricks Jim into believing the storm never happened, then points to all the "rubbish" littering the raft. For the first and last time Jim gets angry with him, because Huck has toyed with Jim's fears for his friend. As Jim says, immortally, "Dat truck dah is *trash*; en trash is what people is that puts dirt on de head er dey fren's en makes 'em ashamed."[30] That's a succinct definition of how white shaming dirties black people, inside and out.

Deeply ashamed, Huck lowers himself to someone even more inferior in social status. As most readers can probably recite from memory, "It was fifteen minutes before I could work myself up to go and humble myself to a nigger; but I done it, and I warn't ever sorry for it afterward, neither." Huck has learned to see himself through Jim's eyes. More important, he feels as Jim feels: "I didn't do him no more mean tricks, and I wouldn't done that one if I'd a knowed it would make him feel that way."[31] Thereafter honor, which surfaces primarily in white aristocrats such as Colonel Grangerford and Colonel Sherburn, seems at a vast distance from Huck's sensibility. For him, shame becomes a curative emotion, while the performance of honor prompts spectacles of adult brutality.

On the other hand, how big is Huck's step from honor to shame when he is already white trash? Moreover, despite Huck's various small moments of courage, he defers to five forceful males, at least three of them preoccupied with honor. Colonel Grangerford's obsession with a community feud leads to the death of his son. Later Colonel Sherburn kills the town drunk, then faces down the lynch mob by calling them cowards. As with Colonel Grangerford, his honor thrives on cruelty. After the shameless Duke and Dauphin conscript Huck for their fraudulent schemes, Huck follows the lead of yet another manipulative authority figure, Tom Sawyer, who reenslaves Jim to serve his own bookish notions of decorum and glory. Huck's courage becomes a follower's unease. When Colonel Sherburn kills Boggs before the deadline and shames the angry mob, Huck voices only momentary sensations of discomfort without responding to the spectacle of amoral authority. Huck quickly gets on the right side of shaming by going to the circus, where the ringmaster pretends to get "fooled" and Huck feels deliciously "sheepish" in his empathy.[32] But Colonel Sherburn's mixture of calm, control, and violence doesn't quite get exorcised. The ruthless authority figures of Twain's later fiction are in the offing.

Thereafter Huck's sound heart goes into hiding. As he retreats to his go-along self, he becomes a good child coping with a world populated mostly by frauds and racists, and he makes no further mention of furthering Jim's desire for freedom. They've drifted south of the Ohio River and that's that, so why bother? Though Huck remains inwardly appalled at the manipulative antics of the Duke and the Dauphin, he voices his disdain with a mix of racist convention and disengagement: "If ever I struck anything like it, I'm a nigger. It was enough to make a body ashamed of the human race."[33] Yet he follows their leadership except for his belated resistance at the Wilkses, until the Duke and the Dauphin exit, suitably tarred and feathered.

Huck's "sound heart" does become momentarily visible again, in one anomalous instance that readers and critics have seized on with relief. His attempt to be "washed clean of sin" by writing to Miss Watson about Jim leads to his celebrated resolution: "'All right, then, I'll *go* to hell,' and tore it up."[34] For a moment he reaffirms his fellowship with Jim, even at the cost of being damned to hell, the site of eternal shaming. Yet it's an unintegrated blip as the racial chasm widens. As over a hundred years of criticism attest, the end leaves readers stranded with incompatible responses. Are the last eleven chapters a satire, or do we abandon Jim to relish Tom's stylish audacity?

Either way, ideals of honor have degenerated into the manipulative dramas of heartless leaders and nervous or craven followers, whether they are boys or men. At the end, Huck continues to voice his aloneness in a white fog. Meanwhile the rough rural justice that has tarred and feathered the Duke and the Dauphin shows that blackening has became a public, visible stigma, worse than putting Hester in the stocks. When Huck ends by saying he'll light out for the territory, to readers in 1885 he'd probably be heading for Oklahoma, where Indians were being dispossessed. Sadness at abandoning Jim doesn't seem to enter his mind.

Published forty years later, at the high point of scientific racism's popularity, F. Scott Fitzgerald's *The Great Gatsby* seems on first reading to be ambivalently progressive about race. Nick Carraway, feeling "uncivilized," hears Tom Buchanan "violently" hold forth about his fears that "the white race will be—will be utterly submerged." Daisy agrees but winks at Nick. Then, Tom insists that "we're Nordics." As an afterthought he includes his audience—sort of. "After an infinitesimal hesitation he included Daisy with a slight nod, and she winked at me again." Perhaps Tom hesitates because he has already turned his wife's knuckle "black and blue." Nick finds "something pathetic" in these postures of racist purity.[35]

Nick also recoils from Tom's mistress, Myrtle Wilson, and her friend, who recalls that "'I almost married a little kike. . . . I knew he was below me." These conversations display the blatant racism in the "Valley of Ashes." Later, after the accident in which Gatsby's car kills Myrtle, Fitzgerald takes care to balance these examples of stereotypic white racism with the appearance of a "pale, well-dressed negro" who gives what Joe Biden might have called a clean and articulate report about the accident. The "pale" black man's standard English contrasts with a "Greek" witness's heavy vernacular.[36]

Four years earlier, when Fitzgerald wrote a letter to Edmund Wilson after coming back from his first trip to Europe, he expressed a more bilious version of Tom's racism. "The negroid streak creeps northward to defile the nordic race. Already the Italians have the souls of blacka-moors. Raise the bars of immigration and permit only Scandinavians, Teutons, Anglo Saxons + Celts to enter. . . . I think it's a shame that England + America didn't let Germany conquer Europe. It's the only thing that would have saved the fleet of tottering old wrecks. My reac-tions were all philistine, anti-socialistic, provincial + racially snobbish. I believe at last in the white man's burden. We are as far above the modern Frenchman as he is above the negro. Even in art!"[37] When Fitzgerald wrote *The Great Gatsby*, he distanced himself from such views by projecting them into the mouth of a boor. Yet other aspects of the narrative betray Fitzgerald's covert contempt for class and race mixture.

The plot continuously emphasizes the tawdriness of class mixing. Aristocratic Tom is having a sordid affair with the wife of the man who runs the gas station. Impoverished Jay Gatz remakes himself as rich, aristocratic Jay Gatsby by becoming a bootlegger whose success owes a great deal to Meyer Wolfsheim, a Jew. As Nick says at the start, Gatsby "represented everything for which I have an unaffected scorn."

Nick's own racism momentarily erupts when he mocks "three modish negroes" riding in a limousine "driven by a white chauffeur.... I laughed aloud as the yolks of their eyeballs rolled toward us in haughty rivalry. 'Anything can happen now that we've slid over this bridge,'" he concludes. The heavy-handed metaphors of "yolks" and "bridge" expose his disgust at upwardly mobile black people who intrude on his world as if they claimed equality. As Ann Douglas notes, they're "Gatsby's rivals, perhaps his superiors, if only in audacious pretense."[38] But they're black.

More subtly, Nick's narration of various skin and car colors betrays his recoil from the social mixtures that define his adult life. When Nick meets Jordan Baker, she seems ballooned in white, and soon she rests her "slender golden arm" inside his. "We're all white here," she murmurs later, as Tom rails against racial mixture. Yet earlier Nick mentions her "brown hand" as she waves goodbye. Jordan's skin is of a piece with her "gray sun-strained eyes" and the rumors of her "bad lie"—a pointed pun—on the golf course. As they become more intimate, Nick sees more mixture: "Jordan's fingers, powdered white over their tan, rested for a moment in mine." After their loveless affair has ended, her face has "the same brown tint as the fingerless glove on her knee."[39] His darkening representations of her suggest that he's not as far from Tom's fears of racial contamination as he supposes.

The differences in descriptions of the color of Gatsby's car also show Nick's quiet disgust for tainted blends. Gatsby's car is "a rich cream color, bright with nickel," Nick says. Yet Myrtle's working-class husband, George Wilson, describes it as "'a nice yellow one,'" as does the well-dressed negro and even Tom Buchanan. Michaelis, the "Greek" whose "coffee joint" stands beside the ash heaps, tells a policeman that it might be "light green."[40] No one but Nick sees the car's creamy whiteness, and conflicting color perceptions leave readers with a mix that Nick, like Gatsby, is trying to transcend.

Nick's disdain for Jordan's increasingly brown skin balances Gatsby's reverence for Daisy's pure whiteness. As Jordan tells Nick, when she first met eighteen-year-old "Daisy Fay" in Louisville, she was "dressed in white" and had innumerable suitors and phone calls. Gatsby was sitting in her "little white roadster" with her, and they were "so engrossed in each other" that she didn't even see Jordan. Yet Gatsby's rapture is solipsistic, of a piece with his "Platonic conception of himself" as a "son of God" who can reinvent himself at will. Nick recalls Gatsby saying to him that one evening in Louisville, "they came to a place where . . . the sidewalk was white with moonlight." As Gatsby prepares to kiss "Daisy's white face" for the first time, he sees the sidewalks as a "ladder" that he could climb to "suck on the pap of life, gulp down the incomparable milk of wonder."[41]

But that ladder has to be climbed "alone," Gatsby realizes. "He knew that when he kissed this girl, and forever wed his unutterable visions to her perishable breath, his mind would never romp again like the mind of God."[42] Gatsby's racialized solipsism appears at the moment he loses it. The many Keatsian transformations throughout the narrative make it easy to overlook the mourning for infantile narcissism that suffuses Gatsby's yearning. Intensifications of whiteness imply the constant fear of its loss. Reluctantly, he yields to his more prosaic desire for Daisy's embodied difference as a somewhat older woman of much higher social status.

Nick reflects, "I disapproved of him from beginning to end." Yet Nick cherishes his friend's failed pursuit of wonder and imagines him "concealing his incorruptible dream" as he stands in a pink suit "against the white steps" of his mansion.[43] The mixture of cynicism and sadness in Nick's eloquent meditations fends off what other aspects of his narrative betray: his disgust at more specific threats of race mixing, often displaced into disgust with class mixing.[44]

For Daisy, too, the tackiness and "raw vigor" of West Egg "offended her," and she quietly recoils from Gatsby's lower-class status, as Nick notices. By the end, after Daisy and Tom have returned to the upper-class bonding that grounds their marriage, Nick tells Jordan that "I'm five years too old to lie to myself and call it honor."[45] By implication, all whites are without honor, at least in the Valley of Ashes. Nick retreats to the Midwest, the world of his father, perhaps to restore a semblance of the honor that he associates with fathers, and more centrally with Gatsby. Yet when Gatsby's own midwestern father appears for the funeral of his son, he seems haplessly out of place.

Honor is less visible in this narrative than in Twain's novel, and shameful adult behavior has become the norm. That's part of Gatsby's appeal to Nick, that his dream of wonder seems impossible to sustain. Nor does Huck's near-paralytic lack of response to Colonel Sherburn's conflation of honor, brutality, and manliness have any echo or parallel in Fitzgerald's narrative. These categories are emptying out. Under the mournfulness of this exceptionally well-formed fiction, Fitzgerald fears the deformations wrought by the threat of racial equality and the incipient loss of white social privilege and power. Literary form, too, fends off contamination.

What remains is a nostalgia as specious as Huck's attempt to resurrect his sound heart by saying he'll go to hell. At the end, Nick wistfully evokes a vanished time, "a fresh, green breast of the new world." That line remains memorable partly because it's so strange. Is that breast made of money, as Gatsby says of Daisy's voice? In seeking to recapture a lost pastoral purity, Nick taints it. His fantasy of a "green breast" reduces the first Dutch explorers to an infantile yearning even more blatant than Gatsby's hunger for "the incomparable milk of wonder." Moreover, the compromised color merely "pandered" to every man's "capacity for wonder."[46] Ashes seep into Nick's language, against his will. Despite what the iconic last sentence claims, time in this narrative pushes him not into a God-like white past but into a mixed-race future. So his "we" beats on, doggedly masturbatory, borne ceaselessly into nostalgia by contaminated waters.

"Lolita had been safely solipsized." That's what Humbert Humbert thinks as he builds toward ejaculation while his nymphet wriggles happily on his lap. Here Nabokov's narrator is shameful from the first paragraph onward and ideals of honor have turned into farce. Long before Lolita enters his life, Humbert is enraged with his wife's Parisian lover, a Russian cab driver, not because he's her lover but because the man doesn't flush the toilet in Humbert's apartment. Then Humbert reflects that what looks like a "crowning insult" may have been "middle-class Russian courtesy . . . so as not to underscore the small size of his host's domicile with the rush of a gross cascade on top of his own hushed trickle."[47] In the narrative's even more farcical end, Humbert pursues Clare Quilty, ostensibly to defend his honor by attacking Lolita's subsequent lover. But he ends up in jail as Quilty's murderer. Two ridiculous failed duels with men who have taken his wife or lover frame his pursuit of Lolita. Shameful Humbert chases even more shameful Quilty, while shameful readers like me are wondering, Where did the sex go?[48]

Throughout, Humbert delights in Lolita's brownness. "I do love that intoxicating brown fragrance of hers," he thinks at the start, and her hair color oscillates between "auburn" and "brown." When she's naked before him at last, he looks at "her honey-brown body," and soon she "hastily" removes "her brown shoulder from my lips." In a scene framed by "a handsome young Negress" and an "Uncle Tom" at the inn, they first talk of "incest," as Lolita calls it. Much later he achingly recalls her "apricot midriff" and "her gaspingly young and adorable apricot shoulder blades" as she played tennis. He calls her "my brown flower" as he tries to hector her into obedience. Most memorably, Humbert wishes they could have gone to Mexico "to lie low for a couple of years in subtropical bliss until I could safely marry my little Creole."[49]

His eagerness to "lie low" with a "Creole" shows Humbert's avidity for racialized slumming. Right after he has first "solipsized" her, Humbert thinks of himself as "a radiant and robust Turk" who is about to enjoy "the youngest and fairest of his slaves." Much later, before he turns toward brutal physical abuse as he's about to lose her, he sees Lolita as a "spoiled slave-child" who has "adapted" well to her surroundings.[50] These racial musings license his sexual exploitation of a lower-class girl.

Strangely, Humbert's own race seems a little questionable, though solidly European. The pretentious introduction by "John Ray, Jr., Ph.D." begins by stating Humbert's title for his posthumous memoir: "Lolita, or the Confession of a White Widowed Male." Yet on the first page of Humbert's own narrative, he says his father was "a salad of racial genes: a Swiss citizen, of mixed French and Austrian descent, with a dash of the Danube in his veins." There's nothing about his mother except for one sentence: "My very photogenic mother died in a freak accident (picnic, lightning) when I was three." The laconic parenthesis has been a red flag for Freudians, the first of many such lures. Meanwhile

Humbert reduces his complex racial lineage to whiteness by colonizing his ideal nymphet. When he first sees her, she's a mixture of "golden and brown, kneeling, looking up" at him.[51]

Is Lolita just tanned or has she absorbed Latina hues, perhaps by osmosis from her conception in Vera Cruz? Does she verge on black? More important, does Humbert's obsessive colorizing debase her or him? Either way, they expose the sexual desires often latent in paternalistic white intimacies with people of color. Published in 1955, the same year Emmett Till was murdered in Mississippi for whistling at a white girl and Rosa Parks refused to take a segregated seat on a Birmingham bus, *Lolita* turns Humbert's lascivious pleasure in racial mixing into one of his badges of shame.

Challenging White Honor

To compare these narratives' treatment of vengeance reveals the hollowing out of white honor. In *The Scarlet Letter*, Roger Chillingworth has the revenger's role, as befits a man who discovers he's a cuckold. Yet his honor is a pretext, an empty gesture toward reputation. Chillingworth aims at possessing the minister, not repossessing his wife. From the moment of his entrance, he resembles a misshapen devil, more Indian and "Black" than white and driven by covertly homoerotic energies to penetrate the minister's secret. As early as 1850, this narrative turns the Old World tradition of avenging a husband's honor into a sadistic quest for dominance. The whiteness of both men in the love triangle masks dishonor, while Hester finds strength in her mixtures. Outwardly, her black hair and eyes make her more strikingly beautiful than conventional white women. Inwardly, her sense of shame seems inseparable from her pride.

The next three novels challenge honor more directly. In *Adventures of Huckleberry Finn*, the feud between the Grangerfords and the Shepherdsons begins with a cause no one can remember and spills over into pointless violence. The clans' passion for collective honor, embodied in the formidably austere Colonel Grangerford, only leads to the death of his son, Buck Grangerford. Later a revengeful mob tries to lynch Colonel Sherburn but gets humiliated, and still later another revengeful mob tars and feathers the more tackily amoral Duke and Dauphin. That branding says, "You look like them now."

In *The Great Gatsby*, George Wilson has the revenger's role. He kills Gatsby to avenge his wife's death and destroy the man he imagines was his wife's lover. But he shoots the wrong killer. From start to finish, he's a hapless cuckold who seems more ridiculous than pitiful. Finally, at *Lolita*'s stagily melodramatic climax, Humbert's ridiculously sexualized shooting only leaves him all the more nostalgic for pederastic desire.[52]

Taken together, these four narratives illuminate the decline of the basis for traditional honor in localized relationships. Initially shamed and forsaken, Hester ends even more starkly alone, since her lover is dead and her daughter has left her. After rejecting his father, Huck develops a bond with Jim so intense that he accepts several kinds of shame as the price for their friendship. For that affirmation modern readers honor him greatly, perhaps too greatly. Then we're left in the lurch as his relational self all but disappears. At the end he's ready to "light out for the territory" as just another American bent on national expansion.

Similarly, Nick begins alone and aimless, then forges an intense bond with Gatsby (or at least with his idealization of Gatsby), only to end alone and aimless. He returns to the Midwest in defeat, not in rediscovery. Humbert has almost no relational subjectivity, except with his own desire. Toward the end he does claim to love Lolita, if only in retrospect, and he seems more attentive to her thoughts and feelings during their last conversation than he ever was when his lust was riding high.[53] Critics have made far too much of his belated claims that he loved her. At the end, Humbert's self-absorption degenerates to an automaton-like role that makes his pursuit of Quilty look farcical. Nabokov seems almost to be taunting readers with a silly climax.

All four narratives try to separate honor from fear. In *The Scarlet Letter*, Dimmesdale seems terrified mostly of being exposed. Until his public revelation of his own scarlet A, he mixes guilt for his one sexual act with shame for being hypocritical and desiring a married woman. Chillingworth thinks far more about Dimmesdale's honor than the minister does. In *Adventures of Huckleberry Finn*, Jim is so terrified of getting caught that he lets himself be imprisoned by Tom Sawyer, with Huck's help, so that Tom can pretend to gain the honor of freeing him. Fear governs the lives of Dimmesdale and Jim, but the vengeful honor of others is what brings it on.

James Gatz hides his fear of getting caught. This pseudo-aristocrat has risen from the contamination of being ordinary to gain the wonder of Daisy's pure whiteness. Like Dimmesdale, he loves an adulterous woman, but unlike Dimmesdale, he revels in his dishonor. Dimmesdale's self-exposure takes him to Gatsby's white heaven; Gatsby's exposure leaves him floating in a pool of his own red blood. Finally, Humbert seems to have come directly from "centre court," or at least central casting. He's a handsome European cosmopolitan who arrives in the American provinces to pursue his colonizing desire. But he ends in jail, and worse, he remains a slave to his desire. As with Gatsby, who used Oxford to enhance his self-image, Humbert's claims to quasi-aristocratic status seem fraudulent from the first. He mostly fears getting caught or growing old.

In all four novels, honor remains in the wings while shame takes center stage. What Chillingworth does to punish Dimmesdale, what Tom and Huck do to enslave Jim, what Gatsby does to get money and Daisy, what Humbert does to bed Lolita are all self-dishonoring. Their whiteness protects an increasingly compromised sense of superiority.

What about Tocqueville's insight that Americans relocate honor from localized hierarchic relations to individuals in a nation-state? In *The Scarlet Letter*, there's almost no sense of nation-state and barely a regional consciousness. The dynamics remain localized in Puritan Boston. Occasionally thoughts of England and Europe intrude, but only on the edge of Hester's awareness. There's no mention of the American South or Midwest and only one mention of the "heathen-folk to the southward" who held Chillingworth captive for a year.[54]

Hawthorne's novel helped define and market New England by foregrounding its cozy villages and less cozy Puritan history. Its ambivalent regionalism betrays a more unequivocal disdain for being part of a nation. In "The Custom-House," Hawthorne muses on being fired by "Uncle Sam's government" after serving under a threatening "American eagle," who "is apt to fling off her nestlings, with a scratch of her claw, a dab of her beak, or a rankling wound from her barbed arrows." The nation-state seems irksome, onerous, and dismissable.[55] Soon Hawthorne quietly seceded from his region, nominally to serve as a consul in Liverpool but really to take a long vacation, ironically, on government pay.

By the 1850s, many abolitionists were loudly calling for New England's secession from their enslaving county. Wendell Phillips writes in his 1845 preface to *The Narrative of the Life of Frederick Douglass* that "New England, cutting loose from a blood-stained Union, shall glory in being the house of refuge" for escaped slaves. No abolitionist, Hawthorne wrote an 1852 campaign biography of his friend Franklin Pierce that all but jettisons the South and its problems with slavery. In 1830 Daniel Webster's famous peroration in his reply to a South Carolina senator—"Liberty *and* Union, now and forever, one and inseparable!"—spurred national resolve to overcome the threat of South Carolina's secession. Twenty years later, Webster's defense of the Fugitive Slave Act along those same lines inflamed northern anger, not agreement. Hawthorne wanted to say goodbye to all that. In 1853, when Pierce became president, the newly famous national author lit out for Europe as soon as he could.[56]

Thirty-five years later, *Adventures of Huckleberry Finn* displayed a much more capacious regional consciousness, though restricted to the Midwest and Southwest. Again there's almost no attempt to locate the individual in a nation-state, except for Huck's browsing among magazines on an Arkansas coffee table. Instead, after Huck and Jim drift south of Cairo, he abandons Jim's hope of going up the Ohio River to freedom. The rest of the novel retreats from that national possibility into regional picaresque.

By 1925, *The Great Gatsby* had a national cast of characters. James Gatz hails from Minnesota, a background he tries to erase. Nick Carraway comes from the Midwest and retreats there. Daisy Buchanan meets Gatsby in Louisville, Kentucky, and Meyer Wolfsheim epitomizes unscrupulous, ethnic New York City. At one point, when a business phone call interrupts Gatsby's ecstatic reunion with Daisy, he barks into the receiver, "Well, he's no use to us if Detroit is his idea of a small town."[57] Villages and regions recede into nostalgic or contemptuous memory. Maybe it's just the East, Nick muses, in his own passive-aggressive version of secession. "Tom and Gatsby, Daisy and Jordan and I, were all Westerners," so "perhaps we possessed some deficiency in common which made us subtly unadaptable to Eastern life."[58] Embodying the valley of ashes, ashen-faced George Wilson kills Gatsby's dream of Platonic whiteness.

The second half of *Lolita* describes a still more national scene. Travel and fucking constitute almost all of the action, while states become a blur. Nabokov inventories the motels that Humbert and Lolita briefly inhabit, the shops they visit, the inquisitive people they fend off, and the moralists who condemn Humbert's pursuit of the nymphet. If my responses are any guide, readers become partly complicit with Humbert's transgressions, unless we allow Lolita's feelings to puncture his narcissism. The tension between his frenetic mobility and his fixity of shameful desire makes him seem disturbingly vital.

Yet the novel's saturation in shame brings some degree of hope about the decline of white people's ability to enforce racial superiority in America. My hope may seem almost as perverse as the novel. Nevertheless, as narratives reach for national and global scope, however tawdry, the union between whiteness and honor becomes more visibly untenable. The progression from Hawthorne's provincial Puritans through Gatsby's national web of corruption to Humbert's globe-trotting lasciviousness suggests that honor and shaming thrive best when individuals can't escape their localized relations.

These novels reflect and critique stages in the emptying out of white honor. From *Adventures of Huckleberry Finn* onward, white honor can't contain the threat of racial mixture and equality. Nor can it contain white people in a coherent group. A gripping 2002 movie, *8 Mile*, empties out the category entirely. Eminem triumphs as a white rapper by shaming himself in front of a black audience. His success depends not on any claim to white honor but on his ability to bond with black people by dissing himself better than his black rival could have done. That performance would have been inconceivable just twenty years earlier.

Even among the country's most honor-bound citizens, its military warriors, the imagined congruence between honor and whiteness started to disintegrate, especially after President Harry S. Truman integrated the armed forces in 1948. Yet for many Americans, black as well as white, dark skin continues to signify shame. For people who continue to identify their personal honor with a dominant racial group, their sense of shared privilege remains unsafely solipsized.

CHAPTER 5

TWO WARS

Growing insecurity about white cohesiveness wasn't restricted to canonized novels. American foreign policy reveals similar tensions. Racial shaming has played a key role in gaining support for wars, though the targets have shifted from Barbary pirates, Mexicans, and Filipinos to "Japs" and "gooks." Recently, as contempt for black people became less acceptable at home, three American wars in the Middle East consolidated American contempt for Muslims abroad, at least until the cascade of Arab protests and revolutions in early 2011 reopened American sympathies for a "them" who suddenly seemed more like "us."

This chapter compares U.S. responses to the Barbary Wars and the second war in Iraq. Both wars thrived on the rhetoric of vengeance and humiliation. But the rhetoric changed from relative tolerance to desperate stridency. As if anticipating 9/11, Samuel Huntington's mid-1990s book *The Clash of Civilizations* encapsulates the change. Indebted to the "culture wars" of the 1980s, Huntington redirects othering from black people to Muslims and rests his case for the West's superiority on Anglo-European culture instead of light skin color.

Humiliation and American Wars

Since the advent of nation-states, one motive for waging war has been to shame another country, often in retaliation for real or alleged humiliation. Whether fighting Barbary pirates or "Japs" or Osama bin Laden and Saddam Hussein, the rhetoric of racial retribution has justified American battles with darker-skinned peoples. After the Japanese attack on Pearl Harbor and Al-Qaeda's attack on the World Trade Center, the metonyms of December 7 and 9/11 became instant triggers for rage as well as mourning. When white Americans have felt victimized by nonwhite peoples inside our borders, racial shaming has quickly turned into localized violence. When humiliation has come from beyond our borders, especially from peoples of allegedly inferior colors, the rhetoric of vengeance often draws on racial stereotypes.

As with our national expansion against the Indians or the war for territorial aggrandizement against Mexico from 1846 to 1848, calls to defend national honor in more distant wars have used claims of racial supremacy to alleviate regional and class conflicts. But revenge and national unity haven't been the only American motives. Honor and shame have been crucial domestic props for military ventures overseas. Lyndon Johnson frequently invoked honor as the rationale for sending more and more soldiers to Vietnam.[1]

Despite—or perhaps because of—multicultural affirmations on the home front, the imagined honor of displaying international dominance has continued to spur imperial wars, though more for civilizing than for colonizing. From Cuba and the Philippines to Iraq, the United States has proclaimed its mission to remake the savages in our own idealized image of democracy and private enterprise. Especially during the Bush-Cheney years, the wars reflected a variant of what Renato Rosaldo has called "imperialist nostalgia." The term applies to people who have a guilty longing for an "innocent" culture their colonizing country has destroyed, while their comfort depends on the colonizing of that culture.[2] My variant suggests that many architects and supporters of our second war in Iraq harbored a longing for imperialism itself. From that vantage point, the second war in Iraq begins to look like nostalgia for an idealized golden age of global white supremacy.

In *Fighting for American Manhood*, Kristin Hoganson shows how incessant invocations of national honor justified the Spanish-American War. Combat for empire would fend off white men's "degeneracy" by building manly character as well as avenging the invented humiliation ascribed to the explosion of the battleship *Maine*.[3] Charges that

Filipinos were "bestial rapists" intensified desires to export white supremacy, despite evidence of widespread American brutalities in the Philippines. As in white perceptions of American black men, the Filipino rapists were also portrayed as babies. In the Vietnam War, the shaming word "gook" came from "goo-goo," Americans' label for Filipinos during their occupation of the Philippines. The term suggested "goo-goo eyes" and "gaga" and implied infantilized subjects. "Gook" also evokes glop, gunk, or shit.[4]

Surprisingly, American racism checked the country's imperial ambitions. Eric Love audaciously argues that throughout the nineteenth century, anxiety about maintaining white supremacy at home thwarted America's imperialist plans of annexing more tropical countries from Mexico to the Caribbean to the Philippines. Political leaders had to be content with seizing little pieces of Cuba and Panama. After 1898, reluctantly abandoning their agendas for colonial expansion, they retreated to a strategy that established indirect political and economic controls over what John Hope Franklin mordantly called the "Negro Empire." One exception was the annexation of Puerto Rico, but its inhabitants weren't given full voting rights, since otherwise they might threaten white dominance. Voters enthusiastically accepted Texas and Alaska because those states were already white and grudgingly accepted Louisiana and Hawaii because of the expectation that they would become white. In 1870, President Ulysses Grant wanted to annex Santo Domingo so that the newly freed black people in the South could be deported there, but too many white Americans opposed even that move. Yet again, they were afraid that an influx of nonwhite voters might threaten their collective dominance.[5]

Love persuasively challenges assumptions that racism supported imperialism. For over two centuries, fears about loss of white supremacy at home have blocked expansionist ambitions except within America's widening borders. The recurrent drive to civilize backward peoples became a fallback position once fears of too much racial mixture had dashed hopes for direct colonial rule.[6]

With Lincoln's 1863 emancipation of black slaves in the Confederacy, Americans took a big step toward the radical ideal in Jefferson's Declaration of Independence that "all men are created equal." But white fears undermined the ideal's promise. As the threat of an emerging black middle class became more immediate, American shaming practices drastically intensified on the home front. Wars for empire helped secure whiteness as a race-based category that justified the push for worldwide dominance. For the United States, which came late to the game, it was marginally more acceptable to attack peoples of color overseas than to suppress challenges from black people at home. Rudyard Kipling's now-infamous 1899 poem "The White Man's Burden" urged the United States to seize and develop the Philippines on behalf of "Your new-caught, sullen peoples, / Half-devil and half-child." As Love points out, Kipling's poem is riddled with fears of being defeated and shamed.[7]

In a speech to white missionaries, Teddy Roosevelt declared that "the expansion of the peoples of white, or European blood" has given "lasting benefit to most of the peoples" now ruled by Europe and America. In practice Roosevelt backed away from his earlier colonialist ardor. But he remained a master at transforming fear into bravado through symbolic displays of white superiority. When Roosevelt deployed his "Great White Fleet" in 1907, that world tour marked America's emergence as a world power. A decade earlier, Mark Twain had ironically concluded that "the world was made for man—the white man."[8]

Many Americans resisted the onset of imperial wars for reasons of morality, practicality, isolationism, or simple racism. One year after Kipling's poem, when Twain introduced Winston Churchill at a New York gathering, he compared the United States in the Philippines to the United Kingdom in the Boer War. Both countries are "kin in sin." In 1901, Twain wrote a poem imagining President William McKinley's last thoughts while dying. McKinley realizes he's worse than Benedict Arnold. Arnold's treason "concerned a garrison" but "Mine . . . peddled out a Nation & its honor" to make the United States a "Conqueror of helpless tribes, Extinguisher of struggling liberties!" He begs forgiveness of the land he has "brought to shame" and contemplates his blackening of the flag's whiteness: "The White Bars are Black—Hide it from my sight!" Other public figures opposed wars of annexation because colored people weren't worth the effort or because they were unassimilable. Since Cubans or Filipinos were hopelessly uncivilized, they couldn't manage democracy, so the argument went.[9]

Nevertheless, from McKinley to Douglas MacArthur to George W. Bush, many American leaders have presented their wars as the missionary crusades of a redeemer nation. If we uplift the Filipinos or the Japanese or the Vietnamese, the logic ran, we can keep thinking of ourselves as both dominant and benevolent. We're doing it for their own good, not for our markets or our territorial expansion. Meanwhile we can continue to think of black Americans as not quite upliftable.

The rhetoric of war did more than displace domestic anxieties about race. It also helped reinforce the fraying bonds between whiteness, honor, and national pride. Faced with black demands for equality, Americans could reconstitute the purity of a white national imaginary through wars against more distant peoples of allegedly inferior colors. Along the way, vexed mixtures of personal honor and shame could be eased into simpler yearnings for white dominance at home and imperial dominance abroad.

For the World War II generation, augmenting American honor through war felt like rooting for the Yankees. There were similar presumptions of prowess and similar oscillations between pride and anxiety. More generally, whether threatened by Barbary pirates, Mexico, Cuba, Japan, North Vietnam, Communist China, the USSR—or black protesters from the 1950s through the 1970s—many Americans responded to attacks or alleged attacks with a craving to regain whitened honor through war. Vengeance impelled such wars, and winning resurrected the pinstripe complacency of champions—until the next humiliation.

Oscillating between hesitancy and braggadocio, American leaders sustained the rhetoric of imperial entitlement until President Barack Obama's June 2009 speech in Cairo. Breaking sharply with previous presidents in tone as well as message, he reached out to respect Arab nations and find common ground. Instead of featuring terrorism, Obama emphasized four times that everyone deserves "dignity." More-over, several times he located the "dead end" of violence in the rage that comes from being on the receiving end of incessant shaming. Muslims in Gaza, for instance, "endure the daily humiliations—large and small—that come with occupation." That has to stop, he said, just as Americans stopped "the humiliation of segregation" for black people. Obama made it clear that humiliation, too, is a dead end. Its sword injures the wielder as well as the victim.[10]

From 1979, when revolutionary Iran humiliated Jimmy Carter by holding fifty-two Americans hostage for over a year, to 2011, when many revolutions suddenly toppled or threatened Arab dictators, Muslims were Americans' international bogeymen. Three wars reflected that presumption. At home, too, most white citizens considered Muslim Americans more alien than African Americans. In *Almost All Aliens*, Paul Spickard recounts a disturbing test that he has given "over one hundred times" to his Berkeley students and other American audiences. He asks them to rank ethnic American groups as Americans. He takes care to emphasize that all the groups are American. Nevertheless, whenever there are more than twenty-five people present, each audience invariably comes up with this ranking:

1.   English American
2, 3. Swedish or Irish American
4.   Polish American
5.   Jewish American
6, 7. Black or Indian American
8.   Mexican American
9.   Japanese American
10.   Arab American.

From the late 1970s onward, over a decade before the various acts of terrorism leading up to 9/11, American Arabs became unAmerican.[11]

The Barbary Pirates, 1783–1815

The word "Barbary" may have come from the Greek *barbaros* or the Latin *barbarus*, meaning non-Greeks or non-Romans, and therefore uncivilized peoples. Or the word could have come from an Arab word, *berbera*, meaning African tribes who mumble or can't communicate.[12] In either case, the label began as a put-down.

Perhaps more neutrally, an American admiral invented "the Middle East" in 1902 to describe the region from Morocco to Turkey and Iran.

Until then Europeans and Americans had called it "the East" or "the Orient." The need for a more discriminating name reflected Americans' commercial and political ambitions in the area. From the start, however, as Michael B. Oren says, eighteenth-century Americans saw the "Musselmen" of that region "as the ultimate Other . . . primitive, sordid, and cruel."[13]

That generalization fits our current conflicts with Muslim countries better than it fits our first encounters.[14] As a weak postcolonial country, the United States frequently tried to dramatize its independence and unite its states by demonizing a common enemy. Yet early American narratives about Muslims also show remarkable diversity. Until 1794, an enlightened relativism characterizes many of the plays, novels, and newspaper accounts featuring American engagements with Muslim cultures.[15]

Susanna Rowson's 1794 play *Slaves in Algiers* and Royall Tyler's 1797 novel *The Algerine Captive* both feature the white slavery of American captives. Under cover of that fashionable appeal, Rowson dramatizes feminist bonding and some antislavery leanings, while Tyler presents religious relativism and sympathy for both Muslim points of view and Africans on slave ships.[16] One of Benjamin Franklin's last editorials adopts the persona of an Algerian official who justifies enslaving Christians by using southern arguments that justify U.S. slavery. From the early seventeenth century on, Franklin's persona notes, thousands of European Christians had been enslaved in Algiers to cultivate crops, just as Africans had been captured to labor for white plantation owners in the South. So what's the problem?[17]

On the other hand, James Cathcart's posthumous narrative of his captivity in Algiers from 1785 to 1796 pleads for redemption of U.S. honor after the national humiliation personified in his captivity. Paradoxically, he adroitly used his skills to gain riches and status. He rose from prisoner to owner of a prison tavern and ended his captivity as chief Christian secretary to the Algerian dey. When the dey sent him to the United States to negotiate a treaty in 1795, Cathcart traveled in a ship he had bought, helped by a loan from the Algerian ruler. Like Tyler's narrator, Cathcart developed a strategic friendship with a devout sheik, a "Hadgi," though Cathcart presents his own knowledgeable "harangue" about Islam to Muslims as his greatest mistake, since it almost got him imprisoned again.

Throughout, Cathcart recounts his steady rise while bemoaning the "indignities" and "humiliations" he received. As he launches successful negotiations on the dey's behalf, his journal entry fervently urges the United States "to extricate us with honor, from this state of incomprehensible misery . . . unhuman beyond expression, and barbarous in a superlative degree."[18] Both narratives articulated widely shared vacillation between cosmopolitan adaptability and provincial anger at the insults to white entitlement.

For the first thirty-two years of its existence, the United States tried and failed to manage conflicts with the Barbary pirates, or more accurately privateers who were agents of the Barbary states (present-day Algiers, Libya, Tunis, and Morocco). From 1776 on the British had withdrawn the support of their navy, the most dominant in the world. In 1778 a treaty with France gained temporary naval protection for American ships. But in 1783, wary of American competition for Mediterranean trade, France refused to honor that agreement. The Revolutionary War had reduced the American navy to almost nothing, and the United States did not have a strong central government.

Suddenly American merchant ships were defenseless anywhere near the four Barbary countries. In 1783 Algerian pirates harassed a convoy, and in 1784 Moroccans captured a ship, though they soon freed the crew. In 1785 Algiers captured two American schooners and enslaved twenty-one crew members. From 1784 to 1815, North African pirates seized thirty-five American ships and 700 American captives. There were a few respites, partly because Algeria fought Portugal from 1790 to 1793. Britain helped end that war, and after that Algerian ships could get to the Atlantic and attack American ships again. Almost immediately, Algerians captured at least eleven American merchant vessels with 119 crew members.[19]

While the U.S. government wavered between accommodation and conflict with North African rulers, growing anger at white slavery exercised citizens up and down the East Coast. By the mid-1790s a wide variety of plays, newspapers, and novels featured the plight of white American captives. By 1790 the United States already had 694,000 lifetime slaves within its own borders. But the outrage at what a recent anthology has called "White Slaves, African Masters" became a much more galvanizing issue.[20]

Monetary tributes also felt humiliating in the extreme. Americans had been spurred toward revolution by a sense that taxation and honor were incompatible, and now tributes were even worse. As Frank Lambert notes, by 1797 the government was allocating "over 20 percent of the federal government's annual budget," or "about $1.25 million," to the Barbary states, and Europeans started complaining that U.S. extravagance was "driving up the cost of ransoms."[21] From 1790 on, Secretary of State Thomas Jefferson called for war to give America an "erect and independent attitude" on the world's stage.[22] Throughout the 1790s the Senate rejected that call. It earmarked more and more money to placate Muslim rulers and ransom American captives.

Yet who was the enemy? Many Americans voiced more anger at England than at North Africa, in part because of the code of honor. Shortly before the War of 1812, a U.S. representative from North Carolina put the issue succinctly: "Honor is a rule between equals only." Therefore, Israel Pickens argued, honor demands going to war with England, not against "savage" North Africans. Besides, as Lawrence Peskin notes in *Captives and Countrymen*, by 1793 there was a "widespread belief" that Britain was "behind the Algerian captures." Britain seemed bent either on preventing American provisions from coming to France or on freeing Portuguese ships for assistance in the war. Either way, the Portuguese-Algerian truce emboldened North African privateers.[23]

Eight years later, Libya declared war on the United States. That four-year combat cost $3 million, "a sum far greater than the tribute America paid to all four Barbary States in those same years." Michael Kitzen puts the sum at $4 million, plus nearly 100 American deaths. In 1805 the First Barbary War ended without much peace and with another tribute. The cost rivals the expense that Americans remember with triumph, Jefferson's $3 million down payment for the Louisiana Purchase in 1803.[24]

While American leaders raged at being shamed, European governments saw the tributes as what Richard Parker calls "necessary commercial expenses."[25] Americans saw humiliation; Europeans saw business opportunities. As Gordon Wood summarizes the situation, Britain and France "simply bought them off . . . and used them to rid the Mediterranean of smaller rival trading peoples, such as the Danes or the Italian city-states." The United States soon joined that hapless list. Jockeying for competitive advantage, France paid the equivalent of $200,000 each year, and Britain paid up to $280,000 each year. Denmark fought a war with Tripoli but yielded to the bashaw's terms. Meanwhile the United States paid and paid, though sometimes it took the new republic two years to do so.[26] North African rulers fulminated against American disrespect and American leaders fulminated against "extortion" and "blackmail." President Washington called it "the highest disgrace" to pay "banditti" who should "be exterminated from the Earth." In 1801, as the new president, Jefferson reiterated that he was "an enemy to all these douceurs, tributes and humiliations."[27]

In 1815, after President James Madison reluctantly agreed to declare war on the Barbary Coast countries, Stephen Decatur achieved sweet national revenge. He captured 500 North Africans in several naval battles and lost only seven Americans when a cannon misfired. In June, Decatur sailed ten U.S. warships into the harbor at Algiers, where he forced the dey to release its ten American captives and pay a $10,000 indemnity. His triumphant visits to Tunis and Tripoli had similar results. Decatur returned "with seven Tripolitan prisoners who were exhibited as 'real bona fide imported Turks' in several New York theaters."[28]

It was worth all the cost in lives and money, most Americans thought. As Michael Oren concludes, battling an alien enemy brought "a galvanized sense of identity" and asserted the country's "national character."[29] Almost two decades earlier, Tyler had ended *The Algerine Captive* with a plea for national unity "to enforce a due respect among other nations."[30] Now the United States had international stature, despite its inconclusive second war with Britain from 1812 to 1815. Until the 1790s, the confederation had been a provincial array of separated settlements, more "states" than "united." But ongoing humiliations—from England, from France, from the Barbary Coast—drew Americans together. The conflict created both an imperial nation and a navy.

One private joke emerged from this protracted conflict. Annette Gordon-Reed recounts the story. In 1806, after the first war had ended, the ambassador from Tunis came to Washington. Dressed in silks and a twenty-yard turban, he presented his credentials to the secretary of state, James Madison, and requested concubines for himself and his entourage. Madison agreed and provided the services of "Georgia a Greek" and other women, all at State Department expense. As Gordon-Reed says, Madison had to have consulted President Jefferson beforehand, since a scandal might have erupted if the expenditures were publicized. A few days after the ambassador left, Madison joked about it in a letter to Jefferson, underlining "appropriations to foreign intercourse."[31] No doubt Jefferson read the letter with amused tolerance, or perhaps contemptuous superiority, despite his public seething about Arab humiliations and his private liaison with Sally Hemings.

At least three other legacies of the Barbary Wars persist in cultural memory, in addition to the twenty towns and cities named for Decatur. First, America's military hero distilled the new national spirit in an 1816 toast, usually misquoted: "Our Country! In her intercourse with foreign nations may she always be in the *right*; and always *successful*, *right* or *wrong*." Decatur was an audacious young commander, quick to avenge any slight to his honor. He had already fought and won two duels by the time he won the war. In 1820 he died after another duel, with a man whom he had shamed by court-martialing him.[32] Another well-known quotation, "Millions for defense, but not one cent for tribute," emerged from the XYZ Affair as part of the undeclared war with France in the late 1790s.[33] That new pride in U.S. pugnacity reflected American resentment about Barbary slaveries and tributes. Already, long before Tocqueville noticed it, Americans were starting to associate honor with a swaggering national independence, sometimes at the cost of moral integrity.

Second, two songs remain very popular, though only one is singable. The Marine Corps hymn begins, "From the halls of Montezuma / To the shores of Tripoli." The song celebrates the marines' willingness to "fight our country's battles" from ancient Mexico to the Barbary Coast. Ironically, the marines never got to Tripoli; they settled for Derna. More surprisingly, the song that became our national anthem was written in 1805 for Decatur's return from the First Barbary War. Many Americans know that Francis Scott Key set his lyrics for "The Star-Spangled Banner" to the tune of an English drinking song. How many know that his original lyrics celebrated "turbaned heads bowed" to the "brow of the brave"?[34]

A third legacy remains less well known except on the left. In 1797 President John Adams enthusiastically signed a treaty with Tripoli after Congress had passed it with a rare unanimous vote. Article 11 of the treaty began, "As the Government of the United States of America is not, in any sense, founded on the Christian religion."[35]

Here is the full text of the article: "As the Government of the United States of America is not, in any sense, founded on the Christian religion; as it has in itself no character of enmity against the laws, religion, or tranquillity, of Mussulmen; and, as the said States never entered into any war, or act of hostility against any Mahometan nation, it is declared by the parties, that no pretext arising from religious opinions, shall ever produce an interruption of the harmony existing between the two countries." This twelve-part "Treaty of Peace and Friendship between the United States and the Bey and Subjects of Tripoli of Barbary" was negotiated by Richard O'Brien, a former prisoner in Algiers, and signed by Joel Barlow, now better known—if at all—as a literary member of the "Connecticut Wits." The treaty held for only four years, until Tripoli declared war against the United States in 1801.

To resuscitate the fitful tradition of tolerance and respect between the United States and Muslim nations, President Obama's June 2009 speech in Cairo carefully quotes the second clause, "no character of enmity," while ignoring the first. His omission prudently avoids the obvious political dangers. Yet even in an eighteenth-century context, the first clause seems mysterious. Why that ostentatious denial of the nation's Christian roots?

It is possible that Article 11 displays strategic submission from a weak position, or at least a gesture toward equality and respect. But in 1930 a Dutch scholar discovered that the language of Article 11 doesn't appear in the Arab version of the treaty. The article was mysteriously added in translation from Arabic to English, perhaps by Barlow. According to Richard Parker, in 1796 the United States had no one who could translate Arabic.[36] On the web, Yale's Avalon Project reprints the 1805 U.S.-Tripoli treaty, in which Article 14 (of 20) repeats Article 11's wording while doubling its length. For what audience?

Most likely, Article 11 can be added to the many early documents that Isaac Kramnick and R. Laurence Moore reprint in *Our Godless Constitution*. It was probably a trivial instance of what most Federalist politicians took for granted, that civic discourse requires rational challenges to each mind's fallible, limited point of view. Like executive authority, faith needs its checks and balances. Whether written as a bargaining chip or improvised for domestic consumption, Article 11 reaffirmed the Federalist elite's image of the new nation as a place free of aliens' religious fanaticism. In that sense the wording might be a subtle thumb in the eye to flaunt America's secular superiority. Faced with the danger of what some now call a "clash of civilizations," American leaders might have enjoyed sneaking in a subtext: if religious differences don't matter to us, why should they matter to you? Another possibility: the article's proud rhetoric of equality and toleration might have been trying to appease American anger at the spectacle of national weakness, as if to say, "We don't have *this* but at least we have *that*."

Contrast Article 11 with an interview Senator John McCain posted on the Internet in late September of 2007, over a year before the presidential election. At that point he was losing ground in the Republican primaries. When asked whether a Muslim should run for president, McCain responded, "I just have to say in all candor that since this nation was founded primarily on Christian principles, that's a decision the American people would have to make, but personally, I prefer someone who I know who has a solid grounding in my faith." Later he declared that "the Constitution established the United States of America as a Christian nation . . . founded on Christian principles."[37]

In that respect, there's an inverse correlation between American military might and the country's toleration of religious diversity when an alien belief seems to threaten its interests. Among mainstream political commentators, the question of whether the United States was founded on Christian principles has long since moved from "No"

to "Sure, but . . ."[38] Throughout the first American conflict in what is
now called the Middle East, even in the crisis years of 1794–1797, many
U.S. writers and politicians expressed a cosmopolitan sense of the
Muslim world's near-infinite variety. Mixing anger with desperation,
American leaders inveighed against the Barbary States. But they didn't
enhance their popularity, as Ronald Reagan and George W. Bush did,
by referring to an "evil empire" or an "axis of evil."

In Tyler's *The Algerine Captive*, the narrator, Dr. Updike Underhill, journeys through the South then sees the horrors of the Middle
Passage before he becomes an Algerian slave. Underhill sympathizes
with African Muslims as well as southern slaves and gives a sympathetic "Mollah" an exceptionally strong voice. Earlier, Dr. Underhill
reverses stereotypes of "white" and "black" when an African dying on
a slave ship yearns to be "beyond the reach of the wild white beasts."
Later, after being sold as a slave in Algiers, the narrator debates with
the mullah at the request of an Englishman who has converted to
Islam. The mullah's gentleness, sophistication, and artful "sophistry"
almost convert him too, and they become good friends. Tyler doesn't
demonize his captors. Instead he blames the "haughty, exasperated"
British for having "excited the Algerines" to capture U.S. ships, and he
reserves the narrator's greatest anger for a dishonest Jew.[39]

The erosion of that relatively cosmopolitan attitude parallels the
minimization of Article 11 in public discourse. Looking back from the
second Iraq War to the first U.S. conflict with Islamic cultures, I'm
startled by the decline in our religious tolerance. In President Bush's
address to the nation after 9/11, he took care to say that "Islam is a
good religion." Most Americans and more than a few intellectuals,
including Ayaan Hirsi Ali, still don't think that is the case. Today, as we
fight two Muslim nations, we are the world's leading imperial power.
Yet despite President Obama's respectful speech in Cairo, most Americans continue to think Muslims are primitive thugs. When unchecked
might gets wielded by true believers in anything, intolerance becomes
the norm.

Another conclusion highlights a continuity. The Barbary Wars
reflected widespread desires to see America stand tall and "erect," as
Jefferson put it, against African Arabs who exposed American power-

lessness. Not much has changed from then to the time of the second Iraq War. In both wars, real and imagined humiliations mandated a drive to restore national honor by defeating people of darker skins.

The Clash of Civilizations

Five years before what has become known as 9/11, Samuel Huntington's *The Clash of Civilizations* (1996) prepared the way for redirecting domestic racism into anti-Muslim fervor. Ostensibly Huntington's book presents a world of equal and contending civilizations. But a passion for preserving Anglo-Protestant culture animates his polemic against domestic multicultural tolerance. His sophisticated pluralism veils fears of contamination, mixture, and equality. He invites readers to imagine Muslims as a devilish trinity: the New Blacks, the New Barbarians, and the New Communists.

Perhaps inadvertently, his title echoes *The Clash of Culture* [*sic*] *and the Contact of Races*, a 1927 book by George Pitt-Rivers, an Englishman who became a eugenicist. Focusing mostly on Pacific Islanders, Pitt-Rivers sharply contrasts the benefits of "inbreeding" with the "race extinction" brought by miscegenation. Attempts to uplift primitive cultures will lead only to race disintegration and intermixing, he counsels European colonists. Don't try to impose clothing or monogamy either. Just let the inferior races build on their own strengths. Pitt-Rivers seems especially keen about the notion that polygamy is a healthy alternative to "hybridization or extinction." Polygamy had helped keep the Navaho strong as "the only relatively unspoilt Indians left in America," he wrote. Sexual practices in primitive cultures are superior to "the stupid and dysgenic method of our own civilized society which rewards the ability to rise in the social scale with sterility."[40]

Though Huntington doesn't share Pitt-Rivers's enthusiasm for non-monogamous sex, he argues for cultural separation on a much larger scale by translating "races" into "civilizations." Influenced by Bernard Lewis, who emphasized "a clash of civilizations" in 1990, Huntington makes Muslims the primary focus of disparagement and containment.[41] During the Bush-Cheney administration, neoconservatives enthusiastically embraced his world view. In his 1993 article for *Foreign Affairs*, as in his book three years later, Huntington declared that the greatest threat to the West comes from fundamentalist Islam.

Given his conservative supporters and liberal opponents, I was surprised to learn from his 2008 obituary that Huntington was a lifelong Democrat.[42] His cantankerous intellectual integrity led him toward what I'll call ideological whiteness, a challenge to the ascendance of multiculturalism in America. He would reject that racial label, of course. As he repeatedly emphasizes, religion now matters much more than race in fashioning identities. Yet his book presumes white cultural superiority. He resembles the late nineteenth-century New England patricians that people John Higham's *Strangers in the Land*. Like Henry Cabot Lodge, Henry Adams, and Barrett Wendell, he mourns and champions the Anglo-Saxon tradition, now expanded to northern Europe, as the only basis for civilization.[43]

Huntington argues that of the seven or eight major civilizations, "five" (he then lists six) currently contend for dominance in the world. The West, which has descended or fallen from "Western Christendom," is "the only civilization identified by a compass direction" instead of by the name of a "people, religion, or geographical area." In practice, the West means "European civilization," now led by the United States, though it might eventually include Australia. The other core civilizations are the Sinic (China), the Japanese, the Hindu (India), and the Orthodox (Russia). Latin American and African cultures are marginal, since they don't yet have clear core states.[44] And then there's Islam.

Islam from without and multiculturalism from within are the villains of Huntington's story. To him Islam has been violently decentered since the seventh century. In the early 1990s, over two-thirds of "intercivilizational wars" have been between Muslims and others. "Islam's borders are bloody," Huntington wrote in his 1993 article. That line got the most flak, he notes. So he intensified it in his book: "Islam's borders *are* bloody, and so are its innards."[45]

For a thousand years Islam and Christianity have been at war, and twice the Christian West was almost overrun. Both faiths are monotheistic, universalistic "missionary religions" with "parallel concepts of 'jihad' and 'crusade'" as well as near-constant rivalry. "Each has been the other's Other."[46]

Insistently and repetitively, Huntington disparages Islam's tendency to ground identities in small-group identifications and large-scale faith. Huntington calls that retrograde Islamic tendency a "U-shaped" identity, based in "the small group and the great faith, the tribe and the *ummah*." The U begins in family, clan, or tribal bonds, slides down to weak and arbitrarily defined nation-states, and precipitously ascends to a passion for Islam, without any pan-Arab state to match. Muslims simply can't do core states, Huntington claims. Modern Arab nations tend to be "fragile states formed on a Western model alien to the traditions of Islam."[47] Clearly he prefers what Tocqueville described as the democratic model of individuals competing in a nation-state, exemplified in the progress that Ayaan Hirsi Ali would make from one model to the other.

Huntington denies the usefulness of the term "barbarians," which he says was invented in the French Enlightenment as a transient stage toward our current awareness of multiple civilizations. Perhaps, he hopes, the world can transcend "Western arrogance, Islamic intolerance, and Sinic assertiveness." Nevertheless, the West's unique beliefs in "Christianity, pluralism, individualism, and [the] rule of law . . . made it possible for the West to invent modernity, expand throughout the world, and become the envy of other societies."[48] Islam remains the "underlying problem for the West" because it too is universalistic. Like the West, Muslims "are convinced of the superiority of their culture." Unlike Westerners, Muslims "are obsessed with the inferiority of their power."[49]

Despite Huntington's disparagement of the word barbarians, his sophisticated geopolitical analysis climaxes with an apocalyptic vision of universal civilization facing barbarians at the gate. What is worse, the West loses. His early chapter on "the Decline of the West" anticipates that fate. There aren't any barbarians, only multiple civilizations, he asserts. But will there be "a moral reversion as Western power declines?" Yes, he concludes. "On a worldwide basis Civilization seems in many respects to be yielding to barbarism," with "a global Dark Ages" in the offing.[50] It's racial shaming in a different key. Once again, fear of losing "civilized" white entitlements propels the resurgence of "barbarism" in his analysis.

To take his second apocalyptic scenario first, Huntington questions whether modernism has brought progress. Barbarians lurk inside each civilization, waiting to slouch forth. In the 1990s, as transnational corporations undermine the "law and order" enforced by nation-states, "a global crime wave" will burgeon that includes "transnational criminal mafias, drug cartels, and terrorist gangs violently assaulting Civilization." Rootless criminals will mirror rootless corporations. The "increasing anarchy" of contemporary life will reflect the "decay" of present Civilization, a word Huntington suddenly capitalizes. Eventually "a different surging civilization with a lower level of Civilization" will replace it.[51] Huntington's vision replicates Yeats's Second Coming, with a similarly patrician mix of contempt and fear at the prospect of being overwhelmed from below.

His first apocalyptic scenario is more spectacular. He predicts that in 2010, fourteen years in the future, we may be in a "global war" involving all the major civilizations. The war will start with Vietnam versus China, a member state versus a core state. Not having learned anything from the Vietnam War, the West will intervene to help Vietnam. Alliances will kick in as the dominoes start falling, and soon India will battle Pakistan, Japan will join with China, Iran will aid Pakistan, China will invade Russia, and—shades of the 1962 Cuban missile crisis—China and Iran will deploy nuclear missiles to Bosnia and Algeria. Meanwhile Islamic groups will take over Arab states and, seeing Western weakness, conquer Israel. Then Algeria will bomb France with one of those nuclear missiles, NATO will retaliate against northern Africa, and Russia will join NATO before invading China.[52]

By the end of this scenario all of the great civilizations will have been destroyed except for India, which tries "to reshape the world along Hindu lines." The bystanders will then come in to dominate their spheres of influence. Indonesia will rule East Asia, while "Hispanic leaders [will] come to power" in the United States, hoping for a Marshall Plan from "the booming Latin American countries which sat out the war." Africa will colonize devastated Europe after it "disgorges hordes of socially mobilized people to prey on the remains."[53]

That's probably "a wildly implausible fantasy to the reader," Huntington admits. But he doesn't disown it. Only as he thinks about

Africans swamping Europe does his language turn explicitly racist, with references to vultures, coyotes, wild dogs, and jungle ants. Otherwise he's more concerned to make readers learn from the war's ultimate cause, the West's attempt "to humiliate and browbeat China" by intervening in China's "legitimate sphere of influence" instead of adhering to the abstention rule.[54] That's the political equivalent of Just Say No. Keep your own peoples in line, and let other core states dominate their member states.

When Huntington considers internal threats to the dominance of the United States as a core state, his argument shifts from affirming global pluralism to presenting internal diversity as a disaster. Barack Obama's inaugural address declared that "our patchwork heritage is a strength, not a weakness." But Huntington finds "moral decline" everywhere. We tolerate immigrants "who reject assimilation" to preserve their cultural values, and we accept people who devalue the work ethic in favor of "personal indulgence" such as divorce and drugs. The United States "will become a cleft country" if we don't reaffirm "the American Creed . . . liberty, democracy, individualism, equality before the law, constitutionalism, private property." A "multicivilizational United States . . . will be the United Nations." The United States has to have a cultural core. "Rejection of the Creed and of Western civilization means the end of the United States of America as we have known it."[55] His use of the country's full name reminds me of a parent chastising a disobedient child.

Not content with his abstract indictment, Huntington takes that "cleft country" image further. It's implicitly castrated, like the "torn country" image he associates with worldwide weakness. Multiculturalism is self-emasculation. "If the United States is de-Westernized . . . the West becomes a minuscule and declining part of the world's population on a small and inconsequential peninsula at the extremity of the Eurasian land mass."[56] A preoccupation with beset manhood animates this passage. Without America's "moral" leadership, there will be national impotence and global anarchy.

Huntington's image of that anarchic, peripheral peninsula rechannels Richard Nixon's defense of the Cambodia bombings. In Nixon's address to the nation on April 30, 1970, he took on the sixties to defend the Vietnam War: "We live in an age of anarchy, both abroad and at home." Great universities are being attacked, he said: "Small nations all over the world find themselves under attack from within and without. If, when the chips are down, the world's most powerful nation, the United States of America, acts like a pitiful, helpless giant, the forces of totalitarianism and anarchy will threaten free nations and free institutions throughout the world." Therefore we should bomb Cambodia, so that we can protect other nations from being destroyed.[57]

In Huntington's next book, *Who Are We?* (2004), cultural honor looms just under the surface of his call to resurrect what he likes to call "Western Christendom." Implicitly he reverses Frederick Jackson Turner's frontier thesis. All the newer American ethnicities should work to restore the "Anglo-Protestant culture" established by our founders, especially "religiosity." Admittedly, those founders were "few and homogeneous: overwhelmingly white (thanks to the exclusion of blacks and Indians from citizenship), British, and Protestant," but no matter. The basic elements of his creed—equality, rights, the rule of law, the dignity of the individual, the work ethic, conscience, and distrust of big government—all came from "dissenting Protestantism."[58]

Now "multiculturalism and diversity" have eroded that "core" and creed. Opposing white nativists, Huntington even favors interracial marriage to make race matter "less and less." His utopian dream would be that "choosing an ethnic identity becomes like joining a club" as values detach from racial identities. Then nonwhite ethnic groups will see the glory of our Anglo-Protestant foundation, while white people will learn "that their mixed ancestries make them 'All American.'" No more affirmative action and "creeping bilingualism"! At last America can become neither cosmopolitan nor imperial, but "national" once again.[59] Barely masked in that extended fantasy looms Huntington's yearning to extend the power of a white elite.

Ironically, the "clash of civilizations" argument proved useful to two groups of political leaders who indeed had become each other's Other. While Washington neocons invoked *The Clash of Civilizations* to justify their preemptive war, Osama bin Laden liked to refer to Huntington's concept too. As Lawrence Wright notes, bin Laden often said "it was his duty to promote such a clash."[60]

Huntington's book continues the culture wars of the 1980s. Like conservatives who mocked multicultural revisions of the traditional literary canon, Huntington tries to shift the bond between whiteness and honor from skin color to Western culture. Though his emphasis on religious and democratic values seems pluralistic, he champions a Protestant parochialism as the last best hope for preserving national greatness. His retreat from explicit endorsements of white honor bespeaks a noisy desperation.

The Second Iraq War, 2003–?

On December 14, 2008, a young Iraqi journalist threw two shoes at President Bush. The occasion was a press conference with the Iraqi prime minister, Nuri Kamal al-Maliki, during the fourth of Bush's surprise visits to Iraq. American and Arab TV stations replayed the tape again and again, and the American press featured the story for several days. As the *New York Times* reported, when Muntader al-Zaidi threw the first shoe, he shouted in Arabic, "This is a gift from the Iraqis, this is the farewell kiss, you dog!" When Bush ducked, al-Zaidi threw the second shoe, shouting "This is from the widows, the orphans and those who were killed in Iraq!" Bush ducked again.[61] Each time, the throws barely missed.

The American media focused mostly on Bush's quick reflexes and on the absurdity of the attack. Even on *Countdown*, Keith Olbermann's left-leaning MSNBC news show, *Newsweek* correspondent Howard Fineman called it "slapstick" and "trivial." Bush himself dismissed the attack: "That's what people do in a free society, draw attention to themselves." Next day Secretary of State Condoleezza Rice told the Associated Press that the shoe throwing was "a kind of sign of the freedom that people feel in Iraq." Not for the first time, she was playing Echo to Bush's Narcissus.

Only a few reporters emphasized the attack's impact as a public shaming. In the *Times*, Steven Lee Myers and Alissa J. Rubin noted that "hitting someone with a shoe is considered the supreme insult in Iraq. It means that the target is even lower than the shoe, which is always on the ground and dirty." On April 9, 2003, crowds had hurled

shoes at the statue of Saddam Hussein before helping U.S. Marines
pull it down. A day before al-Zaidi's attack, and long after many Iraqis
had turned against the United States, crowds opposing a new security
agreement threw stones at an effigy of Bush, then burned it. In the
United States, al-Zaidi had his fifteen seconds of fame as a ridiculous
hothead, though some admired him for his aim. In the Arab world,
he became an instant folk hero. By the first day of his trial, he had
twenty-five lawyers representing him. In Tikrit, a statue of a large shoe
was erected in his honor, though the Iraqi Parliament ordered it torn
down. A Saudi Arabian offered the equivalent of $10 million for one
of the shoes.[62]

The American response reflects the blinding presumption that characterized most aspects of the U.S. occupation in its early years.[63] At least
for the public record, Bush and Rice proclaimed that a newly liberated
nation-state's democratic freedom explained such behavior. It was just
an Islamic version of aggressive individualism, an old American story,
and a natural way of getting attention in a big nation-state.

The shoe-throwing had a different resonance in the Arab world.
It wasn't an assertion of freedom, it wasn't about self-assertion, and
it wasn't about becoming a somebody in a stable nation-state. It was
an attempt to humiliate an oppressor whose occupation had shamed
Islamic peoples across national borders. It aimed at restoring transnational honor. Iraqis disagreed only about whether it was honorable
or shameful to humiliate a despised guest.

Mark Danner begins *Torture and Truth* with a story that highlights
the Iraqi passion for honor. As he asks a resident of Falluja about attacks
on American soldiers, the young Iraqi interrupts him. In "limited but
eloquent English," the young man "pushed his face close to mine, and
spoke to me slowly and emphatically: 'For Fallujans it is a *shame* to
have foreigners break down their doors. It is a *shame* for them to have
foreigners stop and search their women. It is a *shame* for the foreigners
to put a bag over their heads, to make a man lie on the ground with
your shoe on his neck. This is a great *shame*, you understand? This is a
great *shame* for the whole tribe. It is the *duty* of that man, and of that
tribe, to get revenge on this soldier—to kill that man. Their duty is to
attack them, to *wash the shame*. The shame is a *stain*, a dirty thing; they

have to *wash* it. No sleep—we cannot sleep until we have revenge. They have to kill soldiers.'" Predictably, the insurgents' assaults on American soldiers in Falluja began two weeks after soldiers wore boots into a mosque and roughed up some of the worshippers.[64]

Lawrence Wright's *The Looming Tower* grounds extremist Islamic movements in a doubly specific sense of shame: the loss of Palestine's territory to Israel in 1948 and the humiliation of the Six Day War in 1967. "The profound appeal of Islamic fundamentalism in Egypt and elsewhere was born in this shocking debacle." Americans saw terror; Arabs saw shame. At least three American wars in the region followed from that clash of perceptions. It took President Obama, a man with a partly Muslim heritage, to parse the causes without rancor or bias. In his 2009 Cairo speech, he lists three basic reasons for conflicts in the Middle East: colonialism; the Cold War, in which the West treated Muslim nations as "proxies"; and widespread Islamic revulsion against modernity and globalization. All three reasons grow from multiple humiliations.[65]

Wright begins his book with the history of Sayyid Qutb, the founder of the Muslim Brotherhood. The story opens when the reclusive Egyptian was in his forties. In 1948 Qutb left his mid-level clerkship to get more education in the United States. After Qutb's fourteen-month stay in the District of Columbia, Colorado, and California, he came home convinced that America was racist as well as primitive, and his subsequent writings passionately argued that Islam should oppose all things modern, which is to say, all things white and American. "The white man in Europe or America is our number-one enemy," he wrote. "The white man crushes us underfoot while we teach our children about his civilization. . . . Let us instead plant the seeds of hatred, disgust, and revenge in the souls of these children."[66] These writings had an immense influence on later radicals. Like Qutb, they thought Islam should return to the purity of its seventh-century origins. They aimed at turning the Middle East's modern secular states into theocracies governed by the laws of Sharia, not least to control the sexual behavior of women.

After Wright portrays other radical Islamic leaders, he finally settles on Osama bin Laden, a richer and more nerdy recluse who came to share Qutb's vision. Osama bin Laden had a curious similarity with some right-wing Republicans. He too waged what Lawrence Frank calls "a theological war." It isn't a battle between Al-Qaeda and the United States, bin Laden said. "'This is a battle of Muslims against the global Crusaders.'"[67]

Three weeks after the destruction of the World Trade Center, Al Jazeera broadcast a taped speech by Osama bin Laden. Ostensibly he was enraged at the West because the sacred caliphate had disappeared with the Ottoman Empire after World War I. His rhetoric of revenge seeks to turn that shame and anger toward the West. "What America is tasting now is only a copy of what we have tasted. . . . Our Islamic nation has been tasting the same for more [than] eighty years, of humiliation and disgrace."[68]

On the seventh anniversary of 9/11, the *Times* featured a story about a scholar who spent five years translating over 1,500 Al-Qaeda tapes recorded from 1988 to 2000; twenty were by Osama bin Laden. The tapes reveal the organization's shifting tactics to appeal to recruits and the daily boredom of being on jihad. Various speakers dream of uniting against a common enemy, whether that enemy is communism or Israel or America. All the while, one aspect of Al-Qaeda remained unchanged. Its enduring appeal rests on a vision of resurrecting the past: "a time of chivalry and honor and generosity and manliness and the apex of tribalism."[69]

Ironically, the yearning of extremist Muslims for an idealized age of patriarchal chivalry, now over 1,000 years old, has more than a little in common with the yearning of some American fundamentalists for the Rapture and the conversion of the Jews.[70] On both sides, intense religious affiliation perpetuates a voluntary tribalism voiced with evangelical fervor. When such groups feel humiliated, they yearn to humiliate in return. The Al-Qaeda members who bombed the World Trade Center in 1993 "were hoping to humiliate an enemy" by killing civilians, even though that violated Islamic law. "Revenge for many varied injustices was their constant theme," and they "courted retaliation as a prod to other Muslims." One meaning of "Islam" is submission, but only to God, not to the West or to anyone who has dishonored the believers, as they felt the West did so flagrantly with the imposition of Israel. The U.S. success in the first Iraq War intensified the humiliation.[71]

Arab tortures of dissidents also fueled the flames. In Egyptian prisons, as Wright puts it, "humiliation, which is the essence of torture," turned many Muslim men into "militants whose need for retribution—they called it justice—was all-consuming." They blamed the West, probably rightly, for "enabling" Egypt's repressive treatment of them. Such leaders emerged with "an overwhelming desire for revenge, which was characteristic of men who have been abused in prison."[72] The passion to restore tribal and Islamic honor augmented personal desires for revenge.

Back in the United States, such honor-shame issues seemed far away. Yet again and again in the first days after 9/11, Americans from the president to reporters and commentators tried to brand the bombers as "cowards."[73] Just under the surface of seemingly rational discourse, honor and national manhood were at stake once again. Leaders assured voters and themselves that restoring national honor through military dominance would be easy and cheap, since Iraqis seemed to welcome Americans with open arms. Very few citizens felt any shame about the war as long as the United States was winning. But doubts began to fester as the daily headlines about suicide bombing kept coming.

A simmering sense of national shame reached a boiling point on April 28, 2004, when CBS broadcast photographs of American abuses in Abu Ghraib prison. Male prisoners were forced to be naked and prostrate. Some were leashed. Some had to masturbate in public, watch sexual acts, or perform homosexual acts. The American guards humiliated their prisoners for sport as well as for vindictiveness. Guards photographed their exploits for trophies, much as white southerners liked to send postcards of themselves at lynchings. Most Americans felt shock when they witnessed these sadistic spectacles. To millions of viewers, fellow Americans were humiliating themselves, not their prisoners. American dishonor leaped from the TV screen, as joltingly as it had done during the civil rights years.[74]

Like the neocon planners in Washington, the Abu Ghraib guards in Iraq had been prepped about the Arabs. Their instructors had reduced Raphael Patai's homogenizing book *The Arab Mind* to two even more homogenized points. Patai declares that Arabs understand only force and that Arab men are obsessed with sexual shame and humiliation. To the credit of the Marine Corps, one of their pamphlets informed the troops, "Do not shame or humiliate a man in public." If they have to "cause shame," do it privately, since "the most important qualifier for all shame is for a third party to witness the act." Don't shame detainees by placing hoods over their heads. "Placing a detainee on the ground or putting a foot on him implies you are God. This is one of the worst things we can do." Arabs consider feet or soles of feet unclean. Ditto bodily fluids or "using the bathroom around others." And so forth.[75]

Fine, the guards said to themselves. Let's do the opposite. Unclothe prisoners in front of each other, sodomize them with batons, make them do oral sex, force them to masturbate, pile them in naked pyramids, photograph them covered with shit—whatever. They think dogs are ritually unclean, so we'll put dog leashes on their naked bodies and have dogs bite them. We'll strut our own sexual fluids. Their shame shows our mastery. As Charles Graner said to a fellow specialist, "The Christian in me says it's wrong, but the corrections officer in me says, 'I love to make a grown man piss himself.'"[76]

Over 100 years earlier, a U.S. marching song in the Philippines had celebrated the frequent use of water torture with Filipino prisoners. The song's title is "Water Cure," and the verses display the soldiers' jaunty conviction that torture can cure the Filipinos' slavery. The song begins, "Get the good old syringe boys and fill it to the brim. / We've caught another nigger and we'll operate on him." Then the Charles Graners of their time would chorus, "Shove in the nozzle deep and let him taste of liberty." Another verse urged, "Keep on till the squirt gun breaks or he explodes the slave." That's the way to "fill him full of liberty."[77]

Americans were repelled by the tortures at Abu Ghraib. Yet only a few underlings were punished. President Bush said that the abuses at Abu Ghraib were just "disgraceful conduct by a few American troops, who dishonored our country and disregarded our values."[78] Five years later, Vice President Cheney was unapologetic in his exit interviews, as he continued to be thereafter. Such tortures were necessary, he said. The now-infamous Torture Memo from John Yoo of the Department of Justice to Alberto Gonzales, the attorney general, justified getting information by almost any means necessary, whether in Abu Ghraib or Guantánamo, or through renditions of prisoners to other countries that lacked concerns about torture.

Awareness that torture had been encouraged from the top emerged years after the 2004 election. Most American voters knew (sort of) but did not want to know that at least twenty-eight Abu Ghraib detainees had died, five clearly from torture.[79] In other ways, too, racial shaming was alive and well among American soldiers in Iraq. Casual racism often helped alleviate their anxieties. Soldiers driving past Iraqi civilians would regularly shatter bottles on their heads. Referring to another method of torture, some Iraqis joked, "I always knew the Americans would bring electricity back to Baghdad. I just never thought they'd be shooting it up my ass."[80]

While most Americans initially recoiled from the revelations of what had been taking place at Abu Ghraib, Iraqi responses to the photos that were released were quite muted. They'd seen it all before, and much worse, many times. To them the United States had become just the latest in a long line of dictators. The self-preening, the ineptness, the heartlessness, the ruthlessness—what else is new? If Americans thought they were bringing the freedom and benevolence of a redeemer nation, many Iraqis thought "A tyrant is a tyrant." Each side reduced the other to "they all look alike."

Why did the photos of Emmett Till succeed in 1955 and the photos from Abu Ghraib fail in 2004? The pictures of Till's ripped-up face shocked Americans into awareness of the need for black civil rights. The photos couldn't be translated into the image of a black beast who might have deserved it. He was just a teenager who flirted with a girl. Yet he had been ferociously murdered and mutilated.

Honor-shame issues influenced the reception of the photos. The pictures of Till's mutilation couldn't be justified with the rhetoric of proclaiming white men's honor by "protecting our women." In the 1920s and 1930s, as Glenda Gilmore emphasizes, photos of lynching had circulated "from Melbourne to Moscow" with little national effect. Newspapers mostly ignored sit-ins and other protests. Now, in the midst of the Cold War and with the advent of TV, pictures of a dead boy made white Americans think about black civil rights, as if for the first time.[81] The pictures undermined the imagined opposition between shameful blacks and honorable whites. Race-based hierarchies of perception partially disintegrated, and the group called white people no longer seemed quite so supreme. The larger group called Americans became more inclusive and more willing to shame white racists. The photographs of Till accelerated that transformation.

The American recoil against the Abu Ghraib pictures didn't block President Bush's reelection in 2004. The photos of abuses had surfaced just six months earlier, and reports were already blaming midlevel military management. Yet for most voters, the we/they dichotomy held firm. The pictures didn't threaten group boundaries. The first jolt of "My God, we're just as bad as they are" quickly yielded to "Just a few bad apples among us, and besides, the prisoners were probably terrorists." Fear of bad Muslims trumped shame about bad Americans. With remarkable speed, the public outcry receded to a more muted sense of "Oh dear, we were quite bad, but they deserved it."

I'll hazard the speculation that Bush was reelected not despite the photos but because of them. Three years after 9/11, the sense of national humiliation was still too bitter. Bush was victorious not primarily because of conflicts over abortion or gay marriage but because we were revenging Muslims' attacks. Here, too, honor-shame issues shaped the reception of the photos. The pictures proved that the ostensibly multicultural United States was reclaiming national honor by taking racial shaming overseas. Voters reprised Stephen Decatur's "My country, right or wrong." The photos showed what voters wanted to know, that the administration was kicking some brown butt—it didn't matter whose.

Not until December of 2008 was the blame to be placed squarely at the doors of the White House. A bipartisan Senate report finally pointed at the top leaders, not midlevel commanders and guards, for encouraging the abuses of detainees in Iraq, Afghanistan, and Guantánamo Bay. From Vice President Cheney and Defense Secretary Rumsfeld on down, the administration had urged military personnel to get information by any means necessary and had hired the lawyers who would let them do it.

Did the Bush administration get useful information? Former CIA agents and interrogators argue that torture is rarely effective and often intensifies resistance. Was it for revenge, to display dominance, or just to vent frustration?

I think that in a depressing inversion of Article 11's high-road stance over 200 years earlier, our government's tough-guy stance was targeted for domestic consumption. A majority of the voters felt that their country was in charge again. If some Americans took vicarious pleasure in watching alleged terrorists cringe, more thought, "Well, at least we're doing our damnedest." Getting trustworthy information might have been a plus, at best. Humiliating accused terrorists satisfied American guards, American leaders, and too many American citizens that we were regaining national honor, if only through the dishonor of flaunting amoral power.

In the Barbary Wars, Article 11 celebrated American tolerance. Now torture displayed American vengeance.[82] The Iraq War began in March 2003 as a second effort to regain dominance in the Middle East. The roiling national atmosphere of victimization and humiliation hadn't been at all eased by temporarily defeating the Taliban in Afghanistan. Long before 9/11, President Bush was eager to make Iraq what Michael Oren calls "the test case of his new doctrine." Vice President Cheney enthusiastically shared and inflamed the president's desire to use Iraq to bring exemplary democracy to the Middle East. After success proved elusive, at least Iraqi prisoners were at hand to humiliate.[83]

More surprisingly, only two years later the home front had changed. In 2006 voters elected a Democratic Congress because they saw our occupation of Iraq as inept, expensive, and increasingly pointless as well as lethal to thousands of American soldiers. Most voting Americans had turned against claims that national honor was at stake in this war. The accelerating pace of that shift dramatically contrasts with the twelve or fourteen years it took for public opinion to turn so grudgingly against the Vietnam War. Even then, for decades afterward, many Americans—including John McCain—remained enraged and bitter that we had lost honor by letting ourselves be defeated.[84]

Entrenched metaphors die hard at the top, especially when they justify a war. From 1954 through the Johnson administration, the country's leaders frequently compared Vietnam to Munich, where British prime minister Neville Chamberlain had tried to appease Hitler in 1938. In a 1954 letter to Churchill, President Eisenhower compared Vietnam to Munich, and almost everyone in the Johnson administration repeatedly insisted on "The Munich Analogy."[85] Over thirty years later the analogy came around again for the second war in Iraq.

Paul Wolfowitz, Douglas Feith, and Paul Bremer all passionately believed that the right historical analogy for overthrowing Saddam Hussein was Adolf Hitler. If we don't invade Iraq in a preemptive war, we would be appeasing Saddam, who had become a Hitler with more entrenched power, their argument went. Never mind that Iraq was a "tin-pot little dictatorship by comparison," as an Iraqi emigré told George Packer. Liberating the Iraqis became almost analogous to liberating the Jews from Nazi concentration camps. Bremer dismissed out of hand any comparisons to the civil war in Vietnam, in this case a civil war between Sunnis and Shiites. Only Gen. George Shinseki risked comparing Iraq with Vietnam instead of with Nazi Germany. He was removed from command.[86]

But the Nazi metaphor didn't match Iraqi realities. Thomas Ricks has distilled the problem: "The root cause of the occupation's paralysis may have been the cloud of cognitive dissonance that seems to have fogged in Rumsfeld and other senior Pentagon officials" as well as the two prime movers, Vice President Cheney and President Bush. Perceptions and metaphors couldn't get confirmed. To Cheney's shock, no one found any weapons of mass destruction. Instead, daily "bombings and snipings" greeted American troops, but no big winnable battles.[87]

As so many have said, the lack of effective planning for the postwar occupation didn't help. Douglas Feith, the Rumsfeld deputy who was in charge of the planning, believed Americans would be welcomed as liberators, so Iraq would need only modest assistance after the military victory. As journalists and historians have abundantly detailed, more extensive plans were ignored because of that assumption. The defense secretary went even further. In an early planning session for the Iraq occupation, Rumsfeld closed the meeting by declaring, "We will impose our reality on them."[88]

Soon Iraqis' joy turned to resentment. Once again they felt colonized. By December 2005, according to George Packer, Baghdad had mostly disintegrated into neighborhoods riddled with conflicts between rival groups of Sunnis and Shiites. Displaced families gathered by the thousands. As Packer observes, "It amounted to a campaign of ethnic cleansing in a low-grade civil war." Iraqis had long avoided the label of civil war because it threatened mixed marriages and mixed neighborhoods.[89] But here it was, in the country the Europeans had arbitrarily created sixty-four years earlier. As a professor remarked, Iraq remains "half urban, half bedouin." Now the Bedouin side seemed ascendant. Packer concludes, "Iraq turned out to be more religious, more tribal, more suspicious, and more violent than most outsiders had imagined."[90]

In *The Fog of War*, Errol Morris's 2003 documentary about Robert McNamara, the former defense secretary during the 1960s, McNamara says of the Vietnam War with an air of amazed discovery, "It was a civil war!" That insight was old news as early as 1954, when the Geneva agreements divided Vietnam along the 17th parallel. By that year the United States was already funding about three-fourths of the French war with Ho Chi Minh. In their 1967 history of Vietnam, George M. Kahin and John W. Lewis anticipated McNamara's discovery by over thirty years. They argued that the conflict in Vietnam was a civil war misperceived through a Cold War lens.[91]

Another failure of perception was more profound. Paul Wolfowitz and other American leaders presumed that Al-Qaeda had to have state sponsorship and that Iraq was the sponsor. They held fast to that presumption in the face of mounting evidence to the contrary. As Ron Suskind discovered, President Bush and Vice President Cheney paid $5 million to the former head of Iraqi intelligence to keep him quiet about the lack of weapons of mass destruction. To help win the 2004 election, they also had him sign a fraudulent, backdated letter saying that Mohammed Atta had trained for 9/11 in Iraq.[92]

George Packer sums up the perception problem: "When September 11 forced the imagination to grapple with something radically new, the president's foreign-policy advisers reached for what they had always known." The threat had to be "well-armed enemy states." So the solution had to be "military power and the will to use it."[93] But what should be done as the state of Iraq disintegrated? And why did insurgents keep appearing from other Arab states in the Middle East?

American neoconservatives didn't let themselves see how Islam was the basis for a transnational resurgence of tribal values of honor and shame. At that point Iraq remained less a country than a collection of 150 or more tribes, with thousands of clans. Honor often demanded loyalty to tribes and clans instead of nation-building, and honor required a defense of Islam across the region. American leaders could not imagine that their white-knight liberation might intensify shame that leaped across national borders.[94] Instead they saw good guys and bad guys. In January 2002, Bush's first State of the Union address threw down the chivalric gauntlet: Iraq was a prime member of the "axis of evil."[95] Like Thomas Jefferson, the president and vice-president itched to go to war. Unlike Jefferson, they could do it with impunity.

One final continuity has aggravated American conservatives who still yearn for America to exemplify white honor. Bribes and tributes to Barbary rulers have been transformed into payments for oil. Billions of dollars have vanished into Arab pockets and bank accounts throughout the Middle East. Many Americans see the country's dependence on Arab oil as shameful. In 1980, John B. Kelly implicitly compared the Muslim rulers to the Barbary pirates. For Kelly, the oil prices were "a bold attempt to lay the Christian West under tribute to the Muslim East."[96] "Lay . . . under" implies a sexual feminization, a contemptible fall from Jefferson's demand that America "stand erect."

These changes and continuities have at least three implications. First, dominance can cloud perception. As I mentioned in my first chapter, Hegel's 1807 meditation on the Lord and the Bondsman concludes that the bondsman sees the lord more clearly than the lord sees himself. The Bush administration saw themselves as chivalric rescuers who would overthrow a Hitler-like dictator. After the first spate of wary enthusiasm, most Iraqis saw Americans as yet another colonial oppressor.

Second, as white honor became shakier at home, imperial wars shored it up abroad. Amy Kaplan has made that case for Teddy Roosevelt in the Spanish-American War. To counter stories that black "Buffalo

Soldiers" had rescued white Rough Riders from ambush, Roosevelt tried "to rescue the chivalric mode itself from black counter-narratives and preserve it as an exclusively Anglo-Saxon possession."[97]

Third, the Barbary Wars and what the United States has called the "War on Terror" have been the only two external American wars not fought against states. During the nineteenth century, honor in the United States took on national and racialized dimensions. In its new enlarged format, national honor licensed violent acts to humiliate other large racialized groups. Those shamings were called wars, and the villains were called states. At the end of the twentieth century, demonized Arab states helped unify Americans and refocus the country's imperial resolve.

Nevertheless, by the Second Iraq War, bonds between white honor and power had partially disintegrated. For each Gulf War, the U.S. secretary of state was African American, and in the second war the top general was Latino, while the top military spokesman in Iraq was black.[98] Their visible presence helped Americans take pride in their multicultural superiority to a seemingly homogeneous Arab enemy. Perhaps that pride was a secular form of Article 11. Our tolerant, high-tech civilization would take on the primitives, subdue them, and remake them in our image.[99]

The whiteness in white honor now seems quite tarnished. But the drive to make the nation-state exemplify a collective form of manly honor remains. As Evelin Lindner puts it, "Clashes of civilization are not the problem, but clashes of humiliation are."[100] From the eighteenth century to the twenty-first century, American honor has persisted in its most basic form, as a license for violent revenge to preserve a sense of group superiority. If darker-skinned people are the enemy, the task becomes more inviting.

CHAPTER 6

THE 2008 CAMPAIGN

Near the end of the 2008 presidential campaign, a young white woman working for John McCain in western Pennsylvania appeared with a backward B carved on her cheek. Ashley Todd said she had been sexually assaulted and mutilated by a black mugger six feet, four inches tall who might have been working for Obama. Immediately the Drudge Report featured Ashley Todd's accusation, right-wing blogs trumpeted the story, newspapers published it, and the McCain campaign pushed it. The campaign's Pennsylvania communications director told reporters that the B stood for Barack. By that evening McCain had telephoned Ashley Todd to express his sympathy and Sarah Palin had called her family.

But the next day the conservative *New York Post* had a page-one headline: "B is for Bulls___." Pittsburgh police had discovered the story was a hoax. After taking a lie detector test and giving conflicting stories, the disturbed 20-year-old confessed that she had probably mutilated herself in her car but couldn't remember doing it, so she blamed it on her fantasy of a black Obama worker. The B was backward because she had been looking in the car mirror. Within a day, the story of the black beast and the defenseless white woman had fallen apart.

Or rather, it had a second life. Rebranded, it served left-leaning commentators as a prime example of the race-baiting tactics used by the McCain campaign, especially in its last few weeks. As many people noted, 100 years earlier white people would have lynched someone, anyone, so long as he was black, no questions asked.[1] In Hawaii, too, as my second chapter mentions, the 1931–1932 Massie trials featured a young white woman who claimed that she had been raped by several "black" men. For months, the nation's media and politicians avidly focused on protecting white women, not on questioning her false accusation or even on sympathizing with the dark-skinned youth her white defenders had killed.

So there has been racial progress. The calls to affirm white honor by avenging an unsubstantiated attack on a white woman have a much shorter half-life. Calls for action to defend white purity against black beasts are much more likely to be seen as the product of fantasy than they used to be, though such charges still get cultural traction.

Yet Americans still love to witness flaming and shaming on talk radio and the web, on late-night TV shows, and in runaway movie successes such as *Borat*. What Van Jones has called "the 'gotcha' bullies" get instant media attention.[2] Where such shaming proliferates, concerns about honor loom in the background, now in more race-neutral forms. Though playing the race card now invites public humiliation, the role of shaming in securing the honor of small or large groups persists. The kind of mockery we see from TV "news" comics such as Jon Stewart on the left and commentators such as Bill O'Reilly on the right elevates a cosmopolitan or embattled Us and makes scapegoats of a provincial, hypocritical, or immoral Them.

John McCain's Lineage

The union of whiteness with national honor has had a long political life, and it still has a radioactive presence in the Republican South. The 2008 presidential election became a referendum on its persistence, personified in Senator John McCain. A war hero who survived five years of imprisonment by the North Vietnamese with his dignity mostly intact, McCain has often proclaimed his belief in personal and national honor and vigorously supported the second Iraq War to avenge 9/11. In 2005 he courageously broke with President Bush to assail the administration's de facto sponsorship of torture. McCain had experienced torture personally and knew what humiliation felt like. He was appalled that American leaders could degrade his country's honor to the level of the terrorists.

McCain continues to celebrate America's multiethnic strengths. But running for president can bind a candidate to his base. McCain admirably resisted that pressure in 2000, and failed. In 2008 he won the Republican nomination by appealing to voters who held on tight to racialized honor. McCain's campaign managers tried to inflame voters' anxieties about the prospect of a brown-skinned president without making his supporters feel racist.

The Republican "Southern Strategy" had worked for forty years. It emerged as a canny Republican response to President Johnson's passage of the 1964 Civil Rights Act and the 1965 Voting Rights Bill. After securing the first bill's passage, Johnson said privately, "There goes the South for a generation."[3] Almost immediately, in the 1964 elections, rage against Johnson led to Barry Goldwater's victory in five southern states. During the next five decades, Republicans took full advantage of the white flight from the Democrats. The political shift went nationwide for several generations.

Among the innumerable examples of Republicans' race-based successes is Dan Quayle. He began his political rise at age 29 in 1976 by defeating a five-term Indiana congressman, J. Edward Roush. Quayle campaigned against "big government" and "forced busing." Another example is Jesse Helms, who rose to power in North Carolina in the 1970s by making "Socialism" his hot-button euphemism for a government that would enforce equality and erode white privilege. In 1990 he won reelection with TV ads that graphically voiced white people's anger about racial quotas. Ronald Reagan provides another example. In the 1980 campaign, he frequently denounced a Chicago "welfare queen" and proclaimed "states' rights" in Philadelphia, Mississippi, where infamous civil rights murders had occurred in the 1960s. Reagan won the election and the support of white southerners in part because he promised to "'starve the beast' of big government." The image subliminally evoked what Ivan Evans calls the "black-beast rapist." For white southerners at least, "the racial subtext was clear: in practice, 'starve the beast' was another way to prolong whiteness." Other historians argue that the new conservatism also reflected what

Robert Norrell calls "insulated, all-white suburbs" that had become new "bastions of white privilege."[4]

When an interviewer granted anonymity to Lee Atwater in the early 1980s, the rising young Republican star defined the Southern Strategy with exceptional candor: "You start out in 1954 by saying, 'Nigger, nigger, nigger.' By 1968 you can't say 'nigger'—that hurts you. Backfires. So you say stuff like forced busing, states' rights and all that stuff. You're getting so abstract now you're talking about cutting taxes, and all these things you're talking about are totally economic things and a byproduct of them is blacks get hurt worse than whites."[5] For forty years the relentless Republican call for tax cuts has succeeded in part because of its racist subtext: those lazy blacks and illegal Mexicans don't deserve white people's money.[6]

Race issues stayed on the back burner during the spring and summer of 2008, except when Obama had to deal with the controversy about the Rev. Jeremiah Wright. Instead, the presumptive Republican and Democratic nominees sharply disagreed about the Iraq War. To Obama the war was a "blunder" that should be ended. To McCain, ending it would be "humiliating," akin to the humiliation that prompted the war or to the humiliating American defeat in Vietnam. Much as Nixon repeatedly called for "peace with honor" to prolong the Vietnam War, McCain repeatedly called for "victory with honor" and resisted any pressure to bring troops home.

Again and again McCain branded Obama as someone who would bring shame to our country. In the candidates' second debate, McCain mentioned that he had opposed the incursion that led to the "humiliating" rout of American marines in Lebanon in the early 1980s. His view is that when we go in, we should go in to win. As McCain said twice in that October 7 debate, we should strive for "victory with honor" in Iraq. If the latter stages of the campaign were about race and the economy, the first part focused on the war. The subtext for that discussion asked voters to decide whether the drive to restore national honor and the fear of national humiliation should shape American foreign policy.

In their first debate, McCain challenged Obama on the fiscal crisis by invoking a different aspect of traditional honor. He blamed failures of "character and responsibility" instead of the deregulation he had championed for decades. Here his sense of honor took the rather weak form of moralizing about character. In the second part of that debate, when they jousted about foreign policy, McCain returned to more familiar territory. He mocked Obama's advocacy of a sixteen-month timetable for Iraq withdrawal as an invitation to "defeat." As usual, he repeatedly declared that we must "win" with "honor."[7] For him honor meant victory, the opposite of shameful defeat. Those two strands of honor, which interweave personal moral character with national dominance, have characterized American justifications for imperial interventions from the Spanish-American War to the present.

McCain prides himself on being a "warrior." As David Grann wrote in a post-election assessment of McCain for *The New Yorker*, the senator is "driven less by ideas than an almost chivalrous sense of honor." In McCain's various books written with Mark Salter, honor trumps courage as a basic virtue. Throughout the campaign he privately considered Obama "a nice enough young man" who "lacked guts" as well as other "warrior virtues."[8] Obama hadn't "stood up to his party's leaders," McCain said repeatedly, as if Obama's primary fight with Hillary Clinton had never happened. Perhaps he meant standing up to other men.

The underside of that honor has been McCain's very private sense of shame for the momentary moral crumpling he experienced during his five and a half years of confinement and torture by the North Vietnamese. At one point, having been tortured almost continuously for four days, the captured navy pilot gave a false confession. He thought about suicide because, in his biographer's words, he had "dishonored his country, his family, and himself."[9] McCain has never wanted to talk about those years in his books or in his speeches. He has done so only when pushed by his aides.

Of McCain's five books, *Faith of My Fathers* (1998) most richly explores how honor centers his identity. Like Douglas MacArthur in *Reminiscences*, McCain reveres his military father and grandfather, both four-star admirals in the U.S. Navy. His proclamations of paternal lineage rival Ayaan Hirsi Ali's childhood incantations in their repetitive intensity. The first third of McCain's memoir consists of two long

Leviticus-like bows to his most prominent male forbearers. Little John doesn't take center stage until page 99.

Like Hirsi Ali's father, McCain's father and grandfather were absent during much of his childhood. Nevertheless, he doesn't write much about his mother, except to say that he shares her gregarious personality. Mothers do all the child-rearing, but the absent fathers serve a greater cause. As a child McCain "resented my father's absences," a feeling he now regrets. His grandfather had been at least as absent from his father's childhood. "The relationship of a sailor and his children is . . . a metaphysical one." The children "are taught to consider their absence not as a deprivation, but as an honor." The admired father's absence teaches the son to emulate the father's "stoic acceptance" of his greater duty to his country.[10]

McCain's father was "hard driven by his often oppressive desire to honor his father's name," a desire young John shared. His father and grandfather "were my first heroes, and earning their respect has been the most lasting ambition of my life." To all of them, honor meant service and duty. "An officer must not lie, steal, or cheat—ever. He keeps his word, whatever the cost. . . . His life is ransomed to his duty." He acts responsibly, especially toward enlisted men. In 1971, when his father was testifying before a Senate committee, a senator who opposed the war challenged the admiral's honesty. Enraged, McCain's father "jumped to his feet" and gave a "heated and sarcastic lecture" defending the moral integrity of himself, his father, and the U.S. military.[11]

For McCain, too, honor carries great collective weight. If the navy were to tolerate an officer's dishonorable conduct, it "would shame everyone in the service." When McCain was in prison in Vietnam, he and the other U.S. prisoners faced each day "with a steady resolve that our honor was the extension of a great nation's honor," and such honor always "comes with obligations" to measure up.[12]

Accepting yourself as the personal savior for your country's honor brings baggage. Soon after the two-year-old boy's entrance into his own narrative, contradictions become more arresting than assertions. Yes, the code of honor requires stoic sacrifice, service, and duty, and it probably helped stabilize what he calls his "migrant" childhood. But like MacArthur, both younger McCains honored duty more in the breach than the observance. His father was "expelled from the dormitory" at the Naval Academy for what the father himself called "rebellion and mutiny" against upperclassmen, and young McCain became "a notoriously undisciplined midshipman," with almost enough demerits "to warrant my expulsion." From plebe to prisoner, John constantly challenged authority. He mentions his family's long history of "quick tempers." He also mentions the small size of the men in his family. His grandfather and his father were short, and McCain entitles his chapter on his father, "Small Man with the Big Heart." He's proud that his father would "fight at the drop of a hat." As for the son, his "transient childhood" and "my small stature motivated me . . . to fight the first kid who provoked me." That pugnacity helped to make him a notorious hell-raiser, and proud of it.[13]

McCain's ideal of duty often conflicted with his flagrant disobedi-ence. All his life, he muses, he has tried to balance "liberty and honor." But his desire for "liberty" doesn't quite explain why he once said every senior commander who opposed Washington's lack of full commitment to the Vietnam War should resign. "Obviously, my father was implicitly included in my indictment. It was a callous remark." McCain also tries to muster up respect for his father's decision to order B-52s to bomb Hanoi, "the city where I was held a prisoner. That was his duty, and he did not shrink from it." Without comment, McCain notes that the admiral declined the invitation to welcome his son when the prisoner was released because no other parents of POWs would be present.[14]

Not surprisingly, just as his father had yearned for his own father's approval, McCain yearned for his father's respect, mostly in vain. Rummaging through his father's personal files, he tried to find any hint that his father might have been worried about him when he was a prisoner. He painfully reprints the three half-crumbs he finds buried in his father's formulaic letters to others. The admiral did keep copies of the letters, and later his mother told him that she would hear her husband praying God to "show Johnny mercy"—an ambiguous formulation. McCain also learned that when the admiral was visiting soldiers near North Vietnam, he had a "custom of withdrawing from his company at the end of the meal, walking north, and standing alone for a long time, looking toward the place where he had lost his son." But the admiral never talked about it. Duty to country overrode family concerns.[15]

Forthrightly, McCain acknowledges uglier aspects of both relatives. He partially excuses his grandfather's "racist" hate of the Japanese, since such hate "sustains the fighter" in the ruthlessness of war. He is less charitable about his father's alcoholism. The admiral seems to have been a binge drinker "until the very last years of his life." An absent father, sometimes drunk when home—it's tough to honor such a man, but McCain does, partly to measure up to the code. McCain's shame at breaking under torture also humbled him sufficiently to accept the mixed qualities in himself as well as in his father.[16]

Here and in various interviews, McCain has been blunt and complex about his father's drinking problem and absences while he continues to champion his simple code of honor. Perhaps the code eased his ambivalence about his father and his migrant youth. George Lakoff has argued that conservatives tend to come from families with strong disciplinarian fathers whom they idealize, whereas liberals grow up with nurturing parents and project idealized nurturance onto government policies.[17] Yet under the surface of their starkly different relation to their fathers, Barack Obama and John McCain don't quite follow the Lakoff dichotomy. Both candidates had mostly absent fathers and both wrote memoirs that struggled to make sense of those absences. Both have dedicated their lives to public service. Like McCain, who acknowledges shameful aspects of his progenitors and himself, Obama comes to realize that shame bedeviled his father and grandfather in Kenya. Though the Obamas' shame has more racial aspects than the McCains ever experienced, it reflects a similar sense that they had not measured up to the honor expected of them.

McCain begins his narrative with 94 pages on his lineage; he concludes with 161 pages on his five-year imprisonment. Structurally, that balance weights the scale toward his conflicted mixture of shame and resolve. In the fall of 1968, after four days of severe beatings that cracked several ribs, broke his arm and some teeth, and finally broke his will, he signed a false confession that he'd "bombed a school." When he refused to record it on tape, he was beaten until he consented. At one point he tried to kill himself to avoid confessing, but that attempt failed. Afterward "I felt faithless, and couldn't control my despair." All his feelings of shame focused on his father's regard. Again and again he worried that the confession would "embarrass my father. . . . And I still wince when I recall wondering if my father had heard of my disgrace. The Vietnamese had broken the prisoner they called the 'Crown Prince,' and I knew they had done it to hurt the man they believed to be a king."[18]

McCain proudly resisted every subsequent attempt to torture him into confessions. He also refused repeated offers of early release because he knew how his unearned freedom would affect his father and the other prisoners. Other American prisoners broke too, he recounts, though some didn't, even though they died because of torture. McCain reveres their memories. They were better men than he was. Much later, his father said to him, "You did the best you could, John. That's all that's expected of any of us."[19] That was the only time they talked about it.

Unlike other Vietnam veterans in the Senate such as Chuck Hagel, James Webb, and John Kerry, McCain has soldiered on in his support of the Iraq war. Some of those colleagues have mused about whether McCain's passion for winning with honor is connected to the fact that the five years he spent in prison coincided with the period when they saw the hopelessness of the Vietnam War. But McCain's adherence to honor goes far beyond immediate perceptions of victory or defeat. For him, wars always have to end in victory. His imprisonment also taught him that when honor shifts from self-regard to a cause larger than himself, "no humiliation can destroy it." As his father and grandfather knew, "Glory" comes from being "constant" to that cause. "A filthy, crippled, broken man, all I had left of my dignity was the faith of my fathers. It was enough."[20]

The 2008 Presidential Campaign

The 2008 presidential election campaign seemed to be white honor's last national stand. As my next chapter suggests, the funeral was premature. But the desperation accompanying last stands surfaced in the implicitly racial shaming John McCain tolerated and occasionally encouraged, despite himself.

Why did this man of honor allow his managers to wage such a negative campaign? Some have said he was appealing to his conservative base. I think the explanation goes further than tactics. As a man who had earned his honor in battle and mostly preserved it in prison, he had no respect for his opponent. After the election, several commentators mentioned what Elizabeth Drew called "McCain's open display of disdain for Obama in the debates," using tactics such as rolling his eyes and saying "that one" instead of referring to Obama respectfully by name. A Republican explained McCain's "growing anger" to her: "It's not that he's losing, he's losing to someone he doesn't have any regard for." In McCain's eyes, Obama wasn't a warrior. Obama's skin color didn't matter, but his character did. He was a lightweight inferior who deserved to be put in his place. A TV ad released in early October called Obama "dishonorable," "dangerous," and "too risky for America."[21]

In retrospect, David Grann suggested in *The New Yorker*, McCain's own fall from honor may have spurred his relentless attempts to make Obama the Other. In 2000 McCain ran a galvanizing primary campaign. Reporters relished his candor and informality as well as his integrity. But he lost to George W. Bush in South Carolina because in the last two weeks of the primary, McCain was accused of having fathered a child with a black woman, perhaps a black prostitute, a rumor that was probably inspired by Karl Rove or his operatives. Leaflets and phone calls stated that McCain's darker-skinned daughter, actually an adopted Asian American girl, came from that alleged affair, which of course never happened. Eight years later, McCain carefully cultivated his wary conservative base. As Grann puts it, "The more McCain gave in to the base the more he seemed to need to demonize his opponent, as if to justify his own moral compromises."[22]

That's an astute insight into the psychodynamics of public shaming. From the schoolyard to political campaigns to the self-congratulatory TV sparring of Keith Olbermann and Bill O'Reilly, shaming and humiliating bring a pleasurable simplification—even a purification—of inward conflicts and complexities. Othering people simplifies both them and you and lets you disown what might be shameful or complicated in yourself. You can rest your self-simplification on the imagined superiority of your person or of your group or both.

One factor complicates that assessment. McCain resolutely opposed any suggestion that Obama should be directly shamed because of his race. The racial slanders against McCain in South Carolina still loomed large in his mind, staffers said. Besides, a man of honor doesn't do such things. Though McCain and his supporters did their best to make Obama look alien, he drew the line at using the Rev. Jeremiah Wright or attacking Obama's wife.[23] His campaign's racial shaming took indirect forms. The tactics proliferated as Obama unaccountably kept his lead in the polls.

Among white voters, the widespread distrust of Senator Obama's candidacy seized on various peripheral aspects. Until the latter part of the primaries he didn't wear a flag pin. His wife seemed too strong, too black, and too angry. America had made black people unhappy, and she said so—once! Obama had worked with a former member of the Weather Underground. He had done a fist bump with his wife, and he said some Americans were "bitter." Republicans soon tried to maximize the shaming recoil by implying or saying that Obama wasn't just black, he was a Muslim and friends with terrorists. He wasn't one of us, and he never would be.[24] In July 2008, ads calling Obama an "arrogant celebrity" like Paris Hilton and Britney Spears also feminized the candidate. The all-but-transparent racial subtext of that strategy was centuries old: Barack Obama is an uppity black man who can't be taken seriously and we have to put him in his place.[25]

Toward the end of the campaign, vice-presidential candidate Sarah Palin made the shaming charge explicit. Often linking Obama to Bill Ayers, a "domestic terrorist" who co-founded the Weathermen, Palin said repeatedly that Obama was "not one of us." Introductory speakers who referred to the senator as "Barack Hussein Obama" tried to conflate Obama's blackness and alleged Islamic sympathies as evidence of his un-Americanness.[26] Using thinly veiled displacements, these speeches tried to inflame the racial anxieties of undecided white voters. Always seeking to maximize conflict and drama, reporters and commentators moved race to center stage. By late summer a great many people were talking about the Bradley effect.

The Bradley effect conflates the fates of four African American candidates who ran for office in the period 1978 to 1989. According to this theory, despite what many white people tell pollsters, racism surfaces in the privacy of the voting booth. In 1978, Massachusetts senator Edward Brooke, a Republican incumbent, was ahead by nearly eight points in the polls, but Paul Tsongas beat him by ten points. In 1982, Tom Bradley, mayor of Los Angeles, was comfortably ahead in at least one poll when he ran for governor of California, but he lost by 1.2 points. In 1989, polls said David Dinkins was ahead by over ten points in the race for mayor of New York, but he won by only two points. Also in 1989, Douglas Wilder won the governorship of Virginia with barely 7,000 votes, after having been ahead by fifteen points in the polls. More recently, in a 2006 election in Michigan, polls predicted that a proposal to ban affirmative action would barely pass with 51 percent of the votes, but it received 58 percent. All that led Andrew Hacker in *The New York Review of Books* to urge the Obama campaign, in capital letters, to "ALWAYS SUBTRACT SEVEN PERCENT!"[27]

Poll after poll showed that white racism would have a significant impact on the election. In early September 2008, a poll conducted by AP and Yahoo! with the help of scholars from Stanford University concluded that one-third of all white Democrats and Independents had negative views about black people. Moreover, 40 percent of all white people had at least partly negative views of blacks. This poll predicted that without prejudice, Obama's support would be as much as 6 percent higher than it was at that moment.[28] On his November 2 Public Broadcasting System show, Bill Moyers displayed several racist fliers depicting Obama as a black man with watermelons.

Though Obama tried to minimize the danger by presenting himself as the antithesis of an angry black militant, several primary opponents and various Republican bloggers as well as Fox News tried to maximize the fears. Fear continued to be marketed after the primary elections, when gun sales spiked. By late summer, the McCain campaign was featuring attack ads and attack books. Meanwhile, targeted ads by fringe groups and the steady vituperative patter of right-wing talk show hosts tried to fuel the unease in the groups both sides focused on: suburban whites, working-class and unionized whites, and (to a lesser extent) Jews.[29] Again and again news shows played the clip of Obama's former pastor, Rev. Jeremiah Wright, shouting "God *damn* America! God *damn*

America!"[30] Wright's long-ago attempt at national shaming brought rage that threatened to bring down Obama's campaign.

On July 21, *The New Yorker* ran a cover with a drawing of the Obamas by Barry Blitt that was intended to make fun of white race-based fears. Obama wears a white turban, sandals, and a brown robe; his wife wears camouflage pants and sports an attack rifle with a swath of bullets over her right shoulder. Michelle has an Angela Davis hairstyle, and the two of them are bumping fists. Obama's expression looks resolute and smug, while Michelle smiles at him with grim, tight anger. The depiction of them hovers somewhere between 1960s radicals on the street and the Macbeths at home. Above the fireplace, where an American flag is burning, hangs a picture of Osama bin Laden with a turban that matches that of Obama. They are in the Oval Office. Blitt's title, which almost no one talked about, was "The Politics of Fear."[31]

Ironically, the cover galvanized fear in many liberals. They thought it would inflame white voters' racism. Their unspoken presumption was that shaming white people for ridiculous racial demonization won't work, because racial shaming can go only one way, from white to black. To feature paranoid fantasies about the Obamas makes the fantasies seem legitimate. But Barry Blitt's humor plays with reverse racial shaming. By exaggerating the negative images already in wide circulation, the cover mocked white voters who were stereotyping the Obamas, as if to say, "Relax! Get a life!"

Most liberals were too nervous about the race factor to let the humor work. Column after column analyzed what or who was prompting race-based fears. Matt Bai wrote several *New York Times* articles expressing the hope that Obama represented a "post-race" future. Others were less hopeful. In a late September *Times* column, "The Push to 'Otherize' Obama," Nicholas Kristof noted that 13 percent of the American public thought Obama was Muslim, up from 10 percent in March and 12 percent in June. He declared that "religious prejudice is becoming a proxy for racial prejudice."[32]

A more sharply worded *Times* column by Brent Staples indicted the McCain campaign's uses of code words such as "disrespectful" to describe Democratic assessments of his nominee for vice president,

Alaska governor Sarah Palin. Staples cited a Georgia Republican, Representative Lynn Westmoreland, who called the Obamas "'uppity'" and tried to defend the term. Another Republican congressman, Representative Geoff Davis of Kentucky, said "'That boy's finger does not need to be on the button,'" evoking the South's centuries-old use of "boy" for black men. As Staples concluded, with one month to go in the campaign, Obama remained only one slip away from the "uppity nigger" stereotype.[33]

In response to all the race-baiting, Tim Wise wrote a passionate screed widely circulated on the web. In "White Privilege, White Entitlement, and the 2008 Election," Wise raged against the presumptions that allow white people to brand black people as lazy, irresponsible, and dangerous while they praise Sarah Palin for exactly the same things: a daughter pregnant at seventeen, a relish for guns, a spotty educational record, the claim that she was experienced enough while Senator Obama wasn't, a history of firing people for political and personal reasons, an evangelical pastor far more extreme than Obama's former minister, her endearing ambition versus Obama's overreaching. As Wise sums it up, "White privilege is, in short, the problem."[34]

Jerome Corsi's *The Obama Nation: Leftist Politics and the Cult of Personality*, published in August 2008, voiced an exceptionally naked version of both white fear and white privilege. Attacking Obama as a closet Muslim as well as an extremist liberal, it immediately became the number-one best seller on the nonfiction list of the *New York Times* and stayed high on the list for weeks. As David Remnick says, Corsi "was a bigot, a liar, and a conspiracy theorist" who "had mainstream backing." Again came the media checks and balances. Media Matters listed eight to ten pages of blatant factual errors in Corsi's book.[35] But those correctives seemed to have little effect on the large choir that wanted to be preached to. The book's use of familiar rhetorical dichotomies to raise white fears assured its popularity.

Corsi's attack on Obama ostensibly features the candidate's "leftist politics and the cult of personality." From the start, however, what leaps into view is Corsi's fear of angry black men. His first mention of the "extreme left" leads immediately to the "racial politics" in a 1968 gun battle between an African American and the Cleveland police.

Worse, the leader had a Muslim name. Soon Corsi brands Obama a
Muslim because he went to school in Indonesia from the age of six to
the age of ten.[36]

When Corsi turns to Obama's Kenyan father, the fear factor intensifies. He concludes that Obama's embrace of blackness and the "Far Left"
shows his "resentment"; "he turns out radical, internalizing a black
rage." Here Corsi resurrects *Black Rage*, an iconic book for the Black
Power movement in the late 1960s.[37] In high school, Corsi declares,
Obama experienced "perceived insults" that led him to share "black
anger" with a friend, and he felt "racial angst" that morphed into
"anticolonial" rage when he read Frantz Fanon. Then came Malcolm
X, an alleged communist mentor, and Obama's transformation into a
"Kenyan Tribal Elder."[38] Corsi's parade of radicalizing stages culminates
in Obama's tainted links to Bill Ayers, a cagily half-repentant founder
of the Weather Underground.

Throughout, Corsi's hysterical presumption of Obama's race-based
rage grounds his perceptions of the candidate. His dichotomizing
of Them and Us flares up whenever he encounters the specter of
dangerous black men. In that respect Corsi's book simplifies the more
sophisticated dichotomizing in Samuel Huntington's *The Clash of
Civilizations*. Perhaps unintentionally, Corsi's ambiguous title oddly
reflects and intensifies the election's irreconcilable divisions. Is the
senator an abomination or will the nation be Obama's? Though the
ambiguity of the title as well as the author's cantankerous reputation may have undercut the book's force, *Obama Nation* made lots of
money by recycling white fears that black people will challenge white
privilege.

A week before the election, the polls briefly began to tighten. On
her October 29 MSNBC show, Rachel Maddow featured contradictory
but narrowing polls, and she wondered why McCain was acting so
confident. She also noted that between 3 and 6 percent of early voters
said they "couldn't remember" who they voted for. Though she mocked
them, I thought the obvious conclusion was that they knew and didn't
want to say. The Bradley effect seemed to be moving into high gear,
and the undecideds might be tipping toward McCain.

The same morning as the radio report brought Nicholas Kristof's illuminating column titled "What? Me Biased?" Kristof cited studies that showed unconscious racism in college students. When they were "primed to think of Mr. Obama as a black candidate" rather than as a Democrat or other category, they tended to see Obama as "less American" than Hillary Clinton, John McCain, or even Tony Blair. They did the same with well-known black athletes. As Kristof notes, "most Americans, including Latinos and Asian-Americans, associate the idea of 'American' with white skin." Another study found that students tend to see Kate Winslet as more American than Lucy Liu.[39]

To stimulate such responses, charges associating Obama with Rev. Wright surfaced again, this time in advertisements that McCain hadn't authorized. Simultaneously, five days before the election, someone from U.S. Immigration and Customs Enforcement leaked information that one of Obama's relatives, his Kenyan father's half-sister, was an illegal immigrant in Boston. Once again came the implication: "He's going to help them, not you."

Before those final desperate moves of its allies, the McCain campaign had tried to tar Obama with more culturally acceptable versions of blackness and foreignness. The "celebrity" ads gave way to accusations about his alleged terrorist friend Bill Ayers and then used the word "socialist," an un-American word that had a long political history of awakening what Valerie Jarrett called "the sleeping giant" of race fears.[40] The race-neutral charges that Obama "isn't ready yet" and that he would "raise your taxes" carried more weight, several polls noted. The second proposition was outrageous, since Obama's tax increase would apply only to those earning over $250,000 and would raise their rates only 2 to 4 percent. Once more came the Southern Strategy subtext: if this man is elected, white people's money will be given to black people and immigrants.

Throughout the latter stages of the campaign, McCain and Palin tried to do what Teddy Roosevelt advised Douglas MacArthur to do. The young aide-de-camp once asked the president why he thought he was so popular. Roosevelt replied, "'To put into words what is in their hearts and minds but not their mouths. You must listen to the grass grow.'"[41] McCain and Palin were trying to make the grass grow white.

Palin didn't chastise or correct those in her audience who shouted "Kill him!" or "Treason!" or "Off with his head!" or "He is a bomb!" One Ohio man called Obama a "one-man terror cell," and a voter's young daughter said "You need gloves to touch him!" At that point John Lewis, now a representative from Atlanta, voiced his outrage. On October 12, he turned race-based shaming on its head by accusing McCain's campaign of "sowing the seeds of hatred." He pointedly recalled the violence that George Wallace's similar race-baiting had unleashed in the 1960s. Meanwhile the Secret Service reported to the Obama campaign that there had been "a sharp and very disturbing increase in threats to Obama in September and early October."[42]

John Lewis has impeccable civil rights credentials. In Selma, Alabama, he had been beaten almost to death. Earlier, as I recount at the start of the first chapter, he and James Bevel had been fumigated in a Nashville fast-food restaurant in 1960.[43] At last some white liberal commentators had the angry black man they wanted Obama to become. Ever since the Democratic and Republican conventions, when Obama's lead seemed to be slipping, columnists such as Maureen Dowd had been urging him to get fiery rather than stay calm, cool, and collected. Now Lewis had come forth as Obama's surrogate.

As Brent Staples and other black writers were quick to point out, the worst thing this candidate could do would be to awaken white American fears of aggressive African American males. That would link Obama with Al Sharpton and Jesse Jackson, the "radioactive blacks." In the minds of many white people, those leaders advocate the advancement of black people at the expense of the whole country.[44] Obama had learned how to handle that danger by the time he was a senior in high school. As he recounts in *Dreams from My Father*, he managed his mother's fears with "one of those tricks I had learned: People were satisfied so long as you were courteous and smiled and made no sudden moves. They were more than satisfied; they were relieved—such a pleasant surprise to find a well-mannered young black man who didn't seem angry all the time."[45]

McCain was shocked at Lewis's statement. In *Why Courage Matters*, he had written an admiring chapter about the civil rights leader's bravery. He had praised Lewis for being one of the three "wise" people whose advice and counsel he likes to seek. At subsequent rallies he took care to correct anyone who said slurs about Obama, such as "He's an Arab." Yet McCain's quick response to Lewis's charge hints at the problem. He called the accusation not only "brazen and baseless" but also "beyond the pale."

That phrase originally referred to the paling fences that English settlers used to demarcate English territory in contested regions. One example is the border the English constructed in Dublin in 1446–47 to separate the English "civilized" area from the "savage" Irish area of the city. Those who were within the "pale" were "home"; those who were beyond it were alien. In the United States, the phrase has been neutralized, or whitened. Perhaps involuntarily, McCain used the phrase to signal that his perception of his opponent was based on race and that his perception of himself was that he was "within the pale." The bond between honor and whiteness was alive in himself as well as in his campaign.

Some of McCain's Republican allies indicted the campaign's inflammatory tactics with similar vehemence. Frank Schaeffer is a lifelong Republican, the son of an evangelist who helped create the religious right. McCain had written an admiring blurb for his 2006 book. At about the time that Lewis issued his indictment, Schaeffer wrote a stinging open letter to the Republican candidate. "If your campaign does not stop equating Senator Obama with terrorism, questioning his patriotism and portraying Mr. Obama as 'not one of us,' I accuse you of feeding the most unhinged elements of our society the red meat of hate, and therefore of potentially instigating violence. You are unleashing the monster of American hatred and prejudice."[46] Other Republicans, including Colin Powell, swung to Obama not only because they admired his calm intelligence but also because they were appalled at McCain's tactics.

During the last week of the campaign, both members of the Republican ticket suddenly singled out Obama's friendship with Rashid Khalidi. Khalidi, a Columbia professor, has been a strong critic of Israel. In April the *Los Angeles Times* had run an article about the friendship between Obama and Khalidi, who has criticized Yasser Arafat. When conservative bloggers belatedly discovered the article,

McCain and Palin rushed to feature that un-American association. Palin relished mispronouncing his name as "Rashid Khaladi" and listening to the crowd boo the sound of those Muslim syllables. McCain also emphasized Obama's link to Palestinian donors, whose gifts the Obama campaign had returned.

Yet Senator Obama won, and won by what the *New York Times* kept calling a "commanding" margin of 53 percent to 46 percent for McCain. Wall Street's shocking implosion certainly didn't hurt. Nor did a series of impulsive moves by his opponent. The media started to brand the two candidates as "Mr. Cool" and "Mr. Hot," as a *Times* column by Gail Collins stated and then an October 6 *Newsweek* cover proclaimed. Throughout the bailout crisis Obama seemed much more commanding than the ex-pilot, and his campaign staff took great care to burnish that image. For Obama's top aides, the key moment came then, when Obama acted presidential.[47] The "celebrity" charge slowly lost its force.

Now all that sound and fury seems like ancient, nostalgic history. But the history could have been otherwise. If the economy hadn't gone into a terrifying dive after mid-September, McCain and Palin might have been elected, though polls showed a small electoral college edge for Obama throughout the summer and fall. Economic fears pushed voters beyond racial fears. As the white Democratic governor of North Carolina said, "In difficult economic times, people find the price of prejudice is just a little bit too high." In north Florida, a good old boy in the legal establishment told a liberal judge, "You know what? I'm votin' for the nigger."[48]

Looking back after the election, some commentators concluded that race issues helped Obama considerably more than they hurt him. The Bradley effect proved to be nonexistent. Several commentators pointed out that many more voters reacted more negatively to Senator McCain's age (he was 72) than to Obama's race, and more voters saw his race as a positive than a negative. A story in the *Times* a day before the election carried the headline, "Level of White Support for Obama a Surprise." As the election proved, Obama's support was higher among whites than Bill Clinton's had been in either of his elections, and it was higher than for any other Democratic candidate since 1964. Among white voters aged 18 to 29, 68 percent voted for Obama and only 31 percent voted for McCain.[49] Obama has "likeability," a former chair of the Florida Republican Party said ruefully. As one pollster said, "Maybe he has crossed over into Tiger Woods territory."[50]

The prospect of a progressive black president galvanized African American voters, but millions of other voters yearned for someone who could restore America's moral honor in the world. In 1976 Jimmy Carter had been elected as a similar exorcism of Richard Nixon. Now many voters took pride in a man who could represent America's multi-racial possibilities to a national and global audience. Obama won for nonracial reasons as well, of course, especially his promise of progressive change and what conservative columnist Charles Krauthammer grudgingly called his "first class intellect and first class temperament."[51] Yet he could also regain respect for America. As Obama himself often declared, "In no other country on earth is my story even possible."[52]

Honor Unbound

For many Americans, honor remains a personal imperative. In his acceptance speech for vice-president, Joe Biden equated "honor" with the personal "dignity" that comes from work. Biden's white working-class background gave him that ethic, he said. Personal dignity can challenge the inferiority ascribed by class-based or race-based stigmatization.[53] For example, in the 1940s, black men began using the word "man" to confer honor, dignity, and manliness on each other. The word countered white men's ubiquitous use of "boy" when talking to black men of any age.

McCain's loss seemed to show that such honor was becoming unbound from whiteness. A mayoral election in Chicago twenty-five years earlier suggests some parallels and differences. In a March 2009 episode of National Public Radio's *This American Life*, Alex Kotlowitz found "eerie" parallels between McCain's campaign and the 1983 campaign of Bernie Epton for mayor of Chicago. Like McCain, Epton began as a moderate Republican, although he was more progressive than McCain. He had opposed McCarthyism, marched in Memphis after Dr. King's assassination, and sent his children to mostly black schools. When Epton won the Republican nomination, he and everyone else assumed he would lose. In the previous race for mayor, the Democrat had won with 82 percent of the vote. When Harold Washington, a black state legislator, won the Democratic primary, Epton at first spoke respectfully of his opponent.

Then national Republican managers took charge, just as McCain let his managers take over his campaign. The campaign slogan became "Epton for Mayor—before it's too late." One leaflet proclaimed, "Your vote will stop contamination of City Hall" by a "baboon." Epton thrilled to the huge white crowds chanting "Bernie! Bernie!" and he fired an aide who criticized the campaign's racist edge. One white crowd's ferocious anger at a motorcade that included Washington and Walter Mondale forced Democrats to cancel a rally. Epton lost by only 3 percent.

As Kotlowitz points out, McCain and Epton differed in at least one key respect. McCain's speech conceding defeat was admirably gracious and generous. Epton couldn't bring himself to take the high ground. The next day, refusing to attend a Unity Breakfast, he left town for Florida. As his law practice disintegrated, he blamed the media for his alleged victimization and yearned for the cheers of those white crowds. The good-hearted moderate who was in way over his head had struck a Faustian bargain during his campaign. Four years later he died, perhaps a suicide. He had been seduced by adulation that was really racist desperation, and his inflammatory campaign remains his major public legacy.[54]

In 2008, white fears of a black man's power seemed to be simmering down, as long as the candidate didn't trumpet his blackness. Even white rural and suburban voters showed nearly equal allegiances, except in the South. McCain gained his only clear majorities among conservatives, older Americans, white men, and white Protestants—especially evangelical Christians.[55] According to the post-election voting map, McCain's base east of the Mississippi had constricted to the deep South plus Kentucky, Tennessee, Oklahoma, and Arkansas. Even Indiana, the one northern state with a long history of support for the Ku Klux Klan, edged into the Obama column.[56] Virginia went decisively for Obama and Florida too, and North Carolina—barely. In Ohio and Pennsylvania, white racism remained highly visible, as it was for Appalachian whites in general. But only in a few southern and southwestern states did it command most people's votes as it used to.[57]

Many voters weren't letting go of their prejudices. Our youngest daughter, who campaigned for Obama in North Carolina, reported that after one man drove his pickup truck at two campaign workers to get them off his property, they found an effigy of Obama hanging from a tree. But change had come. McCain's concession speech contrasted this moment with the widespread white outrage when Teddy Roosevelt hosted Booker T. Washington at a White House dinner in 1901. With pardonable exaggeration McCain declared, "American today is a world away from the cruel and prideful bigotry of that time."[58]

"Prideful bigotry"—a memorable phrase. Whether it belongs to McCain or his speechwriter Mark Salter, it rings true. But pride in what, exactly? In superiority, in dominance, in whiteness? Such pride hides fears of equality and difference, while the "ful" implies a need to swell or fill up an inward cavity. And how far had McCain himself come? His repeated contrast between Obama's candidacy and the furor over Booker T. Washington at the White House takes justifiable pride in his country's progress. Yet it also signals his perception that the most compelling aspect of his rival is black skin.

On balance, the 2008 election showed that except in some large pockets of the country, prideful bigotry had grudgingly yielded to more complex assessments of Obama's personal qualities. Whiteness seemed to have been reduced to just another special interest. It was as if white voters were finally letting a partially black man into their dens or living rooms or even bedrooms via the TV screen and allowing him to shake their hands. "You're not half bad," they might have muttered. "But those others . . ." Their wary acceptance illustrates a basic human truth, that stereotypes thrive in the absence of contact between people of equal status. Daily television exposure and the length of the twenty-one month campaign provided a virtual equivalent of that contact. Despite Obama's obvious inexperience, many white American voters got just comfortable enough—and respectful enough—to vote for him.[59]

As many commentators have said, claims that America has become "post-racial" go much too far. Appearing a week before the inauguration in *The Atlantic*, Hua Hsu's "The End of White America?"

asserts that America is already "post-white" in culture, as it will be demographically by 2042, when whites become a minority. Adherence to whiteness will persist only "as a somewhat pissed-off minority culture." Given entrenched structures of privilege, these claims seem drastically overstated, as if the politics of hope were already becoming reality. More intriguingly, Hsu argues that race is becoming just one of many possibilities for one's identity.[60] Obama anticipated the new generation when he made his racial choice voluntarily.

The most extreme statement of postracial possibilities that I heard came on the morning of Obama's inauguration, when Congressman John Lewis was being interviewed on CBS's *Early Show*. He told a reporter that he might have "an out-of-body experience." Perhaps his anticipatory giddiness led him to say, "It is the building of a multiracial democracy in America. I think we're coming to the point where we're laying down the burden of race."[61]

Several African American commentators, notably Tavis Smiley and Orlando Patterson, tried to puncture the hopes for an immediate postracial America. On election night Smiley said that Obama might lose his black "soul" in the rush to achieve national unity. Patterson's early November article in *Newsweek* mused about the increasing chasm between black people's substantial public achievements and their continuing private segregation, now at least partly by choice. Worse, the poverty rate for black people has increased from 21.2 percent in 2000 to 24.5 percent in 2008, and "half of all blacks born to middle class families are downwardly mobile; more than half of them fall to the very bottom of the income ladder."[62] The most intractably racial issues, from immigration to inner-city poverty, were all but unmentioned in the campaign speeches, on both sides.

Nevertheless, the election exposed the fraying bonds between whiteness and honor, particularly in white Americans' perception of their country's wars. On election night, Jeffrey Toobin pointed out on CNN that American war heroes have been defeated in each of the last five elections—John McCain, John Kerry, Al Gore (who enlisted and served in Vietnam), Bob Dole, and George H. W. Bush. Elizabeth Drew noted that "for the first time since it happened, the Vietnam War wasn't a topic."[63]

A concern for national honor persists, but a more modern term has replaced it. "Moral" has become the new five-letter word of choice for Americans' ideal national self-image. Books by Ron Suskind and Kwame Anthony Appiah champion the resurgence of moral vision.[64] For many Democrats and for many moderate Republicans as well, the eight years of the second Bush administration had been a disgrace. The humiliation of 9/11 had slowly been balanced and outweighed by exasperation at Bush's misgovernance. In a strange reversal, white fears of being contaminated by black people partially yielded to anger that a mostly white administration had tainted the nation.[65] Elizabeth Drew summed it up at the end of her article on the election: "People felt cleansed."[66]

Most of the people who champion America's possibilities as a moral example, including Obama, do so without a racial edge. Yet racial shaming has by no means disappeared. In Junot Diaz's Pulitzer Prize–winning novel *The Brief Wondrous Life of Oscar Wao* (2007), the hero returns to his high school, where he had been relentlessly shamed. Now "there were a grip more kids of color—but some things (like white supremacy and people-of-color self-hate) never change."[67] He's right because structures of white supremacy still instill self-hatred in people of various other colors. He's wrong because white supremacy is more challengeable and threats of equality seem less threatening, at least most of the time. To highlight an honor-shame framework, as I've tried to do in this book, exposes the fragility of whites' membership in a threatened but still dominant group.

So how does it feel to be a problem? It's easy for white people to retreat from that question into thinking that lower-class black people are still the problem. But the 2008 presidential campaign compelled many white people to face up to the issue of unconscious bias. The growing presence of black middle-class professionals as equals in the workplace has undermined the demonization on which white honor has depended for its appeal. Seeing Obama at the head of the Democratic ticket, and now in the White House, has made racism's ridiculousness half-visible.[68]

Other white voters may have turned to race as a simplifying signifier. It resolved their uneasiness about this relatively unknown candidate for president, pro or con. In my lifetime no one with as little national experience has ever been elected president. Obama had been in the Senate for less than four years. At least John F. Kennedy had been in Congress before his similarly brief stay in the Senate. Bill Clinton, Jimmy Carter, and Ronald Reagan had all been governors of their states for more than four years. Like many generals before him, Dwight D. Eisenhower had been a familiar public figure long before he became a political candidate. Franklin D. Roosevelt had been governor of New York for four years and secretary of the navy in the early 1920s. Of all the U.S. presidents, only Abraham Lincoln had less national exposure before his campaign. Branding Obama as black secured his identity for white voters uneasy about him on other, more plausible grounds. He became a familiar as well as threatening category.[69]

In the most optimistic scenario, President Obama stands for an idealized land of equal opportunity, and people of every ethnicity cherish the renewed sense of possibility that he represents. He received a premature Nobel Peace Prize for that promise. Such hopes reflect a utopian yearning to overcome still-intractable racial divides. In New Orleans many black residents voiced what David Remnick called "a great wariness, a kind of defense against white self-congratulation."[70] Whites voting for one black man won't transform a country.

But it's a start. Someone struggling out of the mud is conscious mostly of the mud. That's especially true if the mud is inside ourselves. We start to see the mud clearly for the fearful self-imprisonment that it is only when white people edge out of our own race-based "we." Even that last sentence remains within the "our" and "we" that it tries to get beyond.

Americans were lucky the campaign lasted nearly two years. Voters got almost accustomed to the idea of a half-black man as the nation's leader. Even when they thought he was unknowable or un-American, they got to know his intelligence, his calm, his discipline, and his caring. But getting used to Obama as a candidate was relatively easy. Getting used to a black man as president would be more difficult.

CHAPTER 7

TO THE TEA PARTY—
AND BEYOND?

Racial shaming has by no means disappeared in the United States. It focuses on Muslims and Mexican immigrants or pours into the ceaseless cascade of films about aliens. Some argue that it has shifted from race to class. New modes of segregation and policing, such as gated communities and anti-drug laws vigorously enforced against the urban poor, may have made it less necessary. More young black men are now in prison than in institutions of higher education, and 40 percent of black children under the age of five live in poverty.[1] Despite the new white tolerance for interracial hand-holding, in 1997, among the population of whites and blacks in the United States, 97 percent had married a person of the same race. In 2000, that percentage increased to 97.6 percent. Perhaps the tide is turning: preliminary results from the 2010 census show that the number of black-white families has more than doubled in several southern and midwestern states.[2] But the numbers are still small.

On the plus side, institutional counterpressures have more cultural power, corporations are hiring more diversely to gain more varied markets, and new Internet technologies make it easier to shame racist shamers. Don Imus never would have been fired after his racial slur against the Rutgers women's basketball team in the spring of 2007 if black board members and executives had not been volubly present in all the companies involved. His remark would not have gained public notice if Media Matters, a liberal organization that monitors all news broadcasts and syndicated talk shows, hadn't caught Imus's casual 6:15 A.M. remark. Even that information wouldn't have mattered much if bloggers hadn't alerted the mainstream media. In the last few years, similar Internet dynamics exposed racist remarks by Senate Majority Leader Trent Lott and comedian Larry Richards, creating new forms of public shaming. Public counterweights are now available, and public penalties are more severe.

But that's true only when racism is clearly visible.

The Tea Party

The national self-congratulation that followed President Obama's inauguration lasted less than a month. Conservatives seized every opportunity to turn diffuse fears into attacks on the president to restore the nation's honor. By midsummer, the trickle of public shaming had become a cascade. Recurrent displays of contempt for Obama roused white voters to defend "our country" with "tea party" revolts against a foreign tyrant. Many protesters passionately invoked the last sentence of Jefferson's Declaration of Independence: "We mutually pledge to each other our lives, our fortunes, and our sacred honor." On August 28, 2010, the anniversary of Martin Luther King's "I Have a Dream" speech, thousands of Americans gathered at the Lincoln Memorial for Glenn Beck's religious revival, titled "Restoring Honor." It required wishful thinking to believe that such honor was unbound from whiteness.

The Tea Party movement began on February 19, 2009, when CNBC's Rick Santelli went into a self-described "rant" on the floor of the Chicago Stock Exchange. To the cheers of traders who surrounded him, Santelli called for a "tea party" so that ordinary taxpayers could stop paying for "the losers." The government's subsidies were "promoting bad behavior," Santelli claimed. Tax money gets used "to subsidize the losers' mortgages" at the expense of people who can pay their bills. Santelli's speech rocketed across the web. He had touched a nerve.[3]

Within weeks, his speech had birthed a grassroots political party. Almost a year later, Tea Party activists astounded both political parties by propelling a Republican senator to victory for Teddy Kennedy's old seat in Massachusetts, the home of the 1773 Boston Tea Party. In the midterm elections of 2010, Tea Party fervor gave Republicans control of the House of Representatives.

Though some of that anger was directed at Wall Street, there was almost no protest from the right against continuing low taxes for those making more than $250,000. The specter of socialist tyranny bothered Tea Party conservatives more than the reality of bankers who turned government bailouts into personal bonuses. In their minds, Obama was trying to turn wealth-making into wealth redistribution, and he might be African to boot. Almost all of them feared they were losing their country. Almost all of them were white. As Jill Lepore suggests in *The Whites of Their Eyes*, the protesters don't think they're racist. Instead, they have intense nostalgia for an all-white America "before race, *without* race."[4]

In February 2010, David Barstow's *New York Times* report on his interviews with Tea Party members highlighted their loose affiliations with the John Birch Society and the resurgent militia movement. The "overwhelmingly white" audiences responded to calls for the abolition of the Federal Reserve, the income tax, and federal bailouts and stimulus plans. There was enormous anger about health care reform, despite the fact that some protesters had lost jobs or medical benefits. People also argued that Social Security, Medicare, and Medicaid should be eliminated. They responded intensely to Glenn Beck and to Richard Mack, who argued that "only local sheriffs and citizen militias could save the nation from 'utter despotism.'" Beck and Rush Limbaugh often stated that health care reform was stealth reparations to black people.[5] Tony Stewart, a civil rights activist in the inland Northwest, emphasized the "puzzling return of racist rhetoric and violence" as a context. Faced with pervasive economic uncertainties, Tea Partiers wanted someone to blame. Some talked about "another civil war."[6]

Historians such as Jill Lepore, Sean Wilentz, and Kate Zernike conclude that race is an intensifier rather than the cause of Tea Party anger toward big government. Wilentz's *New Yorker* article on the influence of W. Cleon Skousen declares that "'socialist' is not a racial slur." The Tea Party resuscitates "very old themes that have nothing to do with the color of President Obama's skin." In *Boiling Mad*, Zernike says that race is "not the driving force for a large number—and possibly most—of them." Tea Party rage comes from "anti-government sentiment, as old as the nation itself." Lepore argues that Tea Party advocates misread the founding fathers, not least by erasing slavery from their version of history. Only the NAACP's report *Tea Party Nationalism* and Will Bunch's *The Backlash* put race at the center of Tea Party dynamics.[7]

To me, the assertions of Lepore, Wilentz, and Zernike downplay the indirect racism that stimulates more socially acceptable forms of anger. Fears that the Democrats have been expanding "big government" make no rational sense. From 1948 to 2008, the three presidents who dramatically increased the federal deficit were Ronald Reagan, George H. W. Bush, and George W. Bush. Bill Clinton left a surplus. Republican presidents did cut taxes, but the U.S. government never contracted during their tenure, though its expansion slowed domestically. At the end of Reagan's second term, federal spending was still a higher proportion of the gross domestic product (21.2 percent) than it had been in the 1970s. George W. Bush expanded national regulation of state and local education with his "No Child Left Behind" program and added a prescription drug program to Medicare.[8] Except for a few principled libertarians, people didn't protest.

In 2009, however, fears of big government erupted, and the hidden issue sometimes surfaced. The issue wasn't government expansion, and it wasn't even taxes. The issue was government for whom? Who was benefiting? Fantasy had turned fear into righteous anger: Republicans govern for our kind, while Democrats give our tax money to losers, especially lazy scary blacks and illegal freeloading immigrants. Another question rarely surfaced: Who was benefiting from the fears? Beyond the obvious answer—people who wanted to reduce their taxes—loomed race and the resurgence of honor, which was implicitly white, although a few libertarian-leaning black people enthusiastically signed on. It was time to fight for our money and our freedom against slavish dependence on big government, especially since government keeps giving our money to people who don't shift for themselves.[9] It was a new Revolution; it was a new Civil War. David Bromwich has argued that the post-election recoil shows "the southernization of American politics." Bromwich notes that Rush Limbaugh "seldom speaks overtly about race." Instead, he voices contempt and disgust for "the Mammy State" and "Yo Mamma Care."[10]

It wasn't just that Obama seemed alien personally, though his skin color might be hiding danger under his "preternatural calm."[11] Tea Party enthusiasts felt under the thumb of new colonial rule. It was time for another tax revolt. National honor was at stake, and white honor was too. Again and again protesters voiced a modern hallucination of the Black Beast: the president is whipping out his big government and "ramming it down our throats." By the end of his first year in office, Obama had the lowest approval rating among white voters in the 30-year history of such polls.[12]

Nonracial issues played their part, including double-digit jobless-ness, bankers' bonuses, worries that health care reform wouldn't benefit the middle class, fear of increased taxes, and anger that the health care bill would require every adult American to get health insurance. But the nearly unanimous Republican strategy of "Just Say No" appealed to voters itching to turn their fears into anger. Where "race" couldn't be spoken, "socialism" could be shouted. Like race, it provided what T. S. Eliot called an "objective correlative," simplifying inchoate anxi-eties that your government isn't for you and life isn't going your way.[13] On October 30, 2010, at a big Washington, D.C., "Rally to Restore Sanity" (Jon Stewart) or "Rally to Keep Fear Alive" (Stephen Colbert), vendors sold T-shirts with a picture of George W. Bush and the caption, "I screwed up, but thanks for blaming the black guy."

Conservative commentators and leaders adroitly inflamed the fears or struggled to catch up to them. In the 1980s, the Southern Strategy thrived with code words that intimated appeals to a racial backlash. Now, in harder times, the strategy took on new national life. Did Republican leaders choose Michael Steele as the first African American chair of the Republican Nominating Committee to make the backlash look postracial? Were they counting on residual racism to make Obama a one-term president? Through the first two years of his term, the Just Say No strategy worked. Like Ahab's white whale, Obama's otherness became a symbol and a scapegoat for how every-thing felt out of control.

"You Lie!"

The tipping point came on September 9, 2009, during Obama's address about health care to Congress, when a representative from South Carolina shouted "You lie!" With Joe Wilson's shout, the issue of race couldn't be avoided any longer. A few days later, Maureen Dowd's much-quoted column in the *New York Times* suggested that Wilson really meant, "'You lie, boy!'" The birthers, the fears of "death panels" should the health care reform bill pass, the outpouring of rage at the idea that Obama would actually give a speech to students in school, and Glenn Beck's charge that Obama was a "racist" were too much for her. "I've been loath to admit that the shrieking lunacy of the summer—the frantic efforts to paint our first black president as the Other, a foreigner, socialist fascist, Marxist, racist, Commie, Nazi; a cad who would snuff old people; a snake who would indoctrinate kids—had much to do with race." But not now.[14]

Joe Wilson apologized to Obama for the outburst, though not for the charge. He refused to apologize to the House of Representatives, which censured him. His own strategic No-saying brought an outpouring of contributions for his reelection campaign, and he was easily reelected. Weeks of national discussion focused on whether the attacks on Obama had a racial component. Former president Jimmy Carter said yes, and many other commentators agreed.

Carter exaggerated the case when he said on NBC's *Nightly News* that "an overwhelming portion of the intensely demonstrated animosity toward President Barack Obama is based on the fact that he is a black man." In other interviews Carter reduced that charge by citing "a radical fringe element." Many conservatives said liberals were playing the race card to avoid debating the issues. Obama himself publicly discounted race as a major factor in the attacks. He said to *CBS News*, "I think what's driving passions right now is that health care has become a proxy for a broader set of issues about how much government should be involved in our economy." But the more elemental proxy, the target for pervasive disgust and distrust, was Obama himself.[15]

In all the commentaries I read on the incident, the subject of honor never came up. Yet I think it was the white elephant in Wilson's mind.

The congressman represents a mostly white South Carolina district stretching from Charlotte to Beaufort and Hilton Head. In 1999, he declared that "the Confederate heritage is very honorable." A year later he was one of seven state senators to vote for keeping the Confederate flag flying over the state house. He first doubted the claim that Strom Thurmond had a mixed-race daughter and called it a "smear," then said she shouldn't have revealed her parentage, since it diminished Thurmond's legacy.

Wilson's charge of lying did have some plausibility. Obama had just said that illegal immigrants wouldn't be covered in the five proposed health care plans. The president was right. Yet at that point in the tortuous process of bill-making, employers wouldn't be prohibited from insuring illegal immigrants. At least that's what some conservatives argued. From the left, as Brian Lehrer pointed out, it seemed telling that Wilson lost his cool at the prospect of illegal immigrants getting government funding. A black man telling him not to worry about paying for Latinos—that was too much.[16]

In antebellum South Carolina, Wilson's accusation would have provoked a duel, since it was a flagrant shaming. In the twenty-first century, his speech act brought a more complicated mix of local disapproval and cheers. Among some of Wilson's white constituents, the race issue seemed less important than his bad manners. In that respect they resembled honor-bound Iraqis who debated whether Bush's shoe thrower shamed an oppressor or violated rules of hospitality for a distinguished guest. South Carolinians debated whether Wilson's disrespect for a man in authority honored or dishonored their state.

Wilson's breach of national decorum exposed two contradictory aspects of a persistently localized honor code. In the antebellum South, it was good for a man to be aggressive. If a man didn't display his virility, he would lose his reputation. In 1856, an earlier representative from South Carolina had exemplified the southern hothead when Preston Brooks caned Charles Sumner on the floor of the Senate. The use of the cane signaled a double shaming, since the weapon was a sign of contempt for an inferior. Yet hotheads had to be respectful. As Bertram Wyatt-Brown notes, in the early nineteenth century, "a military submissiveness to those in higher authority was part of the training in honor and the avoidance of shame" across all classes. In 2009, South Carolina had another hothead in Congress. But now the man in highest authority wasn't white. Representative Wilson snapped, and many of his constituents felt torn.[17]

The Drumbeat of Public Shaming

The buildup to Wilson's outburst had been increasingly intense. In late July, the "birther movement" gained widespread media and web attention, after it had simmered for months on right-wing radio shows. Many white American citizens enthusiastically embraced claims that Obama had been born in Kenya, not Hawaii. On Chris Matthews's *Hardball*, G. Gordon Liddy said the president might well be an "illegal alien." Jerome Corsi's *Obama Nation* hadn't died after all. Rush Limbaugh blamed Obama for a fight on an Illinois school bus, since "in Obama's America, the white kids now get beat up with the black kids cheering 'yeah, right on, right on, right on."[18]

Amid the vilifications of a black president, a white policeman in Cambridge arrested Harvard professor Henry Louis Gates Jr. for "disorderly conduct" because Gates got angry at being taken for a burglar in his own house. A national furor erupted over whether the policeman was doing his duty with a belligerent suspect or whether Gates was yet another victim of racial profiling.

A couple of weeks later, at town meetings across the country, enraged white citizens attacked Obama's push for health care reform. Some had posters that depicted Obama with Hitler's moustache or as an African witch doctor or in whiteface or with Che Guevara. Other signs called Obama a "lying African." Some signs said "Go back to Africa" or "Go back to Kenya." The crowds were almost exclusively white.[19]

Then came an astonishing outburst of anger that the president would actually give a televised address to children in the public schools. A popular radio talk-show host in Kansas City, Chris Stigall, asserted his rights as a father on the air: "I wouldn't let my next-door neighbor talk to my kid alone; I'm sure as hell not letting Barack Obama talk to him alone." How could his child be "alone" when Obama would be addressing the boy's class on TV? Did he fear child molesting or some kind of seduction? In either case, his chivalric protectiveness trumped respect for the president or trust in his son's agency. On September 9, when Obama gave his speech urging students to persevere and study hard, many school districts chose not to show it and many parents kept their children home.[20]

At that point some web commentators suggested that race fears sparked the anger. On the web magazine *Salon.com*, Joan Walsh concluded that "from the Birthers' obsession with the facts of his birth—which lets them obsess about his origins in miscegenation—to the paranoia that he's coming for the children, there's a deep strand of irrational paranoia that can't be anything other than racial." On the *Huffington Post*, Michael Shaw noted the "racist meme at play. It's something along the lines of: You can't trust your children alone with this man . . . knowing how black men are. Wink, wink." The evidence was skimpy, and conservatives accused liberals of evading the issues. Meanwhile, it began to look as though the summer and fall of 2009 would be known for producing the fear of the week. Whatever the mix of policy and prejudice, many speakers and bloggers delighted in stigmatizing a black president.

The birther movement was the most bizarre, but its popularity reflected a political reality that has festered for at least fifty years.[21] Many white Americans like to think of themselves as angry victims. It's a lucrative market, stimulated by Dobbs, Limbaugh, O'Reilly, and Beck, among others, though O'Reilly condemned what Frank Rich has called "the birther brigades." All four conservative commentators are sophisticated showmen who know what buttons to push. They seek the flare-up issues that spark anger at any imagined loss of white privilege. So far the losses have been more symbolic than tectonic. But the well-managed eruptions of anger about the cultural shift that Obama's presidency represents will continue to shape American politics for the foreseeable future.[22]

In August 2009, fears took another form: explosions of rage about Obama's proposals for health care reform, especially at various town meetings during the congressional recess. Part of the anger came from legitimate anxiety about specific aspects of the bill's proposals. Will health care be rationed? How can it be paid for? How much will I pay? Will I pay for someone else's abortion or for illegal immigrants? Can I keep my doctor? Another fear surfaced only occasionally. Will I have to pay for those aliens who are taking over my world?

That's the same apocalyptic fantasy Samuel Huntington was exercised about at the end of *The Clash of Civilizations*. One constituent shouted at Senator Arlen Specter, "You are trampling on our Constitution!" Another shouted that "Obamacare" puts "the existence of the Republic at risk." South Carolina Republican congressman Robert Inglis reported that one constituent demanded, "Keep your government hands off my Medicare." I kept hearing an unspoken subtext: "No big black man is going to ride my back, or boss me around, or"—as one woman screamed at a Washington protest—"ram socialism down our throats!'" Quoting her, Walsh mused, "Where to start?"[23]

Where to end: with the "choking fear" that Leonard Pitts found at the heart of the Tea Party movement. On February 15, 2010, Keith Olbermann concluded his MSNBC broadcast with a meditation on racial prejudice, his own included. "What we're seeing at the Tea Parties is, at its base, people who are afraid—terribly, painfully, cripplingly, blindingly afraid." The movement is "a backlash" whose "euphemisms" and "rationalizations" veil its racism, he continued. Other commentators, notably John McCain's daughter, Meghan McCain, also called the movement racist. But Pitts went the furthest in his musings about the ongoing political phenomenon.[24]

Responding to Olbermann's wide-ranging discussion of prejudice, the African American columnist wrote that though race is "a major component" of the Tea Party movement's appeal, a deeper issue drives the racism. People "face the realization that their days of dominance are numbered. There is a poignancy to their responsive fury because one senses that the nether side of it is a choking fear." They feel "a crippling sense of dislocation and loss," and they want their country back. Too simply, Pitts concludes that "it is already, irrevocably, gone."[25] Centuries of white supremacy don't yield so easily. Amid the mix of anger, mourning, and fear, presumptions of white privilege remain beleaguered but unbowed.

The Tea Party movement represents a national version of "There Goes My Everything," Jason Sokol's wonderful title for his book on southern whites' reactions to the civil rights movement. But fears of loss aren't the end of the story, because they bring the resurgent power of anger, which fights the loss of a race-based world that makes you feel free, on top, and in control, especially when you're not. The anger restores a sense of entitlement. It makes white people demoralized by the recession feel that they matter again.

As Frank Rich pointed out, the protests paralleled a rise in extremist groups. The number of threats against Obama increased 400 percent from the number of threats against Bush. In late September 2010 someone on Facebook ran a poll asking people to vote on whether Obama should be killed. From April to August of that year, an amusement park in Roseto, Pennsylvania, offered a game called "Alien Attack," in which players could throw darts at an Obama-like black man with the presidential seal on his belt buckle who held a scroll labeled "Health Bill." As the AP reported, players won prizes by "hitting targets on the image's head and heart." In four months, only two people complained.[26]

Books that featured exuberant right-wing shaming leaped to the top of the best-seller list at about the same time, though without a whisper of race. Michelle Malkin's *Culture of Corruption: Obama and His Team of Tax Cheats, Crooks, and Cronies* was number one on the *New York Times* nonfiction best-seller list for weeks. Malkin is Asian American, and she doesn't display any presumptions of white supremacy. She's also a conservative columnist and blogger with several previous books and a penchant for fanning flames. Whereas Jerome Corsi voiced explicit paranoia that radical blacks will take over the country, Malkin presents Obama not as an alien but as an insider. Her view is that he may say he favors change, but he's just a Chicago pol on the take, like all of his multiracial "cronies."

Throughout, Malkin zestfully voices disgust, not fear, as she exposes the gulf between preaching and practice. Like Corsi, she slants the evidence and never mentions equivalent or greater instances of Republican wheeling and dealing. In contrast to *Obama Nation*, which seems bedeviled with hysterical anxieties about black people, *Culture of Corruption* is genuinely postracial, an equal opportunity attacker. Race and fear may be gone, but a more ancient struggle between a dishonorable Them and an honorable Us impels Malkin's public shaming. Images of cleansing frame the book. She begins with janitors "cleaning the drool off laptops and floors" after Obama's election, and she ends by turning that drool into a swamp: "But no one, not even Barack Obama, can drain a swamp by flooding it."[27]

In 2010, another best seller updated Corsi's terror at the thought of black power, though with a different disguise. Dinesh D'Souza's *The Roots of Black Rage* presents Obama as an anti-colonialist who is living his Kenyan father's dream of taking down imperialist capitalism. Sympathy with American blacks doesn't drive the president, D'Souza argues, though "Obama's specific achievement is to restore the credibility of the color-blind ideal in America." Rather, his "contrived" black identity, or what Fanon called a "lactification strategy," hides an Afrocentric drive to reduce the American standard of living by opposing oil drilling, favoring controls of global warming, supporting ACORN, "reducing the American arsenal," and converting NASA to a community outreach program for Muslims. He's "a president who seems to want his country to go the way of Britain." He's a "time machine" trying to resist the colonialism that Africa still needs, just as it needed it in the nineteenth century. D'Souza presents his cosmopolitan background, which is similar to Obama's, to imply that Obama should have taken D'Souza's conservative road but instead stayed imprisoned in a Kenyan mind-state.[28]

All these fanciful transformations of rage, fear, and contempt aimed to restore the power that the Republican right was used to. That's standard American practice for the party out of office. As many commentators have pointed out, Democrats were just as contemptuous of George W. Bush, and Republican attacks on Bill and Hillary Clinton had much more personal venom. Nonetheless, race remained an easily available lightning rod to channel fears. "There is an angst out there and there is a climate of fear right now," said a former chair of the South Carolina Republican Party. "That confusion and chaos creates opportunity." By late September, one columnist for *Newsmax* wrote that he saw no alternative but a "civilized" military coup. By early December, at a New York City rally against the attorney general's decision to try Khalid Sheikh Mohammed there, someone shouted, "Lynch Holder!"[29]

In September 2010, Newt Gingrich echoed D'Souza's claim that Obama was channeling his father's rage by exhibiting "Kenyan, anti-colonial behavior." Jerome Corsi's book had faded, but only into the mainstream.[30] Both Corsi and D'Souza assume that Obama must be driven by terrifying anger at whites. That delusional, dehumanizing perception reflects not just fear and contempt but also a denial that powerful black men can exercise responsible authority. In that frame of mind, racism has nothing to do with the privileges available to all light-skinned people who can seize them.

In the most optimistic scenario, the Tea Party movement may be a watershed moment in American history. Most of its supporters are older white people. Younger white Americans tend to have more multi-cultural tolerance, while many of their elders seem filled with rage and mourning. For some of them, seeing Obama on TV is a daily punch in the gut. If a generational shift is in the offing, the movement may be the last flailing surge of the old guard, the last attempt to defend white honor and the tradition of white entitlement.

Alternatively, Tea Party advocates may be right to say we should restore the America that Franklin Delano Roosevelt destroyed. To paraphrase that view: America was built on freedom, and Big Government is reducing its citizens to slaves who lack responsibility or dignity. In a weak state, plucky people innovate, whereas a strong state saps self-reliance. Race has nothing to do with it. Whoever lacks grit and gumption deserves to be a loser. If some African Americans, Latinos, and poor whites have taken advantage of a culture of dependence, that may say something about their character, but we shouldn't keep enabling them. A few black politicians have welcomed that credo.[31]

From the anti-Catholic, anti-immigrant Know-Nothing Party in the 1850s to the present, nativist recoils have appealed to Americans most intensely in hard times.[32] If that's a basic human response, shaming people perceived as the Other will continue into the far future, when-ever Americans in the dominant group feel they are on the skids.

The Gates Arrest

The "Gatesgate" arrest provokes more vexed and irresolvable thoughts. At noon on July 16, 2009, Henry Louis Gates Jr. and another black man, his Moroccan limousine driver, were struggling to open a stuck front door in his house near Harvard when a passerby phoned in a possible burglary. A policeman arrived quickly. During the past six months there had been twenty-three incidents of breaking and entering in that upscale neighborhood. Gates's lock may have been jammed by an intruder while he was in China, filming a PBS series. When the policeman arrived, Gates was in his foyer and the limo driver had left. Gates was 58 years old, and he walked with a cane.[33]

According to the police report, Gates immediately became "belligerent" when Sergeant James Crowley told him to come outside. Gates claimed that Crowley never identified himself. Crowley claimed that Gates couldn't hear the sergeant identify himself (which he did several times) because Gates was shouting. One example: "Are you not answering me because I'm a black man and you're a white police officer?" When Crowley repeated his request, Gates allegedly replied, "Ya, I'll speak with your mama outside." Gates's Harvard ID card didn't include his address. So Sgt. Crowley arrested him for disorderly conduct. Gates was led away in handcuffs for a seven-hour detention, until the charges were dropped. Four days later the case surfaced in the *Harvard Crimson*. It became a media feast of charges and countercharges, with demands for apologies on both sides.[34]

By all accounts, Gates and Crowley were among the least likely people to have a racial flare-up. Each man had a long history of exemplary racial sensitivity. Yet Gates saw red and talked black to a lower-status white man who threatened him.[35] Crowley heard contemptuous disobedience and shouting from a possible suspect. Gates claimed that when Crowley asked him to step outside, "All the hairs stood up on the back of my neck, and I realized that I was in danger." Yet his actions displayed confident rage, not fear. For both men, their honor was at stake. Race and class fueled the flames.[36]

As further information about the arrest emerged, I confess that my sympathies shifted to the policeman. I found more and more things to dislike in Gates's—well, attitude. He told an interviewer that he expected the policeman to say, "How can I help you, sir?" Did he think the policeman was his servant? According to Crowley, Gates said several times, "You don't know who you're messing with." Gates told his daughter, "He should have gotten out of there and said, 'I'm sorry, sir, good luck. Loved your PBS series—check with you later!'" Later he called Crowley "a rogue policeman," though the sergeant had often taught other police how to handle race relations.[37]

In Gates's narrative of the arrest, Sgt. Crowley "presumed that I was guilty because I was black. There was no doubt about that." President Obama echoed Gates in commenting on the issue at his July 22 press conference. Identifying Gates as his friend, Obama said that "the Cambridge police acted stupidly in arresting somebody when there was already proof that they were in their own home." Obama repeated Gates's claim that the incident intimated racial profiling. African Americans and Latinos have been "disproportionately" stopped by police for a long time, he said several times. "And that's just a fact."

Why then did I sympathize with the white policeman, not the black professor? One answer stared me in my face. I was doing what racists do and what I've been critiquing in this book. As Frank Rich put it, "Threatened white elites try to mask their own anxieties by patronizingly adopting working-class whites as their pet political surrogates—Joe the Plumber, New Haven firemen, a Cambridge police officer." Except for some black policemen, most African Americans agreed with Gates and Obama that it was a classic example of racial profiling.[38] Postracial? After nearly a decade of writing this book, I wasn't even close.

Judging by the hate mail Gates received, I was at the gentle end of vilifications by whites. He had to change his phone numbers and his e-mail address, and Harvard urged him to move. Vicious public shaming erupted on both sides. Four days after Obama smoothed the waters, Glenn Beck called the president a "racist" with "a deep-seated hatred for white people or the white culture."[39]

Another answer complicates the first, again to my discredit: my envy of Gates's professional distinction. A third answer inches me back to the progressive side: my sense of the class war here. I was taking the side of the less entitled man, even though he was a policeman with a gun. Gates's presumption did roil me.

All that analysis fends off a simple stark fact. When race gets involved, anyone can flip out. Here were two good men enmeshed in a reciprocal public shaming. One obviously felt disrespected because of race; the other probably felt disrespected because of class. And that shared state of mind, plus Gates's status, drove them into the headlines.

More surprisingly, President Obama also felt disrespected. He was annoyed about media accounts of his speech to the NAACP on July 16, the same day as Gates's arrest. Obama greeted his audience as a brother who had made it to the mountaintop. He declared that "there probably has never been less discrimination in America than there is today." But the "durable and destructive legacies of discrimination" have persisted, particularly the "structured inequalities that our nation's legacy of discrimination has left behind." What probably looked like boilerplate rhetoric to white people remains vividly real to black people. The barriers are also inside us, he said—"the way we've internalized a sense of limitation; how so many in our community have come to expect so little from the world and from themselves."

Taking responsibility can help overcome these internalized limits, Obama said. "No excuses," he added to his prepared remarks, and repeated, "No excuses." The mainstream media highlighted that part of his speech, especially the interjection. Headline after headline trumpeted "No excuses." White people seemed to be shaking their fingers at African Americans as if to say, "See, even the black president we elected is telling you to shape up. Whatever problems you have now, they're your fault."

Obama was dismayed about the coverage. To Eugene Robinson, an African American columnist, he complained that the media featured his calls for "responsibility" while disregarding "the whole other half of the speech." So Obama was disposed to highlight the racial profiling in Gates's arrest, as he did. Stupidly. Humiliating a policeman and his entire police force didn't sound presidential.[40]

Two days later, he appeared at another press conference. Having just talked with Sgt. Crowley on the phone, Obama admitted that his "unfortunate" words had "ratcheted up" the controversy. Now he called Crowley and Gates "two good people . . . two decent people" who "probably overreacted." Obama hoped that the arrest would become "what's called a 'teachable moment.'" It might nudge people toward "listening to each other," and he urged Americans to "be a little more reflective." He also hoped the sergeant and the professor would join him at the White House for a beer.

Obama's change shows a way to get beyond racial rancor. He had used his authority to shame Sgt. Crowley and the Cambridge police. Now he showed respect and listened attentively, even joking with Sgt. Crowley about the size of their lawns. It worked. The issue simmered down.[41] On Thursday, July 30, Sgt. Crowley and his family met Professor Gates and his family at the White House and sat down with Obama and Vice President Biden for almost an hour. Neither the professor nor the policeman apologized. As Crowley said later, "What you had today was two gentlemen who agreed to disagree on a particular issue."[42]

Gentlemen! No more need for a duel; the honor of both parties had been restored. Crowley's statement may have deliberately echoed the original 9–1–1 call, in which the caller reported that there were "two gentlemen trying to get in a house." In any case, the "beer summit" brought closure. Crowley later gave the handcuffs to Gates, who gave them to the Smithsonian. The professor had the last good sound bite: "When he's not arresting you, Sergeant Crowley is a really likable guy."[43]

Even as I write about the incident, long after the national debate has subsided, I go back and forth. Maybe that's as it should be. On his Boston radio show, Mike Barnicle concluded that "race remains the third rail of American life."[44] In Obama's calming remarks on July 22, he said that we've made "incredible progress," but race "still haunts us." Eric Holder was right to say we avoid talking about it, and the president was brave to move beyond his own attempt at public shaming. He praised the two men's ability to "listen to each other," and he respected their differences. As he talked, I felt my own tensions ease.

Like my narrative of that incident, this book has been an uncertain story of progress and recoil. Race does haunt us. For over 400 years, white presumptions of supremacy have persisted in America. Slavery legitimized the claims, and fears of powerful black men continue to shape our nation's politics. Many if not most Americans still think that light skin color secures social advantage, and fears of losing that advantage continue to prompt racial shaming. Using race to separate insiders from outsiders can feel more comfortable than the jostling that comes from competitors on a level playing field.

Only in the last sixty years has the mask of white pseudo-aristocracy begun to disintegrate. For people who define themselves as white, living in a multiethnic mix requires some detachment from racial claims that are more generic than personal. Lording it over someone else or another social group springs from a fear of inadequacy, and turning a person or a group into the Other disowns a part of ourselves. Yet whiteness is shifting from a privileged fact to a fiction that light-skinned people don't have to inhabit and protect.

Whether our skin color is the lightest of tans or the darkest of browns, many of us still use race to brand others and mask our own complexity. But the United States at its best is alive with checks and balances. So are its citizens. Conflicting group affiliations—some racial, some not—have shaped every American's sensibility. To bring out the strength of our outward equalities and inward contentions, conversations with ourselves may be more important than conversations with each other. I hope the conversations continue.

NOTES

INTRODUCTION

1. Bernard Weinraub, "Pioneer of a Beat Is Still Riffing for His Due," *New York Times*, February 16, 2003, 24, paraphrasing Diddley. See Adam Nossiter's "Unearthing a Town Pool, and Not for Whites Only," *New York Times*, September 18, 2006, A1, 23, the history of a Mississippi swimming pool; and Jeff Wiltse's *Contested Waters: A Social History of Swimming Pools in America* (Chapel Hill: University of North Carolina Press, 2007), which details the social turmoil as swimming pools were desegregated in the 1940s and 1950s.

2. Michael Tesler and David Sears, *Obama's Race: The 2008 Election and the Dream of a Post-Racial America* (Chicago: University of Chicago Press, 2010), especially chapter 7. Melissa Harris-Perry argues that many Americans think Obama is African because he doesn't fit their stereotypes of American blackness; Harris-Perry, "For Birthers, Obama's Not Black Enough," *The Nation*, May 16, 2011, 10.

3. Michelle Alexander notes that "70% of men between the ages of eighteen and forty-five" in one black Chicago neighborhood have criminal records, 60 percent for drug offenses that whites are rarely imprisoned for. She argues that mass incarceration perpetuates Jim Crow patterns of segregation; Alexander, *The New Jim Crow: Mass Incarceration in the Age of Colorblindedness* (New York: New Press, 2010), 181–191, quote on 191. On incarcerated African Americans, 93 percent of whom are men, see also prisonactivist.org. Khalil Gibran Muhammad argues that in the 1890s, white writers began using crime statistics to link black people with pathology and criminality while downplaying similar statistics for white immigrants; Muhammad, *The Condemnation of Blackness: Race, Crime, and the Making of Modern Urban America* (Cambridge, Mass.: Harvard University Press, 2010), 6–8, 35–57 (on the impact of Frederick L. Hoffman's *Race Traits and Tendencies of the American Negro* [1896]), 276–277 (on the continuities in Gunnar Myrdal's seemingly liberal *An American Dilemma: The Negro Problem and Modern Democracy* [1944]). Nell Irvin

Painter concludes that "poverty in a dark skin endures as the opposite of whiteness . . . permanently other and inherently inferior"; Painter, *The History of White People* (New York: W. W. Norton, 2010), 396.

4. Augusto Espiritu, "Transitions and Quotes," *Reviews in American History* 35 (September 2007): 411. I disagree here with Melani McAlister's contention that "the multiple and intersecting structures of race in the United States were never organized on a simple binary"; see McAlister, "Race Worlds: Discrimination, American-Style, in the Middle East," *American Quarterly* 59 (December 2007): 1242. I'm also qualifying Robert Levine's emphasis on contingency, uncertainty, and contestations of white supremacy in *Dislocating Race & Nation: Episodes in Nineteenth-Century American Literary Nationalism* (Chapel Hill: University of North Carolina Press, 2008), 11–12, 240–242. Levine argues that "fixed" stances such as mine "simply confess to our own profound sense of futility and entrapment" (11).

5. On Brigitte Gabriel, see Laurie Goodstein, "Drawing U.S. Crowds with Anti-Islam Message," *New York Times*, March 8, 2011, A1, A3. Gabriel, who grew up as a Maronite Christian in Lebanon during the 1970s and now uses a pseudonym, argues that "'America has been infiltrated on all levels'" by Islamic radicals (A1) who follow the "Islamofascism" of the Koran (A3).

6. David A. Gerber notes that "White" as an ethnic marker "is currently owned confidently and proudly only by the racialist and racial Right"; Gerber, "What's Wrong with Immigration History?" *Reviews in American History* 36 (December 2008): 551.

7. Mark Twain, *Pudd'nhead Wilson* (New York: Signet, 1964), chapter 3. The narrator mocks the ridiculousness of labeling Roxy "black" because this white-looking woman has 1/16 "black blood." Henry Louis Gates Jr. muses that his influential 1986 book *"Race," Writing, and Difference* and the 1985 and 1986 issues of *Critical Inquiry*, both of which he edited, were right to establish race as a fiction but may have encouraged people to avoid confronting the ongoing woundingness of race; see Gates, "Reading 'Race,' Writing, and Difference," in "Comparative Racialization," edited by Shu-mei Shih, special issue, *PMLA* 123 (October 2008): 1534–1539. As Toni Morrison asked him (1537–1538), why does race become a fiction at the moment when black professors are entering the academy and black texts are entering the canon?

8. George Lipsitz argues that since the 1930s, legislation has increased material advantages for whites, continuously abetted by the "politics of exclusion" and the "cowardice and craven opportunism of elected officials"; Lipsitz, *The Possessive Investment in Whiteness: How White People Profit from Identity Politics*, rev. ed. (Philadelphia: Temple University Press, 2006), 5–23, 232 (quote). Tim Wise has written four books against white racism: *Speaking Treason*

Fluently: Anti-Racist Reflections from an Angry White Male (New York: Soft Skull Press, 2008); *Colorblind: The Rise of Post-Racial Politics and the Retreat from Racial Equity* (San Francisco: City Lights Publishers, 2010); *Between Barack and a Hard Place: Racism and White Denial in the Age of Obama* (San Francisco: City Lights Publishers, 2009); and a memoir, *White Like Me*, rev. ed. (Brooklyn: Soft Skull Press, 2008). The memoir's first edition (2005) has an almost Calvinist conclusion, that white racism will probably never be defeated, but "our redemption comes from the struggle itself" (153). "It is, simply put, an honor and a privilege to serve as the threat of a good example" (155) in "a battle you may never win" (152). The second edition deletes the word "honor" from this quote (177).

9. Susan Saulny, "Black and White and Married in the Deep South: A Shifting Image," *New York Times*, March 20, 2011, A4. On the increase by 134 percent of those who say they are both black and white (1.8 million at the last census), see Saulny, "Census Data Presents Rise in Multiracial Population of Youths," *New York Times*, March 25, 2011, A3. Earlier articles about multiracial identities include Ruth La Ferla, "Generation E.A.: Ethnically Ambiguous," *New York Times*, December 28, 2003, Style 1; and Saulny, "Black? White? Asian? More Young Americans Choose All of the Above," *New York Times*, January 30, 2011, A1.

CHAPTER 1 — FEAR, HONOR, AND RACIAL SHAMING

1. As John W. Dower writes of Japanese ethnic brutalities, "In its most extreme form, racism sanctions extermination." Dower, "Race, Language, and War in Two Cultures," in Dower, *Japan in War and Peace: Selected Essays* (New York: New Press, 1993), 260.

2. Charles J. Ogletree Jr. recounts 100 stories of contemporary black men, all successful and many very well known, who have experienced various forms of racial profiling; Ogletree, *The Presumption of Guilt: The Arrest of Henry Louis Gates Jr. and Race, Class, and Crime in America* (New York: Palgrave Macmillan, 2011), 129–241.

3. "Attorney General Eric Holder at the Department of Justice African American History Month Program," February 18, 2009, available at www.justice.gov/ag/speeches/2009/ag-speech-090218.html. In "A Nation of Cowards?" *New York Times*, February 21, 2009, A17, Charles M. Blow muses that white people's fears of appearing to be prejudiced may block candid self-confrontation and discussions about race with others.

4. Orlando Patterson, "The New Mainstream," *Newsweek*, November 10, 2008, 41. See also Orlando Patterson, "Race and Diversity in the Age of Obama," *New York Times Book Review*, August 16, 2009, 23, which contrasts the

rapid assimilation of every other ethnic group with the "chronic hypersegre-gation" of blacks. Patterson argues that residential segregation—which black Americans often choose because of the "politics of identity"—remains the primary cause of racial inequality by excluding black people "from network location and access to cultural capital"; Patterson, "Inequality in America," *The Nation*, July 19–26, 2010, 20. In midsummer of 2008, the *New York Times* featured a poll showing "markedly little change" in race relations from 2000 to 2008; see Adam Nagourney and Megan Thee, "Poll Finds Obama Isn't Closing Divide on Race," *New York Times*, July 16, 2008, A1, A14.

5. *Hardball with Chris Matthews*, MSNBC, February 19, 2009, guest host Mike Barnicle, guests Matt Taibbi and Jonathan Capehart, transcript available at www.msnbc.msn.com/id/29301548/.

6. W.E.B. Du Bois, *The Souls of Black Folk*, in *Three Negro Classics*, edited by John Hope Franklin (New York: Avon Books, 1999), 213.

7. Annette Gordon-Reed emphasizes the uses of race to obscure class divisions among whites; see Gordon-Reed, *The Hemingses of Monticello: An American Family* (New York: W. W. Norton, 2008), 53, 514.

8. Edmund S. Morgan, *American Slavery, American Freedom: The Ordeal of Colonial Virginia* (New York: W. W. Norton, 1975), 386. On the "self-amplifica-tion" available to whites through their slaves, see Walter Johnson, *Soul by Soul: Life Inside the Antebellum Slave Market* (Cambridge, Mass.: Harvard Univer-sity Press, 1999), 15, 149–150. On intellectual justifications for racism in the nineteenth and early twentieth centuries, see John Higham, *Strangers in the Land: Patterns of American Nativism 1860–1925*, 2nd ed. (New York: Atheneum, 1973), 131–157; George Fredrickson, *Racism: A Short History* (Princeton, N.J.: Princeton University Press, 2002); and Nell Irvin Painter, *The History of White People* (New York: W. W. Norton, 2010), among many others. Painter notes American claims to class superiority through race superiority (110, 271, 319; see also 131 on race as aristocracy). As Kelefa Sanneh's review of Painter and other recent writers on whiteness notes, "one of the defining qualities of whiteness is that it needs protection." Sanneh, "Beyond the Pale: Is White the New Black?" *The New Yorker*, April 12, 2010, 71.

9. Robert J. Norrell emphasizes "status competition" between whites and blacks for jobs and land ownership as the key factor in claims to white supremacy; Norrell, *The House I Live In: Race in the American Century* (New York: Oxford University Press, 2005), xii–xiii, 6, 20, 50, 72–73, 167.

10. Gordon-Reed, *The Hemingses of Monticello*, 336 (black race an invention of whites), 43 (Africa the most diverse), 41 (settlers associated whiteness with privilege). See also Winthrop D. Jordan, *White over Black: American Attitudes toward the Negro, 1550–1812* (Baltimore, Md.: Penguin Books, 1968), espe-

cially 3–43. Jordan's still-compelling history opened up the field, though his subtitle, "American Attitudes toward the Negro, 1550–1812," betrays lingering presumptions that "American" means "white" and that "the Negro" indicates a monolithic group. On the invention of the white race in the late 1600s, see Tim Wise's published collection of Internet essays, *Speaking Treason Fluently: Anti-Racist Reflections from an Angry White Male* (New York: Soft Skull Press, 2008), 188–190.

11. Scott L. Malcomson, *One Drop of Blood: The American Misadventure of Race* (New York: Farrar Straus Giroux, 2000), 277 (truly white person is dead), 281, 290–291 (free meant not a slave; white meant not black). Strangely, as Nell Irvin Painter points out, "blue bloods" have been raised above other white people because they don't do outside labor so their veins show through their untanned skin; Painter, *The History of White People*, 94.

12. For an analysis of the usage of the word "white" in *The Pennsylvania Gazette*, see Peter Silver, *Our Savage Neighbors: How Indian War Transformed Early America* (New York: W. W. Norton, 2008). Eric Slauter quotes Silver's conclusion and includes two charts of the frequency of use of various words over time; see Slauter, "Revolutions in the Meaning and Study of Politics," *American Literary History* 22 (Summer 2010): 328–330, midcentury spikes quote at 328. For dynamics of white exclusion and inclusion in the late nineteenth century and beyond, see Matthew Frye Jacobson, *Whiteness of a Different Color: European Immigrants and the Alchemy of Race* (Cambridge, Mass.: Harvard University Press, 1998).

13. Zora Neale Hurston, *Their Eyes Were Watching God* (New York: Harper & Row Perennial, 1990), 136. On melanin and debates about genetics, see Painter, *The History of White People*, 94, 390–392.

14. Henry Louis Gates Jr., "Reading 'Race,' Writing, and Difference," in "Comparative Racialization," edited by Shu-mei Shih, special issue, *PMLA* 123 (October 2008): 1534–1539.

15. On the census, see Margo Anderson and Stephen E. Feinberg, "Race and Ethnicity and the Controversy over the U.S. Census," *Current Sociology* 48, no. 3 (2000): 87–110; and Michael Lind, "Defying Categorization," *The Guardian*, April 1, 2008. See also Painter, *The History of White People*, 104–106, 384–385.

16. Ira Berlin, *The Making of African America: The Four Great Migrations* (New York: Viking, 2010), especially 10–13. See also Grace Hale, *Making Whiteness: the Culture of Segregation in the South, 1890–1940* (New York: Pantheon, 1998); and Anthony W. Marx, *Making Race and Nation: A Comparison of South Africa, the United States, and Brazil* (Cambridge: Cambridge University Press, 1998), 16–17, 274–275. Marx argues that racial dominance in the United States and South Africa diminished conflict among whites. Anne Anlin Cheng argues

that what she calls "white racial melancholia" reflects a denied grieving that rejects and retains racialized others; Cheng, *The Melancholy of Race: Psychoanalysis, Assimilation, and Hidden Grief* (New York: Oxford University Press, 2000). Richard Dyer usefully surveys whiteness studies and issues; Dyer, *White: Essays on Race and Culture* (London: Routledge, 1997), 1–40. Robert Zieger writes about struggles involving racism and the possibility of biracial coalitions in America's labor unions and builds on the current scholarly consensus "that blackness was the negativity that defined whiteness"; Zieger, *For Jobs and Freedom: Race and Labor in America since 1865* (Lexington: University Press of Kentucky, 2007), 2, also 3–4 and 188 on the continuing otherness of black people. Jonathan Scott Holloway argues that the collective memory of their black ancestors became "a memory of those whose very presence made the rest of the country white"; Holloway, *Jim Crow Wisdom: Memory, Identity, and Politics in Black America, 1941–2000* (unpublished).

17. Scott Malcomson argues that "white" and "free" are also double negatives, by which he means words whose positive value comes from negating their devalued opposites; Malcomson, *One Drop of Blood*, 281, 290–291.

18. Alexander Welsh, *What Is Honor? A Question of Moral Imperatives* (New Haven, Conn.: Yale University Press, 2008); Kwame Anthony Appiah, *The Honor Code: How Moral Revolutions Happen* (New York: W. W. Norton, 2010). In his influential article "On the Obsolescence of the Concept of Honor," *European Journal of Sociology* 11 (1970): 339–347, Peter Berger argues that honor has been replaced by dignity and dichotomizes self-defined and institution-defined identities. Frank Henderson Stewart rejoins the two by defining honor as the entitlement to respect, which has both internal and external modes of recognition. Honor codes show people how to get respect, he argues; Stewart, *Honor* (Chicago: University of Chicago Press, 1994).

19. Welsh, *What Is Honor?* 207; Appiah, *The Honor Code*, 87. Appiah highlights the honor code's capacity to bring about moral revolutions, citing as examples the cessation of upper-class dueling in the West, foot-binding in China, and the Atlantic slave trade. Sometimes Appiah's evidence seems skimpy, especially about English and American dueling. As he admits, dueling slowly disappeared not because of a nation's concerns for respect but because the practice ceased to be a status marker as lower classes took it up. Similarly, he argues that China ended girls' foot-binding to save national face. But he rests that claim primarily on one minor bureaucrat's 1898 memorandum, which "played no role" in the emperor's short-lived decree. More generally, rulers who seek international respect can do terrible things. (I kept thinking of Mussolini's craving for Hitler's approval.)

20. Tim Wise comes to a similar conclusion, although he places less

emphasis on multiple group affiliations and more emphasis on freeing oneself from racism by recognizing that "we are made up of many identities"; Wise, *Colorblind: The Rise of Post-Racial Politics and the Retreat from Racial Equity* (San Francisco: City Lights Publishers, 2010), 157; see also 21, 153–194.

21. Gail Bederman dates the first use of "masculinity" as a noun to 1854, in *Bertha and Lily*, a novel by Elizabeth Oakes Smith; Bederman, *Manliness and Civilization: A Cultural History of Gender and Race in the United States, 1880–1917* (Chicago: University of Chicago Press, 1995), 245n78, also 6–19. The *Oxford English Dictionary* cites an anomalous use in 1748, crediting the French, then a spate of uses from 1860 onward. According to the *OED Supplement*, "masculinization" emerged in 1895.

22. Bertram Wyatt-Brown, *Southern Honor: Ethics and Behavior in the Old South* (Oxford: Oxford University Press, 1982), 155. Stewart sharply differentiates European and Mediterranean honor codes from Bedouin codes in the Sinai. He argues that Europeans emphasize class deference as well as personal respect and separate law from violent avenging of insults and that Bedouins emphasize obligations and equality and use judges to try honor disputes. Stewart also argues that in Europe, the "external" honor of medieval times had moved toward "internal" honor by the nineteenth century. Stewart, *Honor*, 130–143, 81, 41.

23. Johnson, *Soul by Soul*, 80 (buy their way into the master class), 13, 103–104 (more preoccupied with slave trade than with duels).

24. On whites and "color blindness," see Thomas J. Sugrue, *Not Even Past: Barack Obama and the Burden of Race* (Princeton, N.J.: Princeton University Press, 2010), 110–124; and Tim Wise, *Colorblind*.

25. On separating humiliation from shame, see Evelin Lindner, *Making Enemies: Humiliation and International Conflict* (Westport, Conn.: Praeger Security International, 2006), xiv, 3, 171. Lindner argues that shame is "a humbling experience a person agrees to" that keeps us within social limits (21). See also William Ian Miller, *Humiliation and Other Essays on Honor, Social Discomfort, and Violence* (Ithaca, N.Y.: Cornell University Press, 1993), 168–169; and Judith Lewis Herman, *Trauma and Recovery: The Aftermath of Violence—From Domestic Abuse to Political Terror* (New York: Basic Books, 1997), 56 (on incest trauma), and 88, 212, 235–236 (on humiliation as terror). In *For Shame: The Loss of Common Decency in American Culture* (New York: St. Martin's, 1998), James B. Twitchell notes that shame's loss of face makes you cover your face (22–25).

26. Lindner, *Making Enemies*, 169. Hosea Easton's *Treatise* quoted in Bruce Dain, *A Hideous Monster of the Mind: American Race Theory in the Early Republic* (Cambridge, Mass.: Harvard University Press, 2002), 192–193. I

learned about *The Negro Digest* columns from Holloway, *Jim Crow Wisdom*, chapter 1.

27. Edmund Morgan argues that "Americans bought their independence with slave labor"; Morgan, *American Slavery, American Freedom*, 5. On antebellum workers' defenses of their independence because they feared workplace dependence as "white slavery," see David Roediger, *The Wages of Whiteness: Race and the Making of the American Working Class* (New York: Verso, 1999), 66.

28. Jackson Lears describes several competing types of white racism that resecured white supremacy after 1876. He concludes that racism stabilized white people's sense of identity amid tumultuous social changes; Lears, *Rebirth of a Nation: The Making of Modern America, 1877–1920* (New York: HarperCollins, 2009), 93, 98–100. Frank Henderson Stewart too simply argues that shame is the binary opposite of pride, not honor. He's right that both shame and pride are emotions, whereas honor implies a shifting amalgam of internal and external respect. But the state of being shamed brings external disrespect too. In practice, Stewart tends to dichotomize them, despite his complex differentiations. As he says, many men are more preoccupied with shame than with honor; Stewart, *Honor*, 128–129.

29. G.W.F. Hegel, *Phenomenology of the Spirit*, sometimes called *Phenomenology of the Mind* (1807). Charles W. Mills notes that Hegel denied that Africa had a history and said that black people were morally impaired by slavery, a claim that contradicts Hegel's argument about Lords and Bondsmen; Mills, *The Racial Contract* (Ithaca, N.Y.: Cornell University Press, 1997), 94. Mills's book passionately simplifies modern Western philosophy to racism and global white supremacy (e.g., 1–3, 27). Walter Johnson shows that slaves knew their white buyers and masters far better than the buyers and masters knew the fantasies they were trying to enact through the bodies of their slaves; Johnson, *Soul by Soul*, chapters 6 and 7, 162–213, also 79–88.

30. Bob Blauner, *Black Lives, White Lives: Three Decades of Race Relations in America* (Berkeley: University of California Press, 1989), 16 (consciousness), 23 ("Florence Grier"). The interviews with sixteen blacks and twelve whites occurred in 1968–1969, 1978–1981, and 1986. See also "Len Davis," who says that blue-collar whites are more racist than a rich white man, since "there ain't a hell of a lot of blacks with that much money that can touch him anyway," or than "the real poor person," who is "kind of being taken care of by some little government or somebody. But the guy that's fending for hisself . . . man, he has a fear that blacks are getting his job" (307).

31. Blauner, *Black Lives, White Lives*, 267–268.

32. Deborah Eisenberg, "Introduction," in Gregor von Rezzori, *Memoirs of*

an *Anti-Semite: A Novel in Five Stories* (New York: New York Review Books, 2008), xxii; Roger Wilkins, *Jefferson's Pillow: The Founding Fathers and the Dilemma of Black Patriotism* (Boston: Beacon Press, 2001), 138.

33. Rita Felski, "Nothing to Declare: Identity, Shame, and the Lower Middle Class," *PMLA* 115 (January 2000): 33–45.

34. Aaron Shaheen draws on the work of Klaus Theweleit to argue that both Germans and white Americans used violence to contain the racial and gender fluidity inherent in democracies; Shaheen, *Androgynous Democracy: Modern American Literature and the Dual-Sexed Body Politic* (Knoxville: University of Tennessee Press, 2010), 134–135, 143. In the United States, Shaheen argues, many white Americans feminized black men, especially male slaves, to fend off fears of their own gender fluidity (112–113).

35. William McKee Evans, *Open Wound: The Long View of Race in America* (Urbana: University of Illinois Press, 2009), 9, also 13–35, "Atlantic Slavery Becomes Market-Driven and Color-Defined."

36. Joyce Appleby, *The Relentless Revolution: A History of Capitalism* (New York: W. W. Norton, 2010), 417–422, 121–136, 160–161. Nell Irvin Painter finds instances of the one-drop rule in 1831 and 1835; Painter, *The History of White People*, 129–130. Robin Einhorn argues that Americans' wariness of big government stems from slaveholding elites who championed states' rights as a defense against strong democracy and that slavery, in the form of human property, shaped U.S. tax policies; *American Taxation, American Slavery* (Chicago: University of Chicago Press, 2006).

37. U. B. Phillips, "The Central Theme in Southern History," *American Historical Review* 34 (October 1928): 31. See also Hale, *Making Whiteness*, on southern segregation from 1890 to 1940.

38. See David Blight, *Race and Reunion: The Civil War in American Memory* (Cambridge, Mass.: Harvard University Press, 2001).

39. Will Bunch emphasizes the fears of change and the Other in many Tea Party sympathizers; Bunch, *The Backlash: Right-Wing Radicals, High-Def Hucksters, and Paranoid Politics in the Age of Obama* (New York: HarperCollins, 2010), especially 11, 337–342. Painter suggests that after World War II, as organized labor weakened and the working class seemed less visible, Americans joined "white" to "middle class" as "a conflation of class and race"; Painter, *The History of White People*, 370.

40. Painter, *The History of White People*, 72–90. Painter recounts how Johann Friedrich Blumenbach's fifteen-page dissertation of 1771 argued for racial differentiations based on skull measurements. He invented "Caucasian" in 1795 for his book's third edition (79) as a substitute for "Georgian" (81–84). Linking

the term to beauty, he included people who lived in North Africa and India. The skull of the probable sex slave had perfect teeth (82–84).

41. Chesnutt, *The Marrow of Tradition*, in *Charles W. Chesnutt: Stories, Novels, and Essays* (New York: Library of America, 2002), 509. Frantz Fanon's *Black Skin, White Masks* (English translation 1967) and *The Wretched of the Earth* (English translation 1962) first explored how hostile white gazes made colonized Africans feel that they were objects of contempt.

42. Michelle Alexander, *The New Jim Crow: Mass Incarceration in the Age of Colorblindedness* (New York: The New Press, 2010), 166–168. Eve Kosofsky Sedgwick argues that especially for queer people, shame has "metamorphic possibilities"; Sedgwick, *Touching Feeling: Affect, Pedagogy, Performativity* (Durham, N.C.: Duke University Press, 2003), 64–65, also 37. See also Sedgwick and Adam Frank, eds., *Shame and Its Sisters: A Silvan Tomkins Reader* (Durham, N.C.: Duke University Press, 1995). As Michael Warner formulates it, "the most compelling form of dignity is not that which requires you to clean up your act but rather that which comes from recognizing that we're all capable of abjection." Annamarie Jagose, "Queer World Making: Annamarie Jagose Interviews Michael Warner," *Genders* 31 (2000), available at www.genders. org/g31/g31_jagose.html. Less transgressively, Miller claims that humiliation makes us human: "The elite are those who know that they are humiliated and feel the humiliation keenly"; Miller, *Humiliation*, 206–207. Miller presumes an already entitled "elite," to which he belongs. His final paragraph uses variants of "we," "us," and "our" thirteen times. Similarly, Warner's "we're all capable" presumes the potential inclusiveness of a universal "we."

43. Mark Twain, *Pudd'nhead Wilson* (New York: Signet, 1964), 67; Du Bois, *The Souls of Black Folk*, 353.

CHAPTER 2 — HOW DOES IT FEEL TO BE A PROBLEM?

1. Taylor Branch, *Parting the Waters: America in the King Years, 1954–1963* (New York: Simon & Schuster, 1988), 379–380, on the "morally transcendent humiliation" of Lewis and Bevel (380).

2. Kristen Caldwell quoted in David Remnick, *The Bridge: The Life and Rise of Barack Obama* (New York: Alfred A. Knopf, 2010), 79. Diana Brantley alerted me to a posting on the *Hendersonville Times-News* forums (website BlueRidgeNow), on April 26, 2010, after President Obama and his family had vacationed at the Grove Park Inn in Asheville, North Carolina. Titled "It's Morning in WNC," by "bacillus," the posting states: "We saw the Emperor and his entourage heading for the airport. It was like being in Uganda. Grove Park will have to be fumigated and de-loused" (accessed May 2, 2010).

3. Branch, *Parting the Waters*, 380. Before the 1950s, whites feared that they

could contract polio by mixing with poor immigrants and black people, especially in swimming pools. Ironically, middle-class habits of cleanliness led to the disease by blocking the development of children's immune systems. See Naomi Rogers, *Dirt and Disease: Polio before FDR* (New Brunswick, N.J.: Rutgers University Press, 1992), 13, 29, 143, 190; and David Oshinsky, *Polio: An American Story* (New York: Oxford University Press, 2005), 1–3, 30–31, 84. Lizabeth Cohen notes white fears of "contamination" in "sites of intimate bodily contact"; Cohen, *A Consumers' Republic: The Politics of Mass Consumption in Postwar America* (New York: Alfred A. Knopf, 2003). Patricia Yaeger urges us to explore "the bizarreness, the inherent uncanniness" of "the somatic knowledge" that developed as whites thought about race; Yaeger, *Dirt and Desire: Reconstructing Southern Women's Writing, 1930–1990* (Chicago: University of Chicago Press, 2000), 6. I may be too benign about possible white reactions to a dog jumping into a pool. As Ann Laura Stoler notes, in colonial Jakarta there were signs on public swimming pools stating, "No dogs or natives allowed"; Stoler, *Carnal Knowledge and Imperial Power: Race and the Intimate in Colonial Rule* (Berkeley: University of California Press, 2002), 18.

4. Brad Snyder, *A Well-Paid Slave: Curt Flood's Fight for Free Agency in Professional Sports* (New York: Viking, 2006), 50. On swimming pools, see Jeff Wiltse, *Contested Waters: A Social History of Swimming Pools in America* (Chapel Hill: University of North Carolina Press, 2007). On segregated Red Cross blood supplies, I'm indebted to Shawn Salvant, "Crossing Blood," paper presented at the annual meeting of the American Studies Association, Atlanta, Georgia, November 11–14, 2004.

5. William Ian Miller, *Humiliation and Other Essays on Honor, Social Discomfort, and Violence* (Ithaca, N.Y.: Cornell University Press, 1993), 168–169; James B. Twitchell, *For Shame: The Loss of Common Decency in American Culture* (New York: St. Martin's, 1998), 22–25.

6. Barack Obama, *Dreams from My Father: A Story of Race and Inheritance*, rev. ed. (New York: Three Rivers Press, 2004), 20 (coloreds), 294 (shamed).

7. Booker T. Washington, *Up from Slavery*, in *Three Negro Classics*, edited by John Hope Franklin (New York: Avon Books, 1999), 57. After she participated in civil rights demonstrations, an African American student said that she gained "a feeling of decency and self-respect, a feeling of cleanliness" for the first time; quoted in Branch, *Parting the Waters*, 532.

8. Frank Fitzgerald recounts an instance that may have been local ethnic cleansing. When the University of Kentucky integrated its football team in 1965, one of the first two African American teammates died "after suffering a paralyzing neck injury in practice." The other player quit the team after his first year, and neither played a varsity game. The university's investigation,

perhaps a whitewash, concluded that the death "had been a freak accident"; Fitzgerald, *And the Walls Came Tumbling Down: Kentucky, Texas Western, and the Game That Changed American Sports* (New York: Simon & Schuster, 1999), 142.

9. Alexis de Tocqueville, *Democracy in America*, 2 vols., translated by Henry Reeve, revised by Francis Bowen, revised and edited by Phillips Bradley (New York: Vintage Books, 1954), vol. 1, 394 (slavery as prejudicial to their interests), 390 (increase repugnance toward blacks), 370–397 (prospects for race war in the South). Tocqueville agrees with white southerners that black men are "alien," "hideous," and stupid (374) and declares that whites who hope for amalgamation "appear to me to delude themselves" (quote on 373, also 396–397).

10. According to Philip Dray, from 1866 on there were many national reports of white brutality in the South, including various congressional investigations and some legislative attempts to control the Ku Klux Klan. The Supreme Court's 1876 decision in *U.S. v. Cruikshank* threw these issues back to the states. Dray, *Capitol Men: The Epic Story of Reconstruction through the Lives of the First Black Congressmen* (New York: Houghton Mifflin, 2008). For details of the Colfax massacre, see Charles Lane, *The Day Freedom Died: The Colfax Massacre, the Supreme Court, and the Betrayal of Reconstruction* (New York: Henry Holt, 2008); and James B. Twitchell, *Look Away, Dixieland* (Baton Rouge: Louisiana State University Press, 2011), 25–30. Twitchell estimates that between 70 and 140 African Americans were killed (25). This "*genetic cleansing*" was "the worst in American history" (28), he says, though the Tulsa riots may have been even worse; Twitchell's italics.

11. On Coushatta, see Twitchell, *Look Away, Dixieland*, 30–40, 147–156, and 26 (for a picture of the sign). After an assassin wounded Twitchell's great-grandfather, Marshall H. Twitchell, a pro-black Yankee, his arms had to be amputated. He called the white killers "the chivalry" (147–149). See also Ted Tunnell, *Edge of the Sword: The Ordeal of Carpetbagger Marshall H. Twitchell in the Civil War and Reconstruction* (Baton Rouge: Louisiana State University Press, 2001), 135–136; and LeeAnna Keith, *The Colfax Massacre: The Untold Story of Black Power, White Terror, and the Death of Reconstruction* (New York: Oxford University Press, 2008), especially 106 and 110 on "beeves," and 94–95 on the plaque. Mary Bryan's *Wild Work: The Story of the Red River Tragedy* (New York: D. Appleton and Company, 1881) emphasized how whites felt humiliated by the war, whereas a recent novel, Lalita Tademy's *Red River* (New York: Grand Central Publishing, 2008), dramatizes black perspectives. See also Dray, *Capitol Men*, 142–150 (on Colfax), and 193–195 (on Coushatta).

12. Dray, *Capitol Men*, 85–86. *The Code of Honor*, an 1878 pamphlet written

by Robert Barnwell Rhett, emphasized that laws and courts don't offer sufficient means to avenge insults (80–81).

13. See Debra Walker King, "Nigger," in *Handbook of the Sociology of Racial and Ethnic Relations*, edited by Hernán Vera and Joe R. Feagin (New York: Springer Science & Business Media, 2007), 101–114, opposing Randall Kennedy's more mixed discussion of the word. See also Stephanie A. Smith, *Household Words: Bloomers, Sucker, Bombshell, Scab, Nigger, Cyber* (Minneapolis: University of Minnesota Press, 2006), 122–148. King's *African Americans and the Culture of Pain* (Charlottesville: University of Virginia Press, 2008), focuses on "blackpain" (163–164), a "visible evidence of a vicious, but denied, race war" (19).

14. Dray, *Capitol Men*, 302, 333. In 1904, Tillman said, "Now that Roosevelt has eaten with that nigger Washington, we shall have to kill a thousand niggers to get them back to their places"; quoted in Remnick, *The Bridge*, 572.

15. Gunnar Myrdal, *An American Dilemma: The Negro Problem and Modern Democracy* (New York: Harper & Row, 1962), 100 (quarantining evil), 103–104 (defending the caste system).

16. Brook Thomas, "Stigmas, Badges, and Brands: Discriminating Marks in Legal History," in *History, Memory, and the Law*, edited by Austin Sarat and Thomas R. Kearns (Ann Arbor: University of Michigan Press, 1999), 271. As Thomas notes, "nowhere did the Court in *Brown* use metaphors of stigmas, badges, or brands" to overturn the 1896 *Plessy v. Ferguson* decision (266). Instead of using marking metaphors, the decision declared that racial separation "generates a feeling of inferiority." Thomas teases out the problems in "generates" and in frequent legal uses of stigmas, badges, brands, or colorblindedness as metaphors.

17. Ibid., 250. When Mark Twain paid for an African American student's expenses at Yale Law School in the 1880s, he wrote to the dean, "We have ground the manhood out of them, & the shame is ours, not theirs, & we should pay for it." The student, Warner T. McGuinn, later mentored Thurgood Marshall. See Shelley Fisher Fishkin, *Lighting Out for the Territory: Reflections on Mark Twain and American Culture* (New York: Oxford University Press, 1997), 101. See also David Leverenz, *Paternalism Incorporated: Fables of American Fatherhood 1865–1940* (Ithaca, N.Y.: Cornell University Press, 2003), 165–168.

18. For the text of the *Loving* decision, see *Loving v. Commonwealth of Virginia*, in *Interracialism: Black-White Intermarriage in American History, Literature, and Law*, edited by Werner Sollors (New York: Oxford University Press, 2000), 26–34.

19. David Brion Davis, "Intellectual Trajectories: Why People Study What They Do," *Reviews in American History* 37 (March 2009): 154–155, quote at 155.

20. Tocqueville, *Democracy in America*, 1:346.

21. Michelle Obama, quoted in Remnick, *The Bridge*, 503.

22. Bruce Dain details the complex tensions in early formulations of race theories by black as well as white writers, paying particular attention to David Walker's *Appeal* in 1829, Hosea Easton's *Treatise* in 1837, and James McCune Smith's columns for *Frederick Douglass' Paper* from 1852 to 1854; Dain, *A Hideous Monster of the Mind: American Race Theory in the Early Republic* (Cambridge, Mass.: Harvard University Press, 2002), 139–148 (Walker), 170–196 (Easton), and 237–249 (Smith). Smith's column of January 1852, mocking whites who make the negro "a hideous monster of the mind," gave Dain his title.

23. Frederick Douglass, *My Bondage and My Freedom*, edited by William L. Andrews (Urbana: University of Illinois Press, 1987), 125 (blacker cloud of religious doubts), 141 (blackest atheism), and 169, 189. For a time Douglass supported the idea of "selective African American emigration" to Haiti; see Robert S. Levine, *Dislocating Race and Nation: Episodes in Nineteenth-Century American Literary Nationalism* (Chapel Hill: University of North Carolina Press, 2008), 180, 179–236.

24. W.E.B. Du Bois, *The Souls of Black Folk*, in *Three Negro Classics*, edited by John Hope Franklin (New York: Avon Books, 1999), 215 (double-consciousness to escape white contempt), 218–219 (a sickening despair). Du Bois distances his cosmopolitan sensibility from the "folk" who have been so disdained. At the end of chapter 6 he dreams in iambic pentameter of a time when "I sit with Shakespeare and he winces not. . . . So, wed with Truth, I dwell above the Veil" (284).

25. Du Bois, *Souls of Black Folk*, vii, quoted in Vernon J. Williams Jr., *Rethinking Race: Franz Boas and His Contemporaries* (Lexington: University Press of Kentucky, 1996), 32. Williams discusses Boas's uses of racial uplift and assimilation to critique racial determinism (e.g., 21, 35, 53, and 106–107 on his belief in African Americans'"defective ancestry" because of their "smaller cranial cavities"). Nell Irvin Painter notes that Boas urged black college students to attack "the feeling of contempt . . . at its very roots"; quoted in Painter, *The History of White People* (New York: W. W. Norton, 2010), 232, also 228–244, 329–330 (on Boas).

26. Pauli Murray, *Song in a Weary Throat*, 128, quoted in Glenda Gilmore, *Defying Dixie: The Radical Roots of Civil Rights, 1919–1950* (New York: W. W. Norton, 2008), 283; see also 264–269, 276–290.

27. Zora Neale Hurston, "How It Feels to Be Colored Me" (1928), reprinted in *The African-American Archive: The History of the Black Experience in Documents*, edited by Kai Wright (New York: Black Dog & Leventhal, 2001), 487–488.

Mia Bay argues that white supremacism has caused a lingering essentialism in black self-definitions, including "black chauvinism"; Bay, *The White Image in the Black Mind: African-American Ideas about White People, 1830–1925* (New York: Oxford University Press, 2000), 45, 219, 224, 228–229.

28. James Weldon Johnson, *The Autobiography of an Ex-Colored Man*, in *Three Negro Classics*, ed. Franklin, 497, 499. Johnson was nearly beaten to death in Florida by members of the National Guard in 1901 because he had been interviewing a woman about a Jacksonville fire. He was freed only because the woman was black. See Jacqueline Goldsby, *A Spectacular Secret: Lynching in American Life and Literature* (Chicago: University of Chicago Press, 2006), 166–172.

29. Richard Wright, *Native Son* (New York: Perennial Classics, 1998), 67 (dumb, cold, and inarticulate hate), 296 (family's naked shame), 347 (Jan's handshake), 448 (free myself of this sense of shame), Wright's italics.

30. James Baldwin, *The Fire Next Time* (New York: Vintage, 1992), 3 (grandfather defeated), 19 (incessant and gratuitous humiliation), 25 (Negroes taught to despise themselves), 82 (whoever debases others), Baldwin's italics. Vengeance will surely come, he concludes, unless whites and blacks admit that that they need and can even "love" each other (104).

31. Zora Neale Hurston, *Their Eyes Were Watching God* (New York: Harper & Row Perennial, 1990), 26–27 (fell in love with Joe), 44 (worked for white folks all his life), 142 (color-struck wishes), 136 (oughta class off; a mingled people).

32. Toni Morrison, *Sula* (New York: New American Library, 1982), 119–120 (free fall beyond herself), 130–131 (mud), 107–109 (freezes her in a gray ball), 174 (dandelion spores in the breeze), 130 (loam is giving you that smell), Morrison's italics.

33. Toni Morrison, *Song of Solomon* (New York: New American Library, 1978), 244 (torn and filthy clothes), 249 (crumble and rot).

34. Toni Morrison, *Beloved* (New York: Signet/Penguin, 1991), 308.

35. For Glenda Gilmore, it was "black success, not black deficiency" that consolidated the white supremacy movement in the United States and South Africa; Gilmore, *Defying Dixie*, 237. According to J. Douglas Smith, the real or imagined erosion of white paternalism in Virginia during the 1920s and 1930s spurred white racist attempts to deny citizenship to black people; Smith, "The Campaign for Racial Purity and the Erosion of Paternalism in Virginia, 1922–1930: 'Nominally White, Biologically Mixed, and Legally Negro,'" *Journal of Southern History* 68 (February 2002): 97, 99, 106. For Joel Williamson, white racial "loathing" intensified long before, as black people challenged paternalistic presumptions after the Civil War; Williamson, *The Crucible of Race:*

Black-White Relations in the American South since Emancipation (New York: Oxford University Press, 1984), 52, 22–24, 82–86, 301, 449–455. Lauren Basson argues that the late nineteenth-century threat of "racially mixed people and places" led to an "abstract Americanism" that restabilized white supremacy; Basson, *White Enough to Be American? Race Mixing, Indigenous People, and the Boundaries of State and Nation* (Chapel Hill: University of North Carolina Press, 2008), 192–193, also 2–4. See also Matthew Frye Jacobson, *Whiteness of a Different Color: European Immigrants and the Alchemy of Race* (Cambridge, Mass.: Harvard University Press, 1998). Douglas Blackmon recounts that from the 1870s through the 1940s, up to 200,000 poor blacks throughout the South were fraudulently imprisoned and then leased to corporations, state or local governments, entrepreneurs, or farmers to work in hundreds of forced labor camps; Blackmon, *Slavery by Another Name: The Re-Enslavement of Black Americans from the Civil War to World War II* (New York: Doubleday, 2008), 7, 19–22, 44–56, 331–333, 353–379.

36. On African American farm ownership, see Ivan Evans, *Cultures of Violence: Lynching and Racial Killing in South Africa and the American South* (New York: Palgrave Macmillan, 2009), 69. Too simply, Bill Ayers and Bernadine Dohrn argue that the core of white supremacy is "exploitation and profit"; Ayers and Dohrn, *Race Course against White Supremacy* (Chicago: Third World Press, 2009), 97. Glenda Gilmore argues that white supremacy in late nineteenth-century North Carolina made race more basic than class; Gilmore, *Gender and Jim Crow: Women and the Politics of White Supremacy in North Carolina, 1896–1920* (Chapel Hill: University of North Carolina Press, 1996), 117–118, 143.

37. Mary Douglas, *Purity and Danger: An Analysis of Concepts of Pollution and Taboo* (Middlesex, Eng.: Penguin Books, 1970), 144–148 (vulnerability at the margins), 153 (ritual an attempt to maintain culture), 148 (group survival). On the role of dirt in creating social boundaries and embodied communities, see Yaeger, *Dirt and Desire*, 65–67, 274.

38. Mark M. Smith, *How Race Is Made: Slavery, Segregation, and the Senses* (Chapel Hill: University of North Carolina Press, 2006), 7, 10. Conversely, the mother of Henry Louis Gates Jr. told him white people smelled bad, especially in swimming pools; see Gates, *Colored People: A Memoir* (New York: Alfred A. Knopf, 1994), 34–36. Orlando Patterson notes that at least until World War I, the French and English "ruling and middle classes were obsessed with the odor of the lower classes, which was obviously a way of defining the poor as dirty and of demarcating class lines"; Patterson, *Rituals of Blood: Consequences of Slavery in Two American Centuries* (New York: Basic Books, 1998), 200. Elise Lemire discusses white antebellum Americans who emphasized the "noxious"

odors of black people as a key argument against interracial mixing; Lemire, *"Miscegenation": Making Race in America* (Philadelphia: University of Pennsylvania Press, 2002), quote at 78, see also 76–79.

39. Whiteness studies began in 1990 with Alexander Saxton, *The Rise and Fall of the White Republic: Class Politics and Mass Culture in Nineteenth-Century America*, rev. ed. (London: Verso, 2003), followed in 1991 by David Roediger, *The Wages of Whiteness: Race and the Making of the American Working Class*, rev. ed. (New York: Verso, 1999) and, in the next year, Toni Morrison, *Playing in the Dark: Whiteness and the Literary Imagination* (Cambridge, Mass.: Harvard University Press, 1992); though Winthrop Jordan had prepared the way with *White over Black: American Attitudes toward the Negro, 1550–1812* (Baltimore, Md.: Penguin Books, 1968). Morrison focuses on how blackness shapes classic American literature; Saxton and Roediger focus on nineteenth-century class dynamics, and Saxton argues against Jordan's psychological analysis (12–13). For him, white supremacy was an ideology that continually managed class conflict, as the lower class used white racism to reduce its economic and social distance from the upper class (385–388, also 17). His sense of its incipient "fall" by 1900 seems overstated. Roediger's more psychological approach emphasizes the hate, sadness, and longing in white working-class racism. More problematically, he argues that quasi-"peasant" immigrant workers "created" white identity because they were afraid of dependence on wage labor and capitalist work discipline (65). For a more complex account, see Robert H. Zieger's *For Jobs and Freedom: Race and Labor in American since 1865* (Lexington: University Press of Kentucky, 2007), 5–8; see 23 on Roediger. See also Reginald Horsman, *Race and Manifest Destiny: The Origins of American Racial Anglo-Saxonism* (Cambridge, Mass.: Harvard University Press, 1981); George Lipsitz, *The Possessive Investment in Whiteness: How White People Profit from Identity Politics*, rev. ed. (Philadelphia: Temple University Press, 2006); and several recent books by Tim Wise: *Between Barack and a Hard Place: Racism and White Denial in the Age of Obama* (San Francisco: City Lights Publishers, 2009), *Colorblind: The Rise of Post-Racial Politics and the Retreat from Racial Equity* (San Francisco: City Lights Publishers, 2010), and *Speaking Treason Fluently: Anti-Racist Reflections from an Angry White Male* (New York: Soft Skull Press, 2008).

40. David Croly's 1863 pamphlet praised what it claimed was Lincoln's advocacy of race mixing to reinvigorate the white race. See Martha Hodes, *White Women, Black Men: Illicit Sex in the Nineteenth Century South* (New Haven, Conn.: Yale University Press, 1997), 144; Lemire, *"Miscegenation,"* 116–118, 124–131, 140–142; and especially Sidney Kaplan, "The Miscegenation Issue in the Election of 1864," reprinted in Sollors, *Interracialism*, 219–265, first published in *Journal of Negro History* (1949). See also Peggy Pascoe, *What*

Comes Naturally: Miscegenation Law and the Making of Race in America (New York: Oxford University Press, 2009), 1–3. Roediger agrees with Kaplan that Croly and his co-author, George Wakeman, pitched the pamphlet to racist Irish Americans; Roediger, *The Wages of Whiteness*, 155–156.

41. Rock 'n' roll was what Brian Ward calls "an innovative hybrid"; see Ward, *Just My Soul Responding: Rhythm and Blues, Black Consciousness and Race Relations* (Berkeley: University of California Press, 1998), 52. See also Ward's *Radio and the Struggle for Civil Rights in the South* (Gainesville: University of Florida Press, 2004) on southern radio during the civil rights movement. Ward contends that the impossibility of segregating access to stations led to "cultural miscegenation via the airwaves" (15, see also 189). He argues that the possibility of fluid or blurred identities, especially among white people, vied with reinforced racial stereotypes (359–360).

42. For overviews of miscegenation history and law, see Lemire, *"Miscegenation"*; and Pascoe, *What Comes Naturally*. On the one-drop rule in various states, see Pascoe, *What Comes Naturally*, 119–122, 141–150; and Hodes, *White Women, Black Men*, 199, among many others. As early as 1889, Charles W. Chesnutt noted the variety in state laws defining whiteness and blackness; Chesnutt, "What Is a White Man?" reprinted in Sollors, *Interracialism*, 38–41, quotes on 38–39. For recent changes, especially in the South, see Susan Saulny, "Black and White and Married in the Deep South: A Shifting Image," *New York Times*, March 20, 2011, A1, A4.

43. On laws prohibiting marriage or sex between black men and white women, see Pascoe, *What Comes Naturally*, 44–60 (1865–1900), and 175–180 and 186–191 (1900–1970). In *White Women, Black Men*, Martha Hodes contrasts the "permissiveness displayed for sex between white men and black women" (3) with the affront to "honor" and "patriarchal power" implied by sexual relations between white women and black men (4). White women were not "engulfed by sexual alarm" when they were alone with slave men during the Civil War and before (140, also 2, 203). Then black men's new "autonomy" disturbed "the vanquished white patriarchs" (147), whose interracial taboo "sought to reassert control over white women" as well as black men (148). On white fears of eating with black people because eating "embodied both intimacy and equality," see Gilmore, *Defying Dixie*, 223.

44. See Bertram Wyatt-Brown, "Honor, Secession, and the Civil War," and "Honor and Revolutionary Rhetoric," both unpublished.

45. Lincoln quoted in Robert J. Norrell, *The House I Live In: Race in the American Century* (New York: Oxford University Press, 2005), 10.

46. Wyatt-Brown, "Honor, Secession, and the Civil War" (power over blacks), and "Honor and Revolutionary Rhetoric." Congressman Heflin quoted in

Norrell, *The House I Live In*, 24; historian Charles Robinson quoted in Annette Gordon-Reed, *The Hemingses of Monticello: An American Family* (New York: W. W. Norton, 2008), 87. Congressman Heflin won reelection and later served two terms in the U.S. Senate; Norrell, *The House I Live In*, 25.

47. Dain concludes that by the 1850s, "A psychosexual economy of repression and projection . . . exonerated lust and greed among white men. Black women came to be seen as hypersexual, so lustful that sexual intercourse with them was always voluntary, never coerced. The black woman could not be raped. The white woman, by contrast, became a flower of chastity to be chivalrously protected and defended from the black male beast, a natural rapist"; Dain, *A Hideous Monster of the Mind*, 235. For claims that black women couldn't be raped because they were promiscuous, see Gordon-Reed, *The Hemingses of Monticello*, 314 and following pages.

48. Melissa Fay Greene, *Praying for Sheetrock* (Cambridge, Mass.: Da Capo Press, 2006), 37; Tocqueville quoted in Eva Saks, "Representing Miscegenation Law," reprinted in Sollors, *Interracialism*, 64; Jean Toomer, *Cane*, introduction by Darwin T. Turner (New York: Norton Critical Edition, 1988), 33.

49. For the story of Harrison's slave children, see Thomas Dyja, *Walter White: The Dilemma of Black Identity in America* (Chicago: Ivan R. Dee, 2008), 10. NAACP leader Walter White was a blond, blue-eyed, fair-skinned grandson of one of the sold slaves. Col. Richard Johnson's story is featured at Dan Quayle's Vice Presidential Learning Center in Huntington, Indiana. Johnson remains memorable because of Edgar Allan Poe's 1839 satire, "The Man That Was Used Up," since Johnson had wounds and replaceable body parts from his service in the Indian wars. An 1880 book by Jane Grey Swisshelm alleged the miscegenation rumor about President John Tyler, a Virginian. Though Werner Sollors and Carter G. Woodson take that allegation for fact (*Interracialism* 13, 43), it hasn't been substantiated.

50. Du Bois, *The Souls of Black Folk*, 375–377.

51. Myrdal, *An American Dilemma*, 1194–1195. Thomas J. Sugrue points out that Myrdal evaded discussing "the depth of racial animosity in the North"; Sugrue, *Sweet Land of Liberty: The Forgotten Struggle for Civil Rights in the North* (New York: Random House, 2008), 61 (quote) and see also 59–63, 82–84.

52. J. Michael Butler, "The Mississippi State Sovereignty Commission and Beach Integration, 1959–1963: A Cotton-Patch Gestapo?" *Journal of Southern History* 68, no. 1 (2002): 115; Edward L. Ayers, *The Promise of the New South: Life after Reconstruction* (New York: Oxford University Press, 1992), 139–140.

53. As David Roediger notes, "The violent and sexually menacing black male of the post–Civil War 'coon song' is largely absent from early minstrelsy";

Roediger, *The Wages of Whiteness*, 121. See also Gordon-Reed, *The Hemingses of Monticello*, 86; and Jackson Lears, *Rebirth of a Nation: The Making of Modern America, 1877–1920* (New York: HarperCollins, 2009), 104–107.

54. Evans, *Cultures of Violence*, 249–250 (welding together the white folk; white men guardians of white women's virtue), 32 (depoliticize internal fault lines; racial divide), 34 (restoring the patriarchal powers, Evans's italics).

55. Ibid., 249–250 (regulation of contact), 20 (used honor to legitimize lynching), 249 (antebellum hierarchy). Scott L. Malcomson links lynching to white people's anxieties about mastery based on "what their skin meant"; Malcomson, *One Drop of Blood: The American Misadventure of Race* (New York: Farrar Straus Giroux, 2000), 352–353. Malcomson also discusses "massacres" by South African agencies (7) and racism by a strong state (153). Malcomson points out that before the Civil War, almost all lynching victims in the South were white men, but from 1889 to 1930, 85 percent of the 3,703 lynching victims were black men (9), though a few were Sicilians (25). In 1919 the white mayor of Omaha, Alabama, was lynched because he tried to protect a black prisoner (87). From the 1860s to the 1950s, the South was the only industrializing region where lynching occurred (vii). The phrase "social death" is Orlando Patterson's.

56. Tocqueville quoted in Eric T. L. Love, *Race over Empire: Racism and U.S. Imperialism, 1865–1900* (Chapel Hill: University of North Carolina Press, 2004), 9 (from *Democracy in America* 1:359–360). For accounts of northern racism, see Bob Blauner, *Black Lives, White Lives*, especially 29–32, and 93. On white northerners who compared protecting their homes to protecting their daughters, see Thomas J. Sugrue, "Crabgrass-Roots Politics: Race, Rights, and the Reaction against Liberalism in the Urban North, 1940–1964," *Journal of American History* 82, no. 2 (1995): 561–562.

57. On the National Association of Real Estate Boards, see Sugrue, *Sweet Land of Liberty*, 154–159 and 203. Robert Zieger agrees with Sugrue that "whites' visceral determination to avoid close contact with African Americans is a force independent of capitalist dynamics"; Zieger, "Northern Exposure," *Reviews in American History* 37 (December 2009): 575.

58. On black men's bodies, sex, and racial segregation, see Wiltse, *Contested Waters*, 123–124 and 132–135. Also in Wiltse, see 107 and 123–124 for the effects of the black migration to the North and 34–35, 97, 124, 148–152 for fears of disease after the discovery of microbes. Page 107 discusses chlorine in the 1920s. For the first integrated pool (in St. Louis in 1913), see 78. Zieger recounts that in 1919 a young black man who "inadvertently" walked into the "white" section of a Lake Michigan beach was stoned and drowned, prompting "several weeks of racial violence, which the Chicago police did nothing to quell." The riots

killed twenty-three blacks and fifteen whites; 500 people were injured; Zieger, *For Jobs and Freedom*, 84.

59. See James S. Hirsch, *Riot and Remembrance: America's Worst Race Riot and Its Legacy* (New York: Houghton Mifflin Harcourt, 2002); and the Wikipedia entry about the Tulsa race riots. James Patrick notes that Dick Rowland and Sarah Page, the young African American man and the white elevator operator, may have had a relationship and that the *Tulsa Tribune* referred to Greenwood as "Little Africa" or "Niggertown"; Patrick, "The Tulsa Race Riot of 1921: Part Two," *Exodus News,* March 20, 2000, available at www.exodusnews.com/news-archives/677-the-tulsa-race-riot-of-1921-part-two.html.

60. I'm indebted to Rodman Webb for information about the Massie case, including Douglas O. Linder's 2007 website, "The Massie ('Honor Killing') Trials, 1931–32," http://law2.umkc.edu/faculty/projects/ftrials/massie/massie.html.

61. Cobey Black gives a good history of both trials and highlights the class conflicts involved; Black, *Hawaii Scandal* (Waipahu, Hawaii: Island Heritage, 1962).

62. See Peter Van Slingerman's *Something Terrible Has Happened* (Harper & Row, 1966); and Linder, "The Massie ('Honor Killing') Trials." Van Slingerman's title quotes what Thalia Massie said when she called her husband.

63. Tim Wise summarizes Darrow's role in the 1926 trial of Dr. Ossian Sweet, his brother, and a few friends; Wise, *Colorblind*, 160–161.

64. Both Darrow's account and Deacon Jones's 1966 confession are available at Linder, "The Massie ('Honor Killing') Trials" and in Slingerman, *Something Terrible Has Happened*. For the confession, see 316–322 in Slingerman.

65. John McCain with Mark Salter, *Faith of My Fathers* (New York: Perennial, 2000), 67–69, quotes on 68 (involving enlisted men in the crime) and 69 (shamed by Massie's conduct). Massie had served on a submarine commanded by McCain's father (67).

66. Gail Bederman argues that "whiteness was both a palpable fact and a manly ideal" in early corporate America; Bederman, *Manliness and Civilization: A Cultural History of Gender and Race in the United States, 1880–1917* (Chicago: University of Chicago Press, 1995), 5; see also 1–5, 8–10 (on Jack Johnson), and 225–232 (on Tarzan). Goldsby considers lynching too broadly as a manifestation of corporate capitalism, consumerism, modernism, and U.S. imperial aggression; Goldsby, *A Spectacular Secret*, 24–27, 284–288. Grace Hale similarly links racial violence, spectacles, and modern consumerism; Hale, *Making Whiteness: the Culture of Segregation in the South, 1890–1940* (New York: Pantheon, 1998), 205–206. Julie Cary Nerad argues that "the crucial white fear surrounding 'miscegenation' was not that 'mulattoes' as a class would rise

in the wake of black political rights but that racially-coded sexual preferences and desires that made whites a racial group and thus ensured white socio-economic superiority would be lost"; Nerad, "Race(y) Words and Pictures: Depicting and Demarcating 'Natural' Preference," *American Quarterly* 55 (June 2003): 330. Nerad's essay is a review of Lemire's *"Miscegenation."*

67. Eric Love summarizes Wells's article in *Race over Empire*, 16. For a fine account of Wells's activist, uncompromising, and mostly defeated life (even Du Bois turned against her), see Paula J. Giddings, *Ida: A Sword among Lions* (New York: Amistad, 2008), especially 177–229.

68. Jacquelyn Dowd Hall highlights the "domesticity and paternalism" of men's chivalric presumptions; Hall, *Revolt against Chivalry: Jesse Daniel Ames and the Women's Campaign against Lynching* (New York: Columbia University Press, 1979), 58, 152, 155. Nancy Maclean argues that both lynching and chivalric rhetoric show that patriarchal hierarchy and paternalism seemed to be on the rocks; Maclean, *Behind the Mask of Chivalry: The Making of the Second Ku Klux Klan* (New York: Oxford University Press, 1994), 25–39, 121, 150. W. Fitzhugh Brundage is one of the few other historians who emphasizes honor-shame dynamics in the collective rituals of lynching. See Brundage, *Lynching in the New South: Georgia and Virginia, 1880–1930* (Urbana: University of Illinois Press, 1993), 50–52, also 5, 62. Brundage points out that honor persisted in the South "long after it had withered elsewhere in the nation" (11), until urban and industrial growth emphasized "self-control and new conceptions of self-worth" (70). He highlights the localized variety of lynching motives and notes that "honor is a very blunt interpretative instrument" (11). More recently, Brundage finds that "lynching gripped the imaginations of black and white Americans precisely because it was such an extraordinarily savage and effective mode of humiliation"; Brundage, "The Ultimate Shame: Lynch-Law in the Post–Civil War American South," in "Humiliation and History in Global Perspective," edited by Bertram Wyatt-Brown and Evelin Gerda Lindner, special issue, *Social Alternatives* 25, no. 1 (2006): 28. Michael Pfeifer argues that a national market emboldened the middle class to undermine codes of personal and familial honor and that the death penalty was a "compromise" between rough justice and due process that preserved "white Americans' obsession with the physical maintenance of racial hierarchy"; Pfeifer, *Rough Justice: Lynching and American Society, 1974–1947* (Urbana: University of Illinois Press, 2004), 132, 64, 149 (quote). Patterson emphasizes the links between violence and honor and argues that lynching was terrorism and ritual sacrifice to rebuild the white South; Patterson, *Rituals of Blood*, 189–191, 172–173.

69. Chambliss quoted in Myrdal, *American Dilemma*, 1194; see also Gilmore, *Defying Dixie*, 3. In *Gender and Jim Crow*, Gilmore notes that North Carolina

Democrats feared black-white fusion politics, not sex between black men and white women (see especially 117–118). On controlling white women and humiliating black men for not being able to protect their women, see Dora Apel, *Imagery of Lynching: Black Men, White Women, and the Mob* (New Brunswick, N.J.: Rutgers University Press, 2004), 25. Joel Williamson argues that lynching "symbolically killed" white men's sexual desires for black women; Williamson, *The Crucible of Race*, 308. William F. Pinar argues that lynching was "gang rape" and that castration literalized the cultural emasculation of black men; Pinar, *The Gender of Racial Politics and Violence in America: Lynching, Prison Rape, & the Crisis of Masculinity* (New York: Peter Lang, 2001), 1136. In chapter 3 of *Souls of Black Folk*, when Du Bois repeatedly accuses Booker T. Washington of being unmanly, his attempt to emasculate Washington replicates as well as challenges that strategy.

70. Greene, *Praying for Sheetrock*, 25.

71. George Fredrickson, *Racism: A Short History* (Princeton, N.J.: Princeton University Press, 2002), 106. Fredrickson applies his argument about scapegoating to Nazi Germany, medieval Spain, and apartheid South Africa as well as to the United States (22).

72. C. Vann Woodward, *The Strange Career of Jim Crow* (New York: Oxford University Press, 1957), 65; Giddings, *Ida*, 226. On the southern mix of honor, shame, and religion, see Twitchell, *Look Away, Dixieland*, 149–152.

73. Du Bois, *Black Reconstruction in America* (Cleveland: Meridian Books, 1964), 52–53.

74. Langston Hughes, *The Ways of White Folk* (New York: Vintage Classics, 1990), 227–230, 246–249.

75. *Mulatto: A Play of the Deep South* was written in 1930–1931 as *Cross* and opened on Broadway in 1935. The producer added a rape scene and other incidents to sensationalize the drama, which received caustic reviews. In 1947 Hughes rewrote it as an opera. See Arnold Rampersad, *The Life of Langston Hughes*, vol. 1, *1902–1941: I, Too, Sing America* (New York: Oxford University Press, 1986), 191–192, 311–320, 324. For autobiographical elements of the play, see 2–3, 192.

76. Bertram Wyatt-Brown, *Southern Honor: Ethics and Behavior in the Old South* (Oxford: Oxford University Press, 1982), and personal communication. In Henry James's *The American* (1879), the aristocratic Valentin makes a fool as well as a corpse of himself by dueling with a brewer's son.

77. Priscilla Wald analyzes the American "outbreak narrative," which presents healthy carriers of disease as dangerous strangers in an interdependent world. To contain that threat, the outbreak narrative "reinforces national belonging"; Wald, *Contagious: Cultures, Carriers, and the Outbreak Narrative*

(Durham, N.C.: Duke University Press, 2008), 16, 53 (quote). To extend Wald's argument, as blackness became associated with contamination, whiteness became another kind of belonging.

78. Du Bois, *The Souls of Black Folk*, 315; Du Bois, "The Shape of Fear," *North American Review* 223 (1926): 294–295, quoted in Maclean, *Behind the Mask of Chivalry*, xi. In his 1933 essay "Negro Character as Seen by White Authors," Sterling Brown surveys the nearly ubiquitous literary stereotype of the strong white man, the weak black woman, and the tragic mulatto and concludes with irony: "The stereotype is very flattering to a race which, for all its self-assurance, seems to stand in great need of flattery." Reprinted in Sollors, *Interracialism*, 280.

79. Baldwin, *The Fire Next Time*, 95; Barack Obama, *Dreams from My Father: A Story of Race and Inheritance*, rev. ed. (New York: Three Rivers Press, 2004), 103 (demons make whites afraid), 277 (white men's fears of inconsequence).

80. Benedict Anderson, *Imagined Communities: Reflections on the Origin and Spread of Nationalism* (London: Verso, 1983), 137, also 139 on the "pseudo-aristocratic derivation of colonial racism." Homi Bhabha disagrees; he argues that racism should be understood "not simply as a hangover from archaic conceptions of the aristocracy, but as part of the historical traditions of civic and liberal humanism"; Bhabha, *The Location of Culture* (London: Routledge, 1994), 248–250, quote at 250. That claim minimizes Anderson's insight about the ongoing appeal of pseudo-aristocracy in colonial and postcolonial contexts. See also critiques in Anthony W. Marx, *Making Race and Nation: A Comparison of South Africa, the United States, and Brazil* (Cambridge: Cambridge University Press, 1998), 25; and Ed White, "Early American Nations as Imagined Communities," *American Quarterly* 56 (March 2004): 49–81, especially 74–76 on land speculators.

81. Richard S. Cooper, Jay S. Kaufman, and Ryk Ward, "Race and Genomics," *New England Journal of Medicine* 348 (March 20, 2003): 1166, drawing on Ashley Montague, ed., *The Concept of Race* (New York: Free Press, 1964). Cooper, Kaufman, and Ward argue against the use of racial categorizations in the emerging science of genomics, "a surveillance practice . . . virtually unique in the world" (1167). They argue that the idea of race itself "is the product of an arranged marriage between the social and biologic worlds" (1169).

82. Frantz Fanon, *The Wretched of the Earth*, translated by Constance Farrington (New York: Grove Press, 1963), quoted in James Wood, "Wounder and Wounded," *The New Yorker*, December 1, 2008, 80; Fanon, *Black Skin, White Masks*, translated by Charles Lam Markmann (New York: Grove Press, 1967), 60. Fanon continues, "In the man of color there is a constant effort . . . to

annihilate his own presence." Fanon's books no doubt influenced Anderson's formulation.

83. Fredrickson, *Racism*, 6 (idioms of religion), 150 (marginality, violence).

84. On the Maryland law, see William D. Zabel, "Interracial Marriage and the Law," 56, reprinted in Sollors, *Interracialism*; Carter G. Woodson, "Beginnings of Miscegenation," 45, reprinted in Sollors, *Interracialism*; Pascoe, *What Comes Naturally*, 19–20; and Eva Saks, "Representing Miscegenation Law," reprinted in Sollors, *Interracialism*. See also Gordon-Reed, *The Hemingses of Monticello*, on the use of Virginia law for "the maximum protection of property rights" (45–46) and on property rights as the basis for southern racism (40, 84–85, and 89). William McKee Evans links such cases to labor shortages; Evans, *Open Wound: The Long View of Race in America* (Urbana: University of Illinois Press, 2009), 30–31.

85. Jefferson, *Notes on the State of Virginia*, Query XIV, in *The Life and Selected Writings of Thomas Jefferson*, edited by Adrienne Koch and William Peden (New York: Modern Library, 1944), 256–259. Dain makes a case for Jefferson's complexity about race; Dain, *A Hideous Monster of the Mind*, 1–6, 18–20, 26–39. Saidiya Hartman emphasizes the continuities of abjection underlying the largely "sentimental" differences between antebellum and postbellum white racism; Hartman, *Scenes of Subjection: Terror, Slavery, and Self-Making in Nineteenth-Century America* (New York: Oxford University Press, 1997), 194–195.

86. According to Eva Saks, in 1853, Count Arthur de Gobineau's *Essai sur l'inégalité des races humaines* first transposed the idea of race from a species difference to a human difference. See "Representing Miscegenation Law," reprinted in Sollors, *Interracialism*, 65. For a summary of racist pseudoscience, see Paul Spickard, *Almost All Aliens: Immigration, Race, and Colonialism in American History and Identity* (New York: Routledge, 2007), 262–273. See also Painter, *The History of White People*, especially 59–342. On the varieties and complexities of racial formation during colonization in Asia and Africa, see Michael Adas, *Machines as the Measure of Men: Science, Technology, and Ideologies of Western Dominance* (Ithaca, N.Y.: Cornell University Press, 1989), especially 272–275 and 338–340. See also 65–66, where Adas argues that "color and physical features have been unduly stressed" (65). Bruce Dain argues that "no race theory . . . existed in America until after the American Revolution"; Dain, *A Hideous Monster of the Mind*, ix.

87. Love, *Race over Empire*, xii–xiii, and 17–18 on whiteness. T. H. Breen and Stephen Innes argue that as a result of Bacon's rebellion, whites used race to split lower-class whites from blacks and used slavery to have a subjugated work force; see Breen and Innes, *"Myne owne ground": Race and Freedom on*

Virginia's Eastern Shore, 1640–1676 (New York: Oxford University Press, 1980). On Dutch New York, see Russell Shorto's captivating book, *The Island at the Center of the World: The Epic Story of Dutch Manhattan and the Forgotten Colony That Shaped America* (New York: Doubleday, 2004).

88. Hannah Arendt argues that European racism explained and excused imperialism while achieving national and class unity. As she notes, "racism has survived libraries of refutations"; Arendt, "Race-Thinking before Racism," *The Review of Politics* 6, no. 1 (1944): 36–73, quote on 39. Joyce Appleby emphasizes the crucial role race and racism played in the rise of colonial capitalism, particularly in what became the United States; Appleby, *The Relentless Revolution*, 121–137, 175–176, 417, 420.

89. George Orwell, "Shooting an Elephant," in Orwell, *A Collection of Essays* (New York: Harcourt, Brace, Jovanovich, 1946), 148 (hated by large numbers of people), 152–153 (futility of the white man's dominion; wears a mask), 156 (did it to avoid looking a fool).

90. Bernard Crick questions whether Orwell actually shot the elephant, since the story can't be verified. See Crick, *George Orwell: A Life* (New York: Penguin Books, 1982), 165–166. According to Bertram Wyatt-Brown, Orwell beat his servants in Burma. He was a bed-wetter at his prep school, a more private source of humiliation (personal communication).

91. Jones's transcript is available in Linder, "The Massie ('Honor Killing') Trials, 1931–32," and in Van Slingerland, *Something Terrible Has Happened*, 316–322. In Darrow's account of the trial, also available on Linder's website, he frequently returns to Hawaii's "brown people," who seemed kind and friendly but (in his view) ignorantly sympathetic with the victim. "A jury of white men would have acquitted," Darrow said. Deacon Jones said that only in "the last day or two" did he tell Darrow that he, not Thomas Massie, was the killer.

92. Though resisting Kenneth Lynn's argument that honor was a "'gentlemanly masquerade,'" Bertram Wyatt-Brown declares that "Southerners' touchiness over virility stemmed from deep anxieties about how others, particularly Northerners and Englishmen, saw them"; Wyatt-Brown, *Southern Honor*, 35.

93. As Patricia Yaeger observes, obsessiveness about pollution depends on fears of the excluded group and generates the power of dirt itself; Yaeger, *Dirt and Desire*, 67. See also Edward Ayers, *The Promise of the New South: Life after Reconstruction* (New York: Oxford University Press, 1992), 139–140.

94. On race as a cultural illusion, see Walter Benn Michaels, *The Trouble with Diversity: How We Learned to Love Identity and Ignore Inequality* (New York: Metropolitan Books, 2006), especially 21–49 and 111 on "the phantasms we call races."

95. Saxton, *The Rise and Fall of the White Republic*, 5.

96. Glenda Gilmore, *Defying Dixie*, 3–5, and 390 on TV. Robert J. Norrell asks why civil rights protests did not succeed until 1955–1966, since they started in the late 1930s; Norrell, *The House I Live In*, xii. (Gilmore dates the beginning of the movement to an earlier period.) Norrell answers that the shock of the Holocaust had made white racist claims more untenable (137–138) and the demise of the sharecropping system had eroded white support (139–140). Then television made the contrast between Martin Luther King's nonviolence and southern white violence inescapable. The American value of equality briefly triumphed over white supremacy until the white backlash against black power in the late 1960s (174–186).

97. Fredrickson, *Racism*, 165–167, also 5, 137 on racism as the word first used to characterize Nazi anti-Semitism. Fredrickson gives credit to Ruth Benedict's 1940 anthropological study, *Race: Science and Politics*, for popularizing the term, which Jacques Barzun had helped introduce in the late 1930s. On "prejudice of color" see Love, *Race over Empire*, 15. On *racisme*, see Étienne Balibar, "Racism Revisited: Sources, Relevance, and Aporias of a Modern Concept," in "Comparative Racialization," edited by Shu-mei Shih, special issue, *PMLA* 123, no. 5 (2008): 1630–1639. Balibar writes, "Magnus Hirschfeld coined the term *racism* and associated it with xenophobia" (1632–1633, his italics). Balibar credits the 1950 and 1951 UNESCO declarations on race with popularizing the term. On racism's nineteenth-century links to imperialism in Germany, France, and England, see Arendt, "Race-Thinking before Racism."

98. Bruce Weber, "Jerry Wexler, a Behind-the-Scenes Force in Black Music, Is Dead at 91," *New York Times*, August 16, 2008, A17. Flynt, the author of *Poor but Proud: Alabama's Poor Whites* (1989), is a retired history professor at Auburn. Wexler, who produced black albums for decades, coined the phrase "rhythm and blues." He requested that his epitaph read "More bass."

99. Emmett Till's mother "staged a counter-spectacle in a new, national, real time"; Hale, *Making Whiteness*, 290. On Till, see Norrell, *The House I Live In*, 174; Goldsby, *Spectacular Secret*, 294–305; Evans, *Cultures of Violence*, 256–257; and Blauner, *Black Lives, White Lives*, 34–35, 181.

100. On the "long civil rights movement," see especially Gilmore, *Defying Dixie*.

101. Grace Hale notes that protesters wore masks of "stoic" and "willed passivity" that "paradoxically belied whites' assumptions of their 'natural' deference"; Hale, *Making Whiteness*, 292. As Taylor Branch puts it, even liberals "grossly underestimated the complexity, the restraint, and the grounding respect for opponents that had sustained King, [Robert] Moses, and count-

less others through the difficult years . . . of lifting a despised minority from oblivion"; Branch, *Parting the Waters*, 920.

102. McCain quoted in David Grann, "The Fall: McCain's Choices," *The New Yorker*, November 17, 2008, 60.

103. Branch's three-volume history of the civil rights movement recounts the media's role in vivid detail. Jason Sokol focuses on the civil rights movement, farm mechanization, and migration from rural to urban and suburban settings as major causes of social change; Sokol, *There Goes My Everything: White Southerners in the Age of Civil Rights, 1945–1975* (New York: Alfred A. Knopf, 2006), 282. Sokol notes that white southerners persistently believed they had good relations with black people. See also Greene, *Praying for Sheetrock*, 188.

104. Baldwin, *The Fire Next Time*, 86. William McKee Evans argues that a racial crisis came after World War II, "when a Jim Crow nation set out to lead a world filled with post-colonial peoples of color"; Evans, *Open Wound*, 2, also 3–5, 220–234. In Baldwin's analysis, the two earlier crises were the struggle of the founding fathers to reconcile freedom and slavery and the Civil War and Reconstruction. See also Melani McAlister, *Epic Encounters: Culture, Media, and U.S. Interests in the Middle East, 1945–2000* (Berkeley: University of California Press, 2001), 72.

105. Eisenhower quoted in David Nichols, *A Matter of Justice: Eisenhower and the Beginning of the Civil Rights Revolution* (New York: Simon & Schuster, 2007), 278. The occasion was a stag dinner. Nixon quoted in Charlie Savage, "On Nixon Tapes, Ambivalence over Abortion, Not Watergate," *New York Times*, June 24, 2009, A1, A3.

CHAPTER 3 — HONOR BOUND

1. Democratic Party agenda quoted in Philip Dray, *Capitol Men: The Epic Story of Reconstruction through the Lives of the First Black Congressmen* (New York: Houghton Mifflin, 2008), 249; Bilbo quoted in Robert J. Norrell, *The House I Live In: Race in the American Century* (New York: Oxford University Press, 2005), 142. After Bilbo's reelection, the Senate refused to seat him because he allegedly incited violence against blacks and took bribes. As the 5-foot, 2-inch senator was dying, Bilbo self-published *Take Your Choice: Separation or Mongrelization* (1947). According to Dray, in 1876, South Carolina Democrats had "imported a campaign 'expert' from Mississippi" to learn techniques. Point 16 declares, "never threaten a man individually if he deserves to be threatened, the necessities of the times require that he should die. A dead Radical is very harmless"; Dray, *Capitol Men*, 249–250. See also William McKee Evans, *Open Wound: The Long View of Race in America* (Urbana: University of

Illinois Press, 2009), 183, quoting Col. A. M. Waddell, the "chief architect" of the 1898 race riots in Wilmington, North Carolina: "If you find the negro out voting tell him to leave the polls. If he refuses kill him, shoot him down in his tracks" (182–183).

2. Edmund S. Morgan, "The Price of Honor," *New York Review of Books*, May 31, 2001, 36. Morgan's review essay traces the development of honor-shame studies from Marcel Mauss in 1950 to Julian Pitt-Rivers, Bertram Wyatt-Brown, and Kenneth Greenberg. He emphasizes the centrality of reciprocal gift-giving as the mode of exchange that secured honor in pre-market economies. Frank Stewart gives a more complex account of Roman words for honor, including *fides, honor, honestas, dignitas, pudor,* and *existimatio.* He also mentions *fama* versus *infamia*; Stewart, *Honor* (Chicago: University of Chicago Press, 1994), 57–61. He doesn't mention the origin of honor in *onus,* though he does emphasize reputation and respect due to rank.

3. Malcolm Gladwell, *Outliers: The Story of Success* (2008, repr., London: Penguin Books, 2009), 187–204.

4. In *The Fate of Schechem; or, The Politics of Sex: Essays in the Anthropology of the Mediterranean* (Cambridge: Cambridge University Press, 1977), on Andalusia, Julian Pitt-Rivers contrasts male honor and female purity (10, 77–80). He links the exchange of women not only to men's pride and status (vii) but also to "a consciousness of social equivalence" (161). "Valour" is "the leading qualification of honour" (3), and "social groups possess a collective honour" (13). See also his discussions of shame, or "accepted" humiliation (21; see also 19–24, 43–44).

5. Peristiany contrasts face-to-face societies with modern life, whose "mobility and urbanization" makes us ask, "*who* are our peers and for how long?"; J. G. Peristiany, "Introduction," in *Honour and Shame: The Values of Mediterranean Society* (Chicago: University of Chicago Press, 1966), 11 (quotes in chapter text), 12 (quote in this note). Evelin Lindner finds four kinds of humiliation in honor cultures: conquest humiliation, which subjugates "formerly equal neighbors"; reinforcement humiliation, including "beatings or killings" to keep subordinated people in their place; relegation humiliation "to push an already low-ranking underling even further down"; and exclusion humiliation, usually involving exiling or killing; Lindner, *Making Enemies: Humiliation and International Conflict* (Westport, Conn.: Praeger Security International, 2006), 28–29. In emphasizing individual dignity and equality, Lindner tends to reduce the honor culture's reciprocal bonds to "duty."

6. Ayaan Hirsi Ali, *Nomad: From Islam to America: A Personal Journey through the Clash of Civilizations* (New York: Free Press, 2010), 221. Hirsi Ali attacks Western feminists such as Germaine Greer whose relativism stops

them from speaking out against honor killings (224–225). Frank Stewart states that across cultures, honor is "mainly something for men" and that women help enhance male honor through their chastity, which shows male control; Stewart, *Honor*, 107–110.

7. On "honor killings" of gay Muslim men, see Dan Bilefsky, "Soul-Searching in Turkey after Killing of a Gay Man," *New York Times*, November 26, 2009, A16. On homosexuality in fifteenth-century Florence, see Richard C. Trexler, *Public Life in Renaissance Florence* (Ithaca, N.Y.: Cornell University Press, 1991), 379–382. Sebastian de Grazia quotes the Florentine magistrate in *Machiavelli in Hell* (Princeton, N.J.: Princeton University Press, 1989), 140.

8. Karen Armstrong, *Muhammad: A Prophet for Our Time* (London: Harper Perennial, 2007), 24–25 (*muruwah*), see also 145–148, 104–105, 167–168 (on polygamy). In *Honor*, Frank Stewart emphasizes the Arabic word *'ird* as the key Bedouin term for honor in the central Sinai, where he did field research for six years. He contrasts *'ird* with more wide-ranging European concepts of honor. It is "a right to respect" (147) based on a man's fulfillment of his obligations as host and protector (81, 99, 103, 143–144) and is linked to the more complex terms *wajd*, or face, and *sharaf*, which mixes rank with equality (102, 132–133, 148). Pre-Islamic versions of *'ird* are closer to European ideas of honor (103), but it is never an internal virtue; rather, it is an external thing, like a mouth or a nose (143–144).

9. Armstrong, *Muhammad: A Biography of the Prophet* (London: Victor Gollancz, 1991), 58–61. Armstrong shows Muhammad's ability to bring believers beyond their allegiances to tribe and traditional manliness, since "Islam" means peace and submission and "Muslim" means one who submits to God. Muhammad also championed women's rights. Armstrong notes that Western ideas of small "clans" or big "tribes" don't catch the fierceness of loyalty to the *qawm* (people), whether large or small. In those egalitarian groups, "the vendetta principle" presumed the members' interchangeability (58–60).

10. Ayaan Hirsi Ali, *Infidel* (New York: Free Press, 2008), 126 (felt good to belong), 131 (suffocating).

11. Ali, *Nomad: From Islam to America*, xvi, also 3–12, 274 (on her dying father), and 23–39 (on her mother). As reviewers pointed out, Hirsi Ali makes few differentiations among Muslims. Though she writes, "I am not a Christian and have no plans to convert" (251), she concludes that Muslims need to be converted not only by public education and feminism but also by "the Christianity of love and tolerance" (xv), and she wonders if the Vatican can "lead the way" (245). Her reference to education, feminism, and the Vatican as "antidotes" implies that to her, Islam is a disease (xx). Yet the alternative leaves

her mother's words echoing in her mind: *"The world outside the clan is rough, and you are alone in it"* (39, her italics).

12. Edward Ayers, "Honor," in *Encyclopedia of Southern Culture*, edited by Charles Regan Wilson and William Ferris (Chapel Hill: University of North Carolina Press, 1989), 1483. Peristiany's edited collection *Honour and Shame* (1966) first emphasized the Mediterranean origins of honor. See also David D. Gilmore's collection, *Honor and Shame and the Unity of the Mediterranean* (Washington, D.C.: American Anthropological Association, 1987), especially his introduction on honor, shame, and masculinity (2–21). Muriko Asano-Tamanoi's essay in this collection, "Shame, Family, and State," contrasts Mediterranean and Japanese codes (e.g., 116–117). Stanley Brandes's essay, "Reflections on Honor and Shame in the Mediterranean," teases out complex regional variations while linking honor "to control over scarce resources," including "female sexuality, with its procreative potential" (122). Bertram Wyatt-Brown first wrote about the concept's importance in the antebellum South; Wyatt-Brown, *Southern Honor: Ethics and Behavior in the Old South* (Oxford: Oxford University Press, 1982). Alexander Welsh focuses on theories of honor as character, self-respect, and moral choices from Aristotle to Kant to the present, though without acknowledging honor's central presence in non-Western cultures; Welsh, *What Is Honor? A Question of Moral Imperatives* (New Haven: Yale University Press, 2008). Welsh briefly considers its gendered dynamics; see for example 108–110 (on *Tom Jones*) and 171–172 (on Adam Smith).

13. Bertram Wyatt-Brown, "Honor and Revolutionary Rhetoric," unpublished.

14. Pericles' Oration is in Thucydides, *History of the Peloponnesian War*, translated by Rex Warner (New York: Penguin, 1972), 144–151, quotes on 148–150.

15. Ibid., 151.

16. Ibid., 80 (fear of Persia leads to honor and interest), also 400–408 ("The Melian Dialogue"), 35 (Thucydides the Athenian), and 36 (the same race of people). Warner's translation has "security, honour, and self-interest"; other translators have "fear, honor, and interest." Thucydides omits his exile from his self-serving account of the battle at Amphipolis. The seven ships he commanded arrived too late on the day the city surrendered to Bracidas (328–329).

17. On honor versus law, see Thomas W. Gallant, "Honor, Masculinity, and Ritual Knife Fighting in Nineteenth-Century Greece," *American Historical Review* 102 (April 2000): 359–382.

18. On defaming paintings, see Samuel Y. Edgerton, *Pictures and Punishment: Art and Criminal Prosecution during the Florentine Renaissance* (Ithaca, N.Y.: Cornell University Press, 1985). Dante is Florence's most famous exile. One could argue that *The Divine Comedy* narrates his attempt to reestablish his sense of belonging in heavenly terms, though the relentless shaming of Florentines throughout *The Inferno* bespeaks not only his anger but also his inability to separate himself from the community that banished him.

19. Niccolò Machiavelli, *The Prince*, translated by Robert M. Adams (New York: Norton Critical Ed., 1977), 72; and Adams, "Historical Introduction," in Machiavelli, *The Prince*, xvi; Jacob Burckhardt, *The Civilization of the Renaissance in Italy*, part 1, 134, and 36 on Machiavelli's idea of *virtù* as a "compound of force and intellect." On honor-shame issues in Renaissance Florence, see Trexler, *Public Life in Renaissance Florence*, 17–19, 290–303, 310–312. See also de Grazia, *Machiavelli in Hell*, 243, on *virtù* as "masculine energy." In American politics, Rudy Giuliani has exemplified *virtù* by mixing bullying, courage, and calculation.

20. Gordon Wood, *Empire of Liberty: A History of the Early Republic, 1789–1815* (New York: Oxford University Press, 2009), 236–238 (drawing on Joanne Freeman's *Affairs of Honor: National Politics in the New Republic* [New Haven: Yale University Press, 2001]), 167; Bertram Wyatt-Brown, *The Shaping of Southern Culture: Honor, Grace, and War, 1760s to 1880s* (Chapel Hill: University of North Carolina Press, 2001), 55. Hamilton saw his final duel as what Freeman calls "a public service and a personal sacrifice" to get Burr out of politics (198). Freeman also notes that "the current resurrection of Aaron Burr" suits "an age of jaded distrust" (283).

21. See Freeman, *Affairs of Honor*, 170: honor meant "much more than a vague sense of self-worth; it represented the ability to prove oneself a deserving political leader." On tax revolts versus honor, I'm paraphrasing Julian Pitt-Rivers, whom Wyatt-Brown credits in *The Shaping of Southern Culture*, 37.

22. In *A Dictionary of the English Language* (1755), Samuel Johnson begins his definition of "author" with two variations on first causes: "1. The first beginner or mover of anything"; and "2. The efficient; he that effects or produces any thing." Not until the third and fourth definitions does Johnson turn to writing: "3. The first writer of anything; distinct from the *translator* or *compiler*"; and "4. A writer in general." The first two definitions look backward to author as a descriptive term for any civic initiative. The last two look forward to our modern sense of the author as a writer of an original published text or as one whose career consists of such writings.

23. See my essay on "Men Writing in the Early Republic," in *A History of the Book in America*, vol. 2, *An Extensive Republic: Print, Culture, and Society in the*

New Nation, 1970–1840, edited by Robert A. Gross and Mary Kelley (Chapel Hill: University of North Carolina Press, 2010), 353–354. See also Freeman, *Affairs of Honor,* on honor as a code that partially united American regions.

24. Wyatt-Brown, *The Shaping of Southern Culture,* 49.

25. Joseph Addison, quoted in Forrest McDonald, *Novus Ordo Seclorum: The Intellectual Origins of the Constitution* (Lawrence: University Press of Kansas, 1985), 198, Addison's italics. McDonald develops Addison's influence on Washington, especially through *Cato,* a drama about stoic leadership (195–199).

26. Ibid., 50–51, and 53 ("love of honor and fear of shame drew the North and South together" against the "British overlords"). See Robin Einhorn, *American Taxation, American Slavery* (Chicago: University of Chicago Press, 2006), on the slaveholders' ability to "portray their own power as victimization" (255).

27. The caning occurred on May 22, 1856, in response to Sumner's vehement speech, "Crime against Kansas," partly ridiculing Brooks's cousin, a day after pro-slavery advocates burned and looted parts of Lawrence, Kansas, a free-state center. See Freeman, *Affairs of Honor,* 170, 172. Dueling became problematic in the North in part because New England's more extensive print culture made a published attack a more "severe wound" (168). See also xvi–xvii, and 169 on southern congressmen who "bullied and taunted" their northern counterparts "because they knew that northerners would resist gunplay." The caning helped precipitate John Brown's massacre at Pottawatomie in late May of 1856. See Williamjames Hull Hoffer, *The Caning of Charles Sumner: Honor, Idealism, and the Origins of the Civil War* (Baltimore, Md.: Johns Hopkins University Press, 2010), especially 14–15 and 27–30 (on the honor-shame issues at stake), and 131–133 (criticizing later sympathy for Brooks as an aspect of "reconciliation" among white people).

28. Edmund Morgan notes that Wedderburn used "language too coarse for newspapers to print"; Morgan, *Benjamin Franklin* (New Haven: Yale University Press, 2003) 202. In *The Americanization of Benjamin Franklin* (New York: Penguin Books, 2005), Gordon Wood quotes Franklin's use of "Bull-baiting" in a letter dated February 19, 1774 (146).

29. Edward Bancroft, quoted in Walter Isaacson, *Benjamin Franklin: An American Life* (New York: Simon & Schuster, 2004), 277–278. Isaacson calls it an "hour-long tirade" in "the Cockpit," an arena used for cockfighting during Henry VIII's rule (276–277).

30. Morgan, *Benjamin Franklin,* 204 (letter to Cushing), 272 (American Revolution a civil war). Franklin's defense of the colonies led to a split with his loyalist son, William, who was governor of New Jersey.

31. Ibid., 200–204; Isaacson, *Benjamin Franklin,* 275–279; Wood, *The*

Americanization of Benjamin Franklin, 146. Wood notes that in February 1778, when France signed two treaties with the United States, Franklin wore the same blue velvet coat—"to give it a little revenge," he said to a friend (191).

32. For Isaacson, Franklin's silence "made him look stronger than his powerful adversaries, contemptuous rather than contrite, condescending rather than cowed"; *Benjamin Franklin*, 278.

33. For Gordon Wood, "Honor was exclusive, heroic, and aristocratic, and it presumed a hierarchical world different from the one that was emerging in America"; Wood, *Empire of Liberty*, 159–160. It fostered an "intimate world of competing gentlemen" before the existence of political parties (ibid., see also 235–238). Wood says honor survives mostly in the hierarchical South and the military (717). Alexander Welsh grounds respect in peer groups, particularly in "seeing and exchanging looks"; Welsh, *What Is Honor?* 6, see also xv, 3, and 211 on "reflection" as mirroring. *Aidōs*, the ancient Greek word for honor, also means shame, and the Latin word *pudor* also carries that double meaning. Welsh writes, "The ultimate sanction that enforces the morality of respect is not strictly punishment but loss of membership in the group" (6–7).

34. On anthropologists, see Jill Lepore, "Rap Sheet: Why Is American History So Murderous?" *The New Yorker*, November 9, 2009, 80.

35. Frank Stewart notes the European shift from external ideas of medieval honor, typified by the victories of medieval warriors, to internal ideals of integrity by the nineteenth century; Stewart, *Honor*, 41; see also 46–47, 54, 69 (on prestige), and 141 (on victory versus the dishonor of defeat). James B. Twitchell notes that honor cultures "tend to be sealed off, island cultures, with a rigid social hierarchy"; Twitchell, *Look Away, Dixieland* (Baton Rouge: Louisiana State University Press, 2011), 149.

36. Raymond Williams suggests that writers such as Charles Dickens, George Eliot, and Jane Austen gave readers the pleasure of imagining "face-to-face" or "knowable communities" that in reality were "harder and harder to sustain"; Williams, *The Country and the City* (New York: Oxford University Press, 1975), 165 (quotes), see also 165–181.

37. Here I draw on several studies by Bertram Wyatt-Brown, especially "Honor and Revolutionary Rhetoric."

38. Recent research shows that when we see someone who looks "different," the amygdala flashes a threat warning. See Nicholas Kristof, "What? Me Biased?" *New York Times*, October 30, 2008, A39.

39. Gail Bederman highlights the rise of masculinity as a cultural anxiety; Bederman, *Manliness and Civilization: A Cultural History of Gender and Race in the United States, 1880–1917* (Chicago: University of Chicago Press, 1995), 6–19, 245n78 (first use). See also John Pettigrew, *Brutes in Suits: Male Sensibility*

in America, 1890–1920 (Baltimore, Md.: Johns Hopkins University Press, 2007); and John Kasson, *Houdini, Tarzan, and the Perfect Man: The White Male Body and the Challenge of Modernity in America* (New York: Hill and Wang, 2001), which analyzes men's obsession with bodybuilding. All three studies focus on the United States after the Civil War.

40. Quoted in Greg Bishop, "Payton's Path Was Winding, His Confidence Never Wavering," *New York Times*, February 9, 2010, B10. The running back is Mike Bell.

41. Jonathan Haidt, "What Makes People Vote Republican?" *Edge: The Third Culture*, September 9, 2008, available at www.edge.org/3rd_culture/haidt08/ haidt08_index.html. Haidt's article is followed by commentaries by various distinguished intellectuals, including Howard Gardner. Will Bunch dates an earlier version of this essay to the 1980s, when Jonathan Haidt was a graduate student; Bunch, *The Backlash: Right-Wing Radicals, High-Def Hucksters, and Paranoid Politics in the Age of Obama* (New York: HarperCollins, 2010), 343.

42. Alexis de Tocqueville, *Democracy in America*, 2 vols., translated by Henry Reeve, revised by Francis Bowen, revised and edited by Phillips Bradley (New York: Vintage Books, 1954), vol. 2, Book 2, chapters 2–4 on "Individualism" (104–113). On the word's history, see Steven Lukes, "The Meanings of 'Individualism,'" *Journal of the History of Ideas* 32 (January–March 1971): 45–66.

43. Frances Fitzgerald, *Fire in the Lake: The Vietnamese and the Americans in Vietnam* (Boston: Little, Brown, 1972), 23.

44. Tocqueville, *Democracy in America*, 2:106.

45. Welsh, *What Is Honor?* 200–201, also 194–195.

46. Ibid., 200.

47. Tocqueville, "Of Honor in the United States and in Democratic Communities," in *Democracy in America*, 2:243 (peculiar rule), 2:245–246, (fidelity to the person of the lord versus patriotism), 2:248 (quiet versus turbulent virtues), 2:247 (replaced by commercial definitions; boldness of enterprise), 2:249 (male chastity), all from Book 3 of vol. 2, "Of Honor in the United States and in Democratic Communities." Tocqueville's observation about southern white elites are tucked into a footnote (2:247), since only the states without slavery give "a complete picture of democratic society."

48. Ibid., 2:250 (northerners see idleness as shameful), 2:249 (strange indulgence for bankrupts). A footnote defines honor in two ways: 1) "the esteem, glory, or reverence that a man receives from his fellow men"; or 2), "the aggregate of those rules" for obtaining such esteem (2:242). Tocqueville emphasizes the second definition.

49. Antonio Gramsci, *An Antonio Gramsci Reader: Selected Writings, 1916–1935*, edited by David Forgacs (New York: Schocken Books, 1988), 293.

50. Tocqueville, *Democracy in America*, 2:254 (inequality), 2:251 (glimpses of the rules of honor).

51. Ibid., 2:254–255.

52. Bertram Wyatt-Brown, "Honor, Secession, and the Civil War," unpublished; Tocqueville, *Democracy in America*, 1:390 (white citizen proud of his race), 1:360 (most grasping nation on the globe).

53. Nell Irvin Painter, *The History of White People* (New York: W. W. Norton, 2010), 201 (enlargements), 201, 209 (property), 211 (Irish, German), 359, 370 (ethnics), 384 (Asians, Latinos). To me, the last two create more complex challenges to white supremacy.

54. Robert S. Levine argues that race was "submerged" at first in antebellum American nationalism, whereas late nineteenth-century writers and politicians made white supremacy more explicit, though always with contestations and competing possibilities; Levine, *Dislocating Race & Nation: Episodes in Nineteenth-Century American Literary Nationalism* (Chapel Hill: University of North Carolina Press, 2008), 6–11, 241–242. Throughout, whiteness precariously depended on "fictions of blood" (8). "Anxieties about whiteness rather than confident assertions of whiteness may have inspired . . . the imperial moment itself" (243). On the growing inclusiveness of whiteness in the twentieth century, see Matthew Frye Jacobson, *Whiteness of a Different Color: European Immigrants and the Alchemy of Race* (Cambridge, Mass.: Harvard University Press, 1998).

55. Deborah Eisenberg, "Introduction," in Gregor von Rezzori, *Memoirs of an Anti-Semite: A Novel in Five Stories* (New York: New York Review Books, 2008), xiv.

56. Though he doesn't mention honor, Peter Coviello emphasizes the privileges that came with whiteness, especially the fitness for "self-government" and "the presumption that . . . they had no race." By 1850 whiteness defined "the very substance of American coherence—of American nation-ness"; Coviello, *Intimacy in America: Dreams of Affiliation in Antebellum Literature* (Minneapolis: University of Minnesota Press, 2005), 34–35 and 26.

57. Ayers, "Honor," 1483.

58. Ibid.; Wyatt-Brown, *Southern Honor*, 155. See also Steven Stowe, *Intimacy and Power in the Old South: Ritual in the Lives of the Planters* (Baltimore, Md.: Johns Hopkins University Press, 1987), which emphasizes the plantation class's celebration of male hierarchy and "showiness." Stowe notes with surprise "the almost complete absence of black people in white accounts of ritual and daily routine" (253). Kenneth Greenberg's *Honor & Slavery* (Princeton, N.J.: Princeton University Press, 1996) features nose-pulling as an antebellum southern strategy of shaming an opponent of equal social status (3–23). Joanne

Freeman's *Affairs of Honor* shows honor's centrality in the national politics of the early republic.

59. Well before the DNA evidence persuaded white historians, Annette Gordon-Reed argued that Jefferson and Hemings had a long sexual relationship. See Gordon-Reed, *Thomas Jefferson and Sally Hemings: An American Controversy* (Charlottesville: University Press of Virginia, 1997), 133–141 (Jefferson's racism), and 207 (Jefferson's freeing of his children via various means). Gordon-Reed's *The Hemingses of Monticello: An American Family* (New York: W. W. Norton, 2008) begins with "Jefferson's monumentally patriarchal and self-absorbed view" of his duties in administering slavery (16), then empathetically speculates about many Hemingses' lives and sensibilities. Jefferson's will freed other Hemingses but not Sally, who nonetheless lived and defined herself as free. Gordon-Reed plausibly conjectures that Jefferson set up her "informal emancipation" so that his will wouldn't spark more gossip (657–659).

60. Patrick Henry quoted in Roger Wilkins, *Jefferson's Pillow: The Founding Fathers and the Dilemma of Black Patriotism* (Boston: Beacon Press, 2001), 137–138. Wilkins's title comes from Jefferson's earliest memory, "of being carried on a pillow by a slave riding on horseback" (4).

61. Ayers, "Honor," 1483.

62. W.E.B. Du Bois, *Black Reconstruction in America 1860–1880* (Cleveland: Meridian Books, 1964), 700–701. Du Bois's phrase is quoted in Roediger, *The Wages of Whiteness*, 12, and is reinforced in Kathleen Cleaver's introduction to Roediger's book (xx). Du Bois adds that whiteness didn't just raise workers' status; it gave them more voting power and better schooling. On "blood" in American law, see Eva Saks, "Representing Miscengenation Law" (1988), reprinted in *Interracialism: Black-White Intermarriage in American History, Literature, and Law*, edited by Werner Sollors (New York: Oxford University Press, 2000), 63–81.

63. For the American South, as for South Africa and for Germany after World War I, "the racial Other came to be identified with national defeat and humiliation"; George Fredrickson, *Racism: A Short History* (Princeton, N.J.: Princeton University Press, 2002), 106. Bertram Wyatt-Brown argues that white people's resentment at having been defeated by the North spurred their humiliation of black people after the Civil War. Analogously, the American occupation of Iraq after the United States had been humiliated by Al-Qaeda led to flagrant "violence and atrocities"; Wyatt-Brown, "Honor, Irony, and Humiliation," 22–27.

64. Kenneth W. Warren, *Black and White Strangers: Race and American Literary Realism* (Chicago: University of Chicago Press, 1993), 63. Warren

includes women and poor Irish along with African Americans "as victims of social injustice" whose "equal rights claims . . . became assaults on the genteel norms" of middle-class American households (62–63).

65. A. Leon Higginbotham Jr. and Barbara K. Kopytoff, "Racial Purity and Interracial Sex in the Law of Colonial and Antebellum Virginia" (1989), reprinted in Sollors, *Interracialism*, 81–140. Higginbotham and Kopytoff conclude that Virginia courts used the same rationale for forbidding interracial sex "for some three centuries" (133). Sollors notes the ironic "exceptionalism" in the United States' continuous enforcement of laws against white-black marriages (12, also 3, 7–12). Even South Africa had such laws "for less than forty years" (8). In 1959 (only eight years before the *Loving* decision), when Hannah Arendt wrote an article opposing the laws against racial intermarriage, *Commentary* refused to publish it and *Dissent* published it but with "two sharp rebuttals" (11). On the 1661 Maryland law, see Saks, "Representing Miscegenation Law," 64. See also William D. Zabel, "Interracial Marriage and the Law" (1965), reprinted in Sollors, *Interracialism*, 56–57. See also Elise Lemire, *"Miscegenation": Making Race in America* (Philadelphia: University of Pennsylvania Press, 2002), which argues that since "race" doesn't exist, "the idea that there is a special kind of sex that is 'inter-racial' is . . . a racist social fiction" (147). Robert S. Levine cites the quotation from Don Fehrenbacher about the Dred Scott case; Levine, *Dislocating Race & Nation*, 291n16, from Fehrenbacher, *The Dred Scott Case: Its Significance in American Law and Politics* (1978, repr. Oxford University Press, 2001), 357, Fehrenbacher's italics.

66. Winthrop Jordan, *White over Black: American Attitudes toward the Negro, 1550–1812* (Baltimore, Md.: Penguin Books, 1968), 253, quoting a footnote in David Hume's 1753–1754 version of his essay, "Of National Characters," first published in 1748. On the invention of "Caucasian" in 1775, see Painter, *History of White People*, 72–90. As the index to James Bradley's *The Imperial Cruise: A Secret History of Empire and War* (New York: Little, Brown, 2009) shows, by 1900 "Aryan," "Anglo-Saxon," and "Teuton" had become interchangeable terms in justifications of white supremacy in the Philippines and elsewhere. On Africans and blackness versus Christian whiteness, see Jordan, *White over Black*, 4–11, also 15–17 on European settlers' need to brand black skin as permanent, whatever the climate. On chimpanzees and apes, which Europeans linked to devils, see 29–33

67. John Higham, *Strangers in the Land: Patterns of American Nativism 1860–1925*, 2nd ed. (New York: Atheneum, 1973), 157, and 131–157 on the convergence of nativism and racism. Higham deftly differentiates the "patrician nativists" (139), who were defensive about the waning of New England's cultural dominance, from those who emphasized Anglo-Saxon or Teutonic ancestry

and naturalists and anthropologists who opposed race mixing on "scientific" grounds. Higham points out that Franz Boas's *The Mind of Primitive Man* (1911) challenged the scientific basis for "race thinking" (153).

68. W.E.B. Du Bois, "The Souls of White Folk," in Du Bois, *Darkwater* (New York: Harcourt, Brace, 1921), 37–38 (World War I horrible only because white men fighting white men), 41 (a war for colonial aggrandizement), 39 (this seeming Terrible), 42 (color the worldwide mark of meanness).

69. In *Race over Empire*, Love shows how racism blocked imperialist expansion. Michael Adas has argued that the carnage of World War I made northern white Europeans question the technological superiority that had justified several centuries of colonial dominance; Adas, *Machines as the Measure of Men: Science, Technology, and Ideologies of Western Dominance* (Ithaca, N.Y.: Cornell University Press, 1989), especially the epilogue.

70. Du Bois, "Souls of White Folk," 45 (competition for labor of people of color), 43 (audacity of imperialism), also 49 on the approaching race war. A later Marxist, Alexander Saxton, concludes the opposite, that the "unparalleled . . . savagery and destruction" of whites against whites in World War I became "a decisive turning point" after which "Euro-American world hegemony, based ideologically on white racism, has progressively disintegrated"; Saxton, *The Rise and Fall of the White Republic*, 390.

71. Du Bois, "Souls of White Folk," 32.

72. Ibid., 33 (census hypothetical), 50 (robbing, hatred), 34 (people rush to the inevitable conclusion).

73. Ibid., 35 (we were never deceived), 46 (sequence rests on degradation), 44 (hatred pays; Du Bois's italics), 48 (white world despises "darkies").

74. Ibid., 48 (hatred and despising of human beings), 50 (it is but the beginning), 49 (protest of raped peoples), Du Bois's italics.

75. Ibid., 50 (Europe's greatest sin), 51 (America trains her immigrants), 52 (Soul of White Folk hanging like Prometheus).

76. David Levering Lewis, *W.E.B. Du Bois: The Fight for Equality and the American Century, 1919–1963* (New York: Henry Holt, 2000), 14. Lewis notes that in its first version in 1910, Du Bois's essay mocked white arrogance "with the fury of a tightly clamped pressure cooker over a building flame" (13). See also vol. 1 of Lewis's biography, *W.E.B. Du Bois: Biography of a Race, 1868–1919* (New York: Henry Holt, 1993), 469–470.

77. Lewis, *W.E.B. Du Bois: The Fight for Equality*, 15. Lewis notes Du Bois's "somewhat derivative economic interpretation" (ibid.).

78. Aaron Shaheen, drawing on the work of Hazel Carby and David Levering Lewis, emphasizes the influence of Johann Gottlieb von Herder on Du Bois's rhetoric of manhood. He notes that "Du Bois places gender in a position

usually reserved in white supremacist discourses of evolutionary advancement for race"; Shaheen, *Androgynous Democracy: Modern American Literature and the Dual-Sexed Body Politic* (Knoxville: University of Tennessee Press, 2010) 114–124, quote on 116.

79. W.E.B. Du Bois, "The Negro Mind Reaches Out," in *The New Negro*, edited by Alain Locke (New York: Atheneum, 1970), 402. His immediate subject is Jan Smuts and the rise of African political consciousness.

CHAPTER 4 — FOUR NOVELS

1. Anne Baker's analysis of U.S. geography schoolbooks links national expansion to a "new emphasis on race as a means of categorizing human beings," since Indians and Mexicans also threatened white rule. As Baker notes, relying on George Fredrickson, "race" as a term originated in the sixteenth century to denote the offspring and lineage of plants, animals, and humans. Only in the eighteenth century did people use it to subdivide humans based on physical characteristics, and not until the first half of the nineteenth century did the term presume innate nonwhite inferiority; Baker, *Heartless Immensity: Literature, Culture, and Geography in Antebellum America* (Ann Arbor: University of Michigan Press, 2006), 121 (quote), 119. See also 118–135 on the textbooks and 120–121 on domestic national expansion.

2. See Lauren L. Basson, *White Enough to Be American? Race Mixing, Indigenous People, and the Boundaries of State and Nation* (Chapel Hill: University of North Carolina Press, 2008), 192–193. Basson, whose book focuses on four case studies featuring various non–African American race mixtures, emphasizes white Americans' abstract commitment to private property as a defense.

3. In *Race over Empire: Racism and U.S. Imperialism, 1865–1900* (Chapel Hill: University of North Carolina Press, 2004), Eric T. L. Love persuasively argues that domestic racism checked imperial ambitions. Yet as Willard B. Gatewood Jr. concludes, "The principal harvest of imperialism for black Americans was an abundance of negrophobia"; Gatewood, *Black Americans and the White Man's Burden 1898–1903* (Urbana: University of Illinois Press, 1975), 323, see also 292–319 on recolonization efforts.

4. Bill Hardwig on Joe Christmas, in conversation. In *A Spectacular Secret: Lynching in American Life and Literature* (Chicago: University of Chicago Press, 2006), Jacqueline Goldsby links Crane's narrative to a lynching in New York State.

5. In the first pages of Jonathan Franzen's *Freedom* (London: Fourth Estate, 2010), late 1980s suburbanites wonder what to say "when a poor person of color accused you of destroying her neighborhood" (4, see also 6, 26 on black dispossession). The question yields to concerns about cloth diapers,

panhandlers, Volvo dashboards, and "life skills" (4). On the pressure to be extraordinary, usually by being competitive, see 9, 22 (Joey), 29–30 and 118 (Patty in sports), and 74, 134–137, 147, 247, 329, 131 and 186 (Walter). On the freedom to excel, see 91–92. Patty's maiden name is Emerson, an irony exposed in a passage about Patty's mother: "She needed to feel *extraordinary*, and becoming an Emerson reinforced her feeling that she was" (516). On the desire for fans, see 77–78, 119, and 248 (Patty), 243–245 (Joey), 208 (Walter and Lalitha), 137 (Walter fan of Richard), and 151, among many other passages. On Patty's desire to be raped, as she was when she first felt "free" as a teenager (35), see 127, 140, 181, 459–460, 508. See 169 on Patty being banged by Richard in the old house of Walter's mother (156, 166, 172), in part because Richard felt "defeated" by Walter (377). On Lalitha as "nigger" see 310; on Richard's black hair, shirt, and room, see 66–67, 162, 103, 162, 177. Richard recurrently feels the "allure of death" (347, 378–379).

Franzen's novel may be a quarrel with himself. His previous book of essays, *How to Be Alone*, declares that "writing is a form of personal freedom. It frees us from the mass identity we see in the making all around us" (95). Writers write "to save themselves, to survive as individuals" (96). See also 77, 81–83.

6. Ayaan Hirsi Ali, *Infidel* (New York: Free Press, 2008), 167–169. Islamic militants in Somalia continue to enforce the traditional punishment of killing women whose sexuality transgresses family control, even young women who have been raped. In late October 2008, a thirteen-year-old Somalian girl was stoned to death on a soccer field before 1,000 spectators. As UNICEF reported, three men had raped the girl as she walked along a road in Mogadishu to visit her grandmother. Her family reported the rapes to the authorities, who charged her with adultery and had fifty men stone her to death in a stadium in Kismayu, as the holy law of Sharia decrees. By early November, none of the three accused rapists had been arrested. See Jeffrey Gettleman, "Somalia: Rape Victim Executed," *New York Times*, October 29, 2008, A9; also "Rape Victim Stoned to Death in Somalia Was 13, U.N. Says," Reuters dispatch, *New York Times*, November 5, 2008. Gettleman erroneously reports the victim's age as 23.

7. Nathaniel Hawthorne, *The Scarlet Letter*, in *The Scarlet Letter and Other Writings*, edited by Leland S. Person (New York: W. W. Norton, 2005), 40–41.

8. Racial issues surface only twice in *Infidel*: when Islamic immigrants to the Netherlands resent being treated as black (224), and when her mother is racist about Kenyans. She sees them not only as "unbelievers, just like Ethiopians," but also as "filthy . . . cannibals." She calls them slaves and stones as well as infidels. To her they are "barely human." Hirsi Ali's grandmother says that the Kenyans "stank." For ten years "the two of them treated Kenyans almost exactly

as the Saudis had behaved toward us" (61). Later in the book Moroccans and Somalians say that Dutch people stink (221, 223).

9. Hawthorne, *The Scarlet Letter*, 48 (Rev. Wilson condemns Hester), 39–40 (town beadle represents Puritan law; dark and abundant hair).

10. Ibid., 126. T. Walter Herbert tries to equalize the naming by calling the minister "Arthur"; Herbert, *Sexual Violence and American Manhood* (Cambridge, Mass.: Harvard University Press, 2002). I've argued elsewhere that in chapter 5, Hester dreams of an eternal union with Dimmesdale in hell "for a joint futurity of endless retribution"; see my *Manhood and the American Renaissance* (Ithaca, N.Y.: Cornell University Press, 1989), 264. The quote is from Hawthorne, *The Scarlet Letter*, 56.

11. Hawthorne, *The Scarlet Letter*, 48.

12. David Greven, *Men beyond Desire: Manhood, Sex, and Violation in American Literature* (New York: Palgrave Macmillan, 2005), 254n8.

13. Hawthorne, *The Scarlet Letter*, 45.

14. Ibid., 44–45.

15. Ibid., 55. Larry Reynolds links the Black Man to fears of voodoo and witchcraft as well as "dark racial Others"; Reynolds, *Devils and Rebels: The Making of Hawthorne's Damned Politics* (Ann Arbor: University of Michigan Press, 2008), 88. Problematically, he defuses the racist charge by interpreting the Black Man as "an amalgamation of superstition and guilt" (166) and as "the fabulous ally" of rebels such as Hester (168). Trying to redeem Hawthorne from his indifference to slavery, Reynolds presents him as a pacifist and notes that Hawthorne once aided runaway slaves, an experience he suppressed (97, also 95–98).

16. Hawthorne, *The Scarlet Letter*, 164 (Dimmesdale's property), 53–54 (he shall be mine).

17. Hirsi Ali, *Infidel*, 210.

18. Herbert emphasizes the "eroticized punishment" of the opening scene and the "emotional rape" or "pornographic manhood" of the Chillingworth-Dimmesdale relationship; Herbert, *Sexual Violence and American Manhood*, 96, 100.

19. Hawthorne, *The Scarlet Letter*, 118 (holy whiteness of the clergyman's good fame), 119–121 (Black Man), 138 (total change of dynasty and moral code), 141 (infectious poison), 154–155 (voice resonates with anguish and pain), 157 (high and glorious destiny).

20. Ibid., 159–160.

21. Ibid., 163–164.

22. Ibid., 107–108. Elsewhere I argue that Hester's seemingly sensitive narrator subdues her spirit; see *Manhood and the American Renaissance*,

259–278. David Greven notes similarities between Hawthorne's narrators and Hannibal Lecter; Greven, *Men beyond Desire*, 124.

23. For the nervous responses of some contemporary American reviewers, see my *Manhood and the American Renaissance*, 277. Leland S. Person's Norton Critical Edition of *The Scarlet Letter* reprints seven major early reviews (237–274).

24. Hawthorne, *The Scarlet Letter*, 166.

25. In chapter 5, Hester dreams of being married to Dimmesdale "for a joint futurity of endless retribution" (56). As he dies, her lover rejects her ambiguous hope (162). See my *Manhood and the American Renaissance*, 264.

26. Hirsi Ali, *Nomad*, xx.

27. Ibid., xx.

28. Mark Twain, *Tom Sawyer Abroad; Tom Sawyer, Detective* (Berkeley: University of California Press, 1983), 60. Taking up Donald Gibson's argument in a 1968 essay, Jonathan Arac chastises critics for calling Jim "Nigger Jim"; Arac, *Huckleberry Finn as Idol and Target: The Functions of Criticism in Our Time* (Madison: University of Wisconsin Press, 1997). That critique is overstated. When Huck writes to the Widow Douglas, he tells her about "your runaway nigger Jim"; Mark Twain, *Adventures of Huckleberry Finn: Tom Sawyer's Comrade* (New York: Signet, 1959), 209) and speaks of "our nigger, Jim" (128) when telling his (fake) life story to the Duke and the Dauphin. Huck also begins *Tom Sawyer Abroad* by reminiscing about "the time we set the nigger Jim free" (1), and he starts *Tom Sawyer, Detective* (first published in 1896) by referring to "our old nigger Jim" (107, also 173).

29. Notebook #35, often quoted; see Henry Nash Smith, *Mark Twain: The Development of a Writer* (New York: Atheneum, 1972), 113–137, quote on 113.

30. Twain, *Adventures of Huckleberry Finn*, 86 (solid white fog), 88 (black speck on the water), 90 (ashamed).

31. Ibid., 90.

32. Ibid., 149.

33. Ibid., 162.

34. Ibid., 209–210.

35. F. Scott Fitzgerald, *The Great Gatsby* (New York: Scribner, 2004), 12–13.

36. Ibid., 34 (almost married a little kike), 139–140 (pale, well-dressed negro).

37. Fitzgerald's July 1921 letter to Wilson is quoted in Greg Forter, "F. Scott Fitzgerald, Modernist Studies, and the Fin-de-Siècle Crisis in Masculinity," *American Literature* 78 (June 2006): 306. Forter emphasizes Fitzgerald's fear of becoming "explicitly 'negroid' and implicitly female" (307).

38. Fitzgerald, *The Great Gatsby*, 2 (everything for which I have . . . scorn), 69

(three modish negroes); Ann Douglas, *Terrible Honesty: Mongrel Manhattan in the 1920s* (New York: Farrar, Straus & Giroux, 1995), 100–101.

39. Fitzgerald, *The Great Gatsby*, 8 (ballooned in white), 43 (slender golden arm), 130 (We're all white here), 52 (brown hand), 11 (gray eyes, also 58), 57 (bad lie), 116 (fingers powdered white), 177 (fingerless glove).

40. Ibid., 64 (a rich cream color), 123 (George: a nice yellow one), 139 (negro), 140 (Tom), 136 (Greek), 137 (green).

41. Ibid., 74 (little white roadster, also 77), 98 (Platonic conception of himself).

42. Ibid., 110.

43. Ibid., 154 (disapproved of him; against the white steps).

44. Here I'm reversing Walter Benn Michaels's argument that Fitzgerald's novel uses race to avoid class conflicts. Michaels argues that "Jimmy Gatz isn't quite white enough"; Michaels, *The Trouble with Diversity: How We Learned to Love Identity and Ignore Inequality* (New York: Metropolitan Books, 2006). 2. On the contrary, he's not quite upper-class enough, and Daisy isn't as white as his dreams would like to make her. See also Michaels's *Our America: Nativism, Modernism, and Pluralism* (Durham, N.C.: Duke University Press, 1995), 7, 23–28.

45. Fitzgerald, *The Great Gatsby*, 107 (upper-class bonding), 177 (lie to myself and call it honor).

46. Ibid., 180 (fresh, green breast of the new world; incomparable milk of wonder), also 120 (voice made of money).

47. Vladimir Nabokov, *Lolita* (New York: Vintage International, 1997), 60 (had been safely solipsized), 30 (middle-class Russian courtesy).

48. Nabokov toys with readers' expectations of sex scenes by arousing our hopes then withholding such descriptions after the first seduction. As Alfred Appel Jr. notes, "Nabokov's final joke on the subject" gives the "desire for high-brow pornography" a further turn of the screw by making pornographer Clare Quilty the reader's double. See Appel's edition of *The Annotated Lolita* (New York: McGraw-Hill, 1970), 428–429.

49. Nabokov, *Lolita*, 43 (intoxicating brown fragrance), 125 (honey-brown body), 133 (brown shoulder), 117–119 (handsome young Negress, an Uncle Tom, also 122), 119 (incest), 231 (apricot midriff, shoulder blades), 173–174 (my little Creole). Leslie Tomson and Louisa, "amiable" Negro servants, frame Charlotte's death (73, 82, 97–98, 102). Lolita's midwestern mother and late father (78) conceived Lolita as one of the "mementoes" of their honeymoon in Vera Cruz (57).

50. Ibid., 60 (radiant and robust Turk), 188 (spoiled little slave-child).

51. Ibid., 3 (title italicized), 9 (salad of racial genes; mother died), 167 (gold

and brown, kneeling). See also Humbert's first vision of Lolita as Annabel Leigh reincarnated, "peering at me over dark glasses" with her "honey-hued shoulders . . . chestnut head of hair . . . the tiny dark-brown mole on her side" (39).

52. On the murder as sexual farce, see ibid., 303 ("I was injecting spurts of energy into the poor fellow") and 299 ("He was naked and goatish under his robe . . . he rolled over me. I rolled over him. We rolled over me. They rolled over him. We rolled over us").

53. For Humbert's claims of love, see ibid., 234, 270, 280, 284, and 287.

54. Hawthorne, *The Scarlet Letter*, 45.

55. Ibid., 8–9. On the marketing of New England regions by consolidating the image of its villages, see Stephen Nissenbaum's superb essay, "New England as Region and Nation," in *All Over the Map: Rethinking American Regions*, edited by Edward L. Ayers, Patricia Nelson Limerick, Stephen Nissenbaum, and Peter S. Onuf (Baltimore, Md.: Johns Hopkins University Press, 1996), 38–61.

56. Wendell Phillips to Frederick Douglass, April 22, 1845, published in *Narrative of the Life of Frederick Douglass*, in *The Classic Slave Narratives*, edited by Henry Louis Gates Jr. (New York: Signet, 2002), 337. Larry Reynolds problematically argues that Hawthorne was a progressive on racial matters, opposing war but sympathizing with black rebels; Reynolds, *Devils and Rebels*, 25–26, 163–169, especially 168.

57. Fitzgerald, *The Great Gatsby*, 93.

58. Ibid., 176.

CHAPTER 5 — TWO WARS

1. See Bertram Wyatt-Brown, "Honor and American Diplomacy in Peace and War," *Clio's Psyche* 10 (December 2003): 82–83. Wyatt-Brown exempts only Jimmy Carter from presidents who sought to avenge humiliations and notes that Carter's decision not to wage war for Iran's hostages may have cost him the 1980 election. President Nixon also tried to placate American voters by reiterating the necessity for "peace with honor."

2. On imperialist nostalgia, see Renato Rosaldo, *Culture and Truth: The Remaking of Social Analysis* (Boston: Beacon Press, 1989). Matthew Frye Jacobson emphasizes the race-based paradoxes that shaped postbellum American imperialism, particularly the urge to regain vitality by appropriating "barbarian virtues"; the mixed desire to uplift and hold at bay inferior peoples, including immigrants; and the "combination of supreme confidence" and "an anxiety driven by fierce parochialism"; Jacobson, *Barbarian Virtues:*

The United States Encounters Foreign Peoples at Home and Abroad, 1876–1917 (New York: Hill and Wang, 2000), 262, 3–4, 265.

3. On the conflation of honor and manhood that legitimated going to war with Spain, see Kristin L. Hoganson, *Fighting for American Manhood: How Gender Politics Provoked the Spanish-American and Philippine-American Wars* (New Haven, Conn.: Yale University Press, 1998), 69–76. A navy inquiry concluded that an external mine of uncertain origin caused the explosion of the USS *Maine* in Havana's harbor on February 15, 1898, though a 1976 investigation concluded that "a spontaneous fire in the coal bunker . . . next to the powder supply" caused it (90). Hoganson questions a subsequent study that holds to the older theory (226–227n1). She notes that although President McKinley attributed his reluctant warrior resolve to a dream from God, widespread aspersions on his manhood may have played a role (104–106).

4. Ibid., 134–135 (Filipinos bestial rapists). Though Americans depicted Cubans as chivalrous (44–55), they portrayed Filipinos as barbarous (184–185) and generated reports about them that included mentions of venereal disease, homosexuality, "contaminated blood," and "miscegenation" (188–189). American brutality bolstered the antiwar case "that imperial policies were debasing American men" (184). On the etymology of "gook," see John Dower, "Yellow, Red, and Black Men," in *The Impact of Race on U.S. Foreign Policy: A Reader*, edited by Michael L. Krenn (New York: Garland Publishing, 1999), 200.

5. John Hope Franklin quoted in Eric T. L. Love, *Race over Empire: Racism and U.S. Imperialism, 1865–1900* (Chapel Hill: University of North Carolina Press, 2004), 8. See also chapter 1, "American Imperialism and the Racial Mountain," 1–26, and the preface and epilogue. The term "racial mountain" comes from Langston Hughes. After 1898 a new policy emerged that favored brief or selective annexation for Cuba, Panama, and Puerto Rico (200). Love contrasts opposition to the Louisiana Purchase and to the Mexican War (21) with the response to the purchase of Alaska (28). On Grant's plans for Santo Domingo, see xvi and chapter 2. In 1862, President Lincoln voiced similar hopes of recolonizing African Americans to solve the problem of the South (xvi).

6. The evidence in Love's *Race over Empire* partially contradicts Michael Adas's argument that white Americans'"can-do confidence" in their technological prowess has complemented "racially charged" assessments of darker-skinned foreigners to buttress imperial policies, especially toward Japanese, Filipino, and Vietnamese peoples; Adas, *Dominance by Design: Technological Imperatives and America's Civilizing Mission* (Cambridge, Mass.: Harvard University Press, 2005), 311. Love emphasizes the racist need to protect white superiority, whereas Adas emphasizes technology as the ultimate justi-

fication for white dominance. Anthony Marx argues that racial dominance functioned "to unify white nationalism and allow for state centralization" in both the United States and South Africa by diminishing class and sectional conflicts among white groups; Marx, *Making Race and Nation: A Comparison of South Africa, the United States, and Brazil* (Cambridge: Cambridge University Press, 1998), 16 (quote), 17, 25, 131 (on South Africa), 138–157 (on the United States). Marx notes that the United States differed from South Africa in defining as "black" anyone who can pass as black or (even more severely) with the one-drop rule. In South Africa, where whites were a minority seeking to expand their numbers, "white" was defined as anyone who could pass as white (73). In Brazil, the Portuguese elite could maintain control and privilege with "a more inclusive nationalism" instead of with "a racial divide" (16).

7. Kipling quoted in Love, *Race over Empire*, 6. Love's analysis of "The White Man's Burden" notes that the "churning irony and cynicism" of the poem ends with apocalyptic images of "servility, exile, and the cold judgment of their countrymen" as well as the "disillusion" of being judged contemptuously by the "'silent sullen peoples'" (6, 198).

8. Roosevelt, "Expansion of the White Races" (January 18, 1909), quoted in Douglas Blackmon, *Slavery by Another Name: The Re-Enslavement of Black Americans from the Civil War to World War II* (New York: Doubleday, 2008), 163; Mark Twain, *Following the Equator* (1897), quoted in Jacobson, *Barbarian Virtues*, 109. Roosevelt's Great White Fleet toured the world from December 1907 to February 1909. John McCain notes that in 1908 his grandfather ended his first navy tour of Asia by sailing for home on its flagship; McCain with Mark Salter, *Faith of My Fathers* (New York: Perennial, 2000), 24. Love teases out Roosevelt's changing stances toward imperialism; Love, *Race over Empire*, 12, 196–200. More problematically, James Bradley blames Roosevelt's secret and unratified pact with Japan in 1905 for encouraging Japanese expansion into Korea and the imperialism that led to Pearl Harbor, as if Japanese agency played a subordinate part; Bradley, *The Imperial Cruise: A Secret History of Empire and War* (New York: Little, Brown, 2009).

9. Mark Twain's poem "My Last Thought" quoted in Susan K. Harris, "Mark Twain and José Rizal," paper presented at the 21st Annual Conference of the American Literature Association, San Francisco, California, May 27, 2010. According to Harris, Twain supported freeing Cuba and initially supported invading the Philippines but turned against U.S. intervention after the United States suppressed the Filipinos' guerilla war for independence (1899–1902). Michael Adas argues that the colonial war in the Philippines became "a vast engineering project" (144) that led to an "ambiguous" variety in American racial assessments; *Dominance by Design*, 144, 157, and 129–182.

10. "Text: Obama's Speech in Cairo," *New York Times*, June 4, 2009.

11. Paul Spickard, *Almost All Aliens: Immigration, Race, and Colonialism in American History and Identity* (New York: Routledge, 2007), 247–248. Spickard argues that white immigrants established their racial dominance as the context for all subsequent entering groups and established racialized hierarchy among whites, especially after the Civil War (see 227–340). The courts equated "Christian" with citizen, especially in the early twentieth century, Spickard says (260).

12. For the etymology of "Barbary," see Paul Baepler, "Introduction," in *White Slaves, African Masters: An Anthology of American Barbary Captivity Narratives*, edited by Paul Baepler (Chicago: University of Chicago Press, 1999), 2–3.

13. Michael B. Oren, *Power, Faith, and Fantasy: America in the Middle East, 1776 to the Present* (New York: W. W. Norton, 2007), 41. In May 2009, Oren—born in upstate New York and raised in New Jersey—was appointed as Israel's ambassador to the United States.

14. For example, Robert Allison uses the phrase "the Specter of Islam" in one of his chapter titles in *The Crescent Obscured: The United States and the Muslim World, 1776–1815* (New York: Oxford University Press, 1995). Frank Lambert argues that "the Barbary Wars were primarily about trade, not theology" and faults Allison and others for presentist interpretations prompted by the 1986 bombing of Libya and the 1991 Gulf War, even before 9/11. Lambert tends to reduce the complexity of early American assessments of North African Arabs to "dyads" between "despicable" pirates and "lofty" Americans or "liberty versus tyranny and good versus evil"; Lambert, *The Barbary Wars: American Independence in the Atlantic World* (New York: Hill & Wang, 2005), 8, 7, and 105–107.

15. Robert Battistini, "Glimpses of the Other before Orientalism: The Muslim World in Early American Periodicals, 1785–1800," *Early American Studies* 8 (Spring 2010): 446–474. Battistini notes that several writers imagined "a complex and fascinating Muslim world, not a monolithic Other" (458), at least until "fear and rage" erupted in 1793 and 1794, when "the capacious, relativisitic position was rejected in favor of a local, biased, and defensive one" (471). Then narratives began to present two Muslim worlds: Persia, Arabia, and Turkey were good, but the Barbary States were bad (460). Throughout, a profusion of articles and translations about Muslims mixed uncertainty, curiosity, "and even delight" (473) in what Battistini called "this blurry Other" (470), as the United States moved from "a pan-European Enlightenment cosmopolitanism" (447) toward an imperial nation-state. I'm indebted to Ed White for this reference.

16. On how Susanna Rowson's *Slaves in Algiers* uses the Algerian Orient "as an enabling sexual space for women" to develop "an emancipatory feminist discourse" while preserving racial hierarchy, see Malini Johar Schueller, *U.S. Orientalisms: Race, Nation, and Gender in Literature, 1790–1890* (Ann Arbor: University of Michigan Press, 1998), 61–67, quotes on 65 and 61. Lawrence A. Peskin notes the antislavery aspects of Rowson's play and other contemporary texts. He points out that the two perfunctory chapters in Royall Tyler's *The Algerine Captive* about the American South have little to say about the slavery the narrator encounters there, except to expose a white parson's brutality and hypocrisy. Tyler's narrator is much more graphic when he describes the horrific abuses of Africans on the slave ship *Sympathy* as a lead-in to his own capture; Peskin, *Captives and Countrymen: Barbary Slavery and the American Public, 1785–1816* (Baltimore, Md.: Johns Hopkins University Press, 2009), 79–80, 93–107. On the complexity of Tyler's "critical transnational consciousness," see Timothy Marr, *The Cultural Roots of American Islamicism* (Cambridge: Cambridge University Press, 2006), 55. See also 50–52 (on Rowson's play), 26–34 (on American humiliation), and 141–146 (on slavery). Marr notes that prisoners from Tripoli were taken to New York theater shows as exotic spectacles (67–68).

17. On Franklin's editorial, which he signed "Historicus," see Baepler, "Introduction," in Baepler, *White Slaves, African Masters*, 8. Europe's navies fought with Barbary pirates from the early seventeenth century on. In the 1620s and 1630s, Algiers had thousands of Christian captives (ibid., 2–3).

18. James Cathcart, *The Captives*, reprinted in Baepler, *White Slaves, African Masters*, 103–104. See also 142–144 (Cathcart's harangue, quote on 143), 110, 141 (indignities), 114 (humiliation), 145 (extricate us with honor). Cathcart, who had a talent for impressing people, began his rise by purchasing a prison tavern (137–138). Later he got loans from the dey and the Swedish consul. After his return he became U.S. consul general to the Barbary States (103). The narrative was compiled by his daughter from his journal entries and was first published in 1899 (104).

19. Michael Kitzen, "Money Bags or Cannon Balls: The Origins of the Tripolitan War, 1795–1801," *Journal of the Early Republic* 16 (Winter 1996): 603–604; Oren, *Power, Faith, and Fantasy*, 22, 34; Baepler, "Introduction," 8. On the Barbary Wars, see Oren, 21–23, 75, and 17–40, 51–79. On the complex politics that led to Tripoli's declaration of war in 1801 (including President Adams's waffling indifference), see Kitzen. For a more detailed history, see Allison, *The Crescent Obscured*; and Lambert, *The Barbary Wars*. See also Caleb Crain, "Introduction by Caleb Crain," in Royall Tyler, *The Algerine Captive; or, The Life and Adventures of Doctor Updike Underhill; Six Years a Prisoner among*

the Algerines (New York: Modern Library, 2002), xxviii–xxxi; see also 252n2, 255n3. Gordon Wood notes that the United States' 1786 peace agreement with Morocco remains our longest continuous treaty; Wood, *Empire of Liberty: A History of the Early Republic, 1789–1815* (New York: Oxford University Press, 2009), 634, also 633–639 and 696 on the wars.

20. On the 1790 census, see Crain, "Introduction by Caleb Crain," xxviii.

21. Lambert, *The Barbary Wars*, 93; Baepler, *White Slaves, African Masters*. On various U.S. payments for ransoms, treaties, and tributes, see Oren, *Power, Faith, and Fantasy*, e.g., 33 ($140,000 in 1790), 37 ($650,000 for ransom in 1797, loaned by "a Jewish businessman in Algiers"), 38 (another $160,000 for the treaty in 1797), and 68 (100 prisoners of war and $60,000 for 297 Americans in 1805). Lambert puts the 1794 treaty with Algiers as $600,000 plus another $600,000 at signing (81). Richard Parker estimates that the cost of the 1797 treaty was $172,500, the equivalent of $2.6 million in 2007; Parker, *Uncle Sam in Barbary: A Diplomatic History* (Gainesville: University Press of Florida, 2004), 42. Lambert puts it at $180,000, along with a $40,000 treaty with Tripoli plus $12,000 in presents in 1796 (92–93) and notes that none of these treaties stopped demands for more (98–99).

22. Jefferson quoted in Oren, *Power, Faith, and Fantasy*, 24, 75. Jefferson wanted war, but he opposed a strong central government. On this point, see also Lambert, *The Barbary Wars*, 79–80; and Allison, *The Crescent Obscured*, 24. He wouldn't declare war until Congress authorized it. He was appalled at the idea that American women captives might be violated in harems, though he continued his sexual relationship with Sally Hemings; Oren, 23–24; Wood, *Empire of Liberty*, 635–638.

23. Israel Pickens quoted in Peskin, *Captives and Countrymen*, 190. See also 104 (on suspicions of England's machinations). Peskin also emphasizes the honor at stake. In the South, "honor culture dictated that planters . . . take umbrage at each slight to their honor. . . . The greatest insult was to be labeled a coward" (138). On the restoration of national honor in 1815, see ibid., 202 and 213.

24. On war expenses, see Oren, *Power, Faith, and Fantasy*, 75; and Kitzen, "Money Bags or Cannon Balls," 624. The Louisiana Purchase cost $15 million dollars—a $3 million down payment in gold, the rest in bonds. One cause of the 1801–1805 war with Tripoli came from an impasse regarding previous treaties between the United States and Algiers. The dey of Algiers, Hassan Bashaw, had guaranteed the 1796–1797 treaties with Tripoli and Tunis. But he died in 1798, and the new dey said he wasn't bound by the treaty. The United States said that a treaty was between nations, not persons. The new dey disagreed and refused to rein in Tripoli's bashaw, especially since Algiers had just been

very successful in wars with Denmark and Sweden. See Kitzen, 609, 611, 613, 615, and 618.

25. Parker, *Uncle Sam in Barbary*, 161.

26. Wood, *Empire of Liberty*, 634; Kitzen, "Money Bags or Cannon Balls," 609. The dey of Algiers, the bey of Tunis, and the bashaw of Tripoli (various historians use different terms for each ruler) negotiated tributes from the United States in 1796–1797, while the bashaw fought Denmark in 1797–1798. Inexplicably, President John Adams rejected an invitation from Sweden and Denmark to join naval forces in 1800. Soon Sweden capitulated to the bashaw, who then declared war on the United States. In 1800 the United States hadn't paid Algiers for two years, though Adams left Jefferson a substantial surplus; ibid., 617–618, 620, 624. Peskin declares that the United States refused to pay any ransom to the dey of Algiers until a 1796 treaty, highlighting globalization as a context; Peskin, *Captives and Countrymen*, 2–3, 211–214. For Wood the real issue was always the conflict with Britain; see *Empire of Liberty*, 639. Lambert argues that the wars "pitted two marginal players in the Atlantic world against each other as each sought to better its position vis-à-vis Europe's maritime powers"; Lambert, *Barbary Wars*, 200. Jefferson said that the Barbary Wars were a "sideshow"; quoted in ibid., 7. Only after the conclusion of the War of 1812 did Congress finally declare war on Algiers; Wood, 696.

27. Oren, *Power, Faith, and Fantasy*, 29 (Washington), 54 (Jefferson). On annual payments by France and England, see David McCullough, *John Adams* (New York: Simon & Schuster, 2001), 352. McCullough takes both sides: "It was extortion and an accepted part of the cost of commerce in that part of the world."

28. On Decatur in 1815, see Oren, *Power, Faith, and Fantasy*, 73–75; and Robert J. Allison, *Stephen Decatur: American Naval Hero, 1779–1820* (Amherst: University of Massachusetts Press, 2005), 175–178. Allison claims that Decatur became "the nation's idol" (177).

29. Oren, *Power, Faith, and Fantasy*, 75, 78.

30. Tyler, *Algerine Captive*, 226. Tyler concludes, in capital letters, "BY UNITING WE STAND, BY DIVIDING WE FALL." Gordon M. Sayre over-states the case for making religion, not nationality, the basis for American and European fascination with captivity narratives (356–357), though he rightly notes "the literary origins of US nationalism, whiteness, and imperialism" in narratives about "white" captives in Barbary (350). See also Brian Edwards's response to Sayre's article, emphasizing that after World War II, Americans projected domestic anxieties about race onto North Africans and Arabs (363–366); Sayres, "Renegades from Barbary: The Transnational Turn in Captivity Studies," *American Literary History* 22 (Summer 2010): 356–359, 350.

31. Annette Gordon-Reed, *Thomas Jefferson and Sally Hemings: An American Controversy* (Charlottesville: University Press of Virginia, 1997), 231–232. Gordon-Reed notes that the prostitute incident appears in a 1950s biography of Madison but not in Dumas Malone's six-volume biography of Jefferson (232). The ambassador was Sidi Suliman Mellimelli, or "Sidi Soliman Mellimelni (or Mellimelli)," as Marr refers to him; Marr, *The Cultural Roots of American Islamicism*, 66–67.

32. For Decatur's toast in Norfolk, Virginia, see Allison, *Stephen Decatur*, 183–185, Allison's italics. The second part of the toast has usually been misquoted (and improved) as "our country, right or wrong," though Allison's versions of the toast are confusing. On Decatur's dictation of peace terms to Algiers, see Daniel Walker Howe, *What Hath God Wrought: The Transformation of America, 1815–1848* (New York: Oxford University Press, 2007), 77–79. On Decatur and duels, see Allison, *Stephen Decatur*, 3–7, 26, 94–95, and 208–217. He was 41 when he was killed.

33. In 1797, after the United States refused to honor the 1778 treaty with France in part because of the French Revolution, French warships captured many American ships. French foreign minister Talleyrand demanded a $250,000 bribe and a $12 million loan to open negotiations. "Not one sixpence," Charles Pinckney replied. American newspapers transformed his response into "Millions for defense, but not one cent for tribute." Later, in an 1815 issue of *Niles' Weekly Register*, Hezekiah Niles applied that quotation to the Barbary War; Peskin, *Captives and Countrymen*, 202.

34. Oren, *Power, Faith, and Fantasy*, 77. Francis Scott Key revised the lyrics of "The Star-Spangled Banner" after watching a night battle with the British in 1814; the song became the national anthem in 1931. In his introduction to *White Slaves, African Masters*, Baepler sums up the attacks and reversals. In 1803, a U.S. frigate ran aground at night in Tripoli's harbor and was captured with 307 sailors. In 1804, 25-year-old Stephen Decatur led a daring assault on the captured ship to burn it so it couldn't be used for raiding. In 1805, the marines captured the fort at Derna, which Oren calls "Darna," (77) and Gordon Wood calls "Derne" (*Empire of Liberty*, 638). See also John Picker, "Two National Anthems," in *A New Literary History of America*, edited by Greil Marcus and Werner Sollors (Cambridge, Mass.: Harvard University Press, 2009), 87–88, quoting Key's description of African Americans as an "inferior race."

35. According to Ed Buckner, the Senate's passage of the 1797 treaty was only its third unanimous vote; Buckner, "Does the 1796–97 Treaty with Tripoli Matter to Church/State Separation?" available at www.stephenjaygould.org/ctrl/buckner_tripoli.html. Neither Lambert's *Barbary Wars* (92) nor Allison's *Crescent Obscured* (22) mentions the treaty except in passing. Jon Meacham

has mentioned it in several *Newsweek* columns, as does Jill Lepore in *The Whites of Their Eyes: The Tea Party's Revolution and the Battle over American History* (Princeton, N.J.: Princeton University Press, 2010), 150.

36. According to Richard Parker, the Arab version survives in a letter from the dey of Algiers to Tripoli's ruler, Yusuf Pasha. Three-fourths of the letter may have been a secretary's "ignorant bombast." Parker speculates that Yusuf Pasha "may have been illiterate, and unaware of the significance of what he signed"; Parker, *Uncle Sam in Barbary*, 257, 134. On Richard O'Brien as the negotiator deputized by Joel Barlow, see xiv, 133. The Dutch Orientalist was Dr. C. Snouk Hugronie.

37. Stephen Labaton, "McCain Casts Muslims as Less Fit to Lead," *New York Times*, September 30, 2007, A21. After the interview, McCain clarified his statement by saying "I would vote for a Muslim if he or she was the candidate best able to lead our country and defend our political values"; "McCain: I'd Prefer Christian President," MSNBC.com, October 1, 2007, available at http://www.msnbc.msn.com/id/21080742/ns/politics-decision_08/t/mccain-id-prefer-christian-president/. Citing Article 11, Jon Meacham critiques McCain's assertions; see "A Nation of Christians Is Not a Christian Nation," *New York Times*, October 7, 2007, WK15.

38. Isaac Kramnick and R. Laurence Moore champion the "wall of separation between church and state" (Jefferson's phrase); Kramnick and Moore, *The Godless Constitution: A Moral Defense of the Secular State*, rev. ed. (New York: W. W. Norton, 2005), 97. Many state governments did affirm their Christian foundations.

39. Tyler, *Algerine Captive*, 100 ("white beasts"), 125–138 ("Mollah"; quote on 136), 161 (blaming the British). Near the end, Tyler's narrative portrays a greedy, deceiving Jew who repeatedly betrays the narrator after he trusted a good Jew; see 200–205 and 194–196. In many chapters the narrative becomes a travelogue, with ample discussion of Islam's history and beliefs; see 154–196.

40. George Henry Lane Fox Pitt-Rivers, *The Clash of Culture and the Contact of Races, an Anthropological and Psychological Study of the Laws of Racial Adaptability, with Special Reference to the Depopulation of the Pacific and the Government of Subject Races* (New York: Negro Universities Press, 1969), 86–114 ("inbreeding" versus "race extinction" through miscegenation), 234–241 ("The White Man's Task" to colonize without uplift), 58 (no clothing), 141, 192 (no monogamy), 115–141 (virtues of polygamy), 268 (polygamy versus hybridity and extinction), 267–269 (the "Navaho"), 134 (sterility), 174 (imitative Africans compared to reasoning whites), 81–82 (all Jews are "narrow-chested"). See the obituary of his son, Julian Pitt-Rivers, who hated him, and whose anthropological work illuminates honor-shame societies ("Professor Julian Pitt-Rivers,"

The Independent, August 25, 2001, available at http://www.independent.co.uk/
news/obituaries/professor-julian-pittrivers-729358.html).

41. Samuel P. Huntington, *The Clash of Civilizations and the Remaking of World Order* (New York: Simon & Schuster, 2003), 213, quoting Bernard Lewis, "The Roots of Muslim Rage: Why So Many Muslims Deeply Resent the West and Why Their Bitterness Will Not Be Easily Mollified," *Atlantic Monthly*, September 1990, 60.

42. Tamar Lewin, "Samuel P. Huntington, 81, Political Scientist, Is Dead," *New York Times*, December 29, 2008, A19. The obituary notes that Huntington "opposed the invasion of Iraq and had little sympathy for the neoconservatives of the Bush administration." See Fareed Zakaria's reminiscence about his mentor, "Sam Huntington, 1927–2008," *Newsweek*, January 12, 2009, 41.

43. John Higham, *Strangers in the Land: Patterns of American Nativism 1860–1925*, 2nd ed. (New York: Atheneum, 1973), especially 136–144. See also Nicholas Kristof, "America's History of Fear," *New York Times*, September 5, 2010, WK10.

44. Huntington, *The Clash of Civilizations*, 45–47. Oddly, Huntington excludes Russia from his big five, then includes Russia in his list (45–46).

45. Ibid., 258. Melani McAlister briefly critiques Huntington's "deeply conservative position"; McAlister, *Epic Encounters: Culture, Media, and U.S. Interests in the Middle East, 1945–2000* (Berkeley: University of California Press, 2001), 267–269.

46. Huntington, *The Clash of Civilizations*, 209.

47. Ibid., 175 (small-group identifications and large-scale faith), 268 (U-shaped identity, also 249), 177 (Western model alien to the traditions of Islam).

48. Ibid., 40 (barbarians), 183 (Sinic assertiveness).

49. Ibid., 217–218

50. Ibid., 321 (yielding to barbarism, global Dark Ages). See also 81–121 on the decline of the West. Huntington argues that though the West is still temporarily triumphant, power will become "increasingly dispersed" in the twenty-first century (91). He urges the United States to reaffirm its core identity and expansive role as "the leader of Western civilization" (308).

51. Ibid., 321.

52. Ibid., 313–316. Huntington doesn't say Third World War, perhaps because he considers World War II "the West's civil war" (144), oddly erasing Japan's role.

53. Ibid., 316.

54. Ibid. Despite his descriptions of competing universalisms, Huntington advances "the *commonalities rule*" that people should "attempt to expand the

values, institutions, and practices they have in common with peoples of other civilizations" (320, Huntington's italics).

55. Ibid., 304–307.

56. Ibid., 307.

57. Richard Nixon, "Address to the Nation on the Situation in Southeast Asia," April 30, 1970, available at www.presidency.ucsb.edu/ws/index.php?pid=2490. As Huntington notes, hypocrisy has been one of the prime attributes of universalism; Huntington, *The Clash of Civilizations*, 184.

58. Huntington, *Who Are We? The Challenges to America's National Identity* (New York: Simon & Schuster, 2004), 67–68 (creed), 68 (dissenting Protestantism). Huntington takes the creed from Gunnar Myrdal's 1944 book on white racism, *An American Dilemma* (Huntington, 66).

59. Huntington, *Who Are We?* 18 (core eroded), 399 (choosing an ethnic identity like joining a club), 303–307 (mixed ancestries), 319 (creeping bilingualism).

60. Lawrence Wright, *The Looming Tower: Al-Qaeda and the Road to 9/11* (New York: Vintage Books, 2006), 237.

61. Steven Lee Myers and Alissa J. Rubin, "Iraqi Journalist Hurls Shoes at Bush and Denounces Him on TV as a 'Dog,'" *New York Times*, December 15, 2008, A6. Some accounts said al-Zaidi was 28; others said he was 29.

62. On March 12, 2009, al-Zaidi was sentenced to three years in jail after the charge had been downgraded from assault of a foreign head of state to assault of an official during the execution of his duties. Riyadh Mohammed and Anwar J. Ali, "Iraqi Who Threw Shoes Is Sentenced to 3 Years," *New York Times*, March 13, 2009, A5. On al-Zaidi's twenty-five lawyers, see Campbell Robertson, "At Trial, Iraqi Calls Shoe-Throwing Payback," *New York Times*, February 20, 2009, A12. He was released in mid-September 2009 after serving nine months.

63. For riveting accounts of presumption and dysfunction in early U.S. governance of Iraq, see Rajiv Chandrasekaran, *Imperial Life in the Emerald City: Inside Iraq's Green Zone* (New York: Vintage Books, Random House, 2006); and Thomas Ricks, *Fiasco: The American Military Adventure in Iraq*, 2nd ed. (New York: Penguin Group, 2007).

64. Mark Danner, *Torture and Truth: America, Abu Ghraib, and the War on Terror* (New York: New York Review Books, 2004), 1.

65. Wright, *The Looming Tower*, 45; see also 11 and 61–67 on humiliation as the basic spark for political jihad. Several *New York Times* columns by Thomas L. Friedman have emphasized humiliation as a key factor in tensions throughout the Middle East. See for example Friedman, "Still Not Tired," *New York Times*, October 4, 2009, WK8. Malini Johar Schueller argues that

universalizing invocations of "transnational" and "global" avoid confronting structures of inequality and domination; Schueller, *Locating Race: Global Sites of Post-Colonial Citizenship* (Albany: SUNY Press, 2009), 166.

66. Wright, *The Looming Tower*, 27. In Colorado, Qutb wondered why Americans called their violent sport football when "the foot does not play any role in the game. . . . Meantime, the fans cry out, 'Break his neck! Crack his head!'"; quoted on 23.

67. Ibid., 237–238.

68. "Bin Laden's Warning: Full Text," *BBC News*, October 7, 2001.

69. Neil MacFarquhar, "Tapes Offer a Look Beneath the Surface of bin Laden and Al Qaeda," *New York Times*, September 11, 2008, A14. The scholar is Flagg Miller.

70. On the "Left Behind" novels by Tim LaHaye and Jerry Jenkins, see Melani McAlister, "Left Behind and the Politics of Prophecy Talk," in *Exceptional State: Contemporary U.S. Culture and the New Imperialism*, edited by Ashley Dawson and Malini Johar Schueller (Durham, N.C.: Duke University Press, 2007),191–220. The apocalyptic series affirms multiracial salvation but omits Palestine, Palestinians, and American Jews while dramatizing the conversion of Israel's Jews (196–197, 210). McAlister notes that the "average buyer . . . is a Southern, white, married female between the ages of twenty-five and fifty-four" (204).

71. Wright, *The Looming Tower*, 203 (revenge for injustices), 48 (submission the meaning of Islam). In *The Clash of Civilizations*, Samuel Huntington notes the pan-national Arab resentments at the "humiliation" of Iraq's defeat in the Gulf War (251).

72. Wright, *The Looming Tower*, 61, 67.

73. Bush vowed to "punish those responsible for these cowardly acts"; quoted in Oren, *Power, Faith, and Fantasy*, 584.

74. After waiting several weeks at the administration's request, CBS showed the photos on April 28, 2004, because Seymour M. Hersh was about to break the story in *The New Yorker*.

75. Quoted in Danner, *Torture and Truth*, 18. Oren notes that GIs were given a "laminated Iraqi Culture Smart Card" with advice about manners and cultural conflicts; Oren, *Power, Faith, and Fantasy*, 591. See also Malini Johar Schueller, "Techno-Dominance and Torturegate," in *Exceptional State: Contemporary U.S. Culture and the New Imperialism*, edited by Ashley Dawson and Malini Johar Schueller (Durham, N.C.: Duke University Press, 2007), 172–173.

76. Charles A. Graner Jr. to Joseph M. Darby, quoted in Danner, *Torture and*

Truth, 215. Graner had been a prison guard in Pennsylvania before he went to Iraq.

77. Bradley quotes the lyrics to this water torture song in *The Imperial Cruise*, 108–109.

78. Bush quoted in Danner, *Torture and Truth*, 23, see also 27.

79. Ibid., 48. Elsewhere in the August 2004 report, James R. Schlesinger, a former secretary of defense, characterized the behavior as just "*Animal House* on the night shift" (28).

80. Ibid., 29. On the ubiquity of casual racism among American soldiers, see Aidan Delgado, *The Sutras of Abu Ghraib: Notes from a Conscientious Objector* (Boston: Beacon Press, 2007); and Delgado's interview with Bob Herbert, "From 'Gook' to 'Raghead,'" *New York Times*, May 2, 2005.

81. Glenda Gilmore, *Defying Dixie: The Radical Roots of Civil Rights, 1919–1950* (New York: W. W. Norton, 2008), 8. Gilmore agrees with Jacqueline Dowd Hall that "the Long Civil Rights Movement" began in the 1920s.

82. See Ali H. Soufan, "What Torture Never Told Us," *New York Times*, September 6, 2009, WK9. Soufan interrogated accused Islamic terrorists after the invasion of Iraq. What the administration called "enhanced interrogation techniques" were counterproductive, Soufan concludes, since they resulted mostly in false information. The program ended in 2005.

83. Oren, *Power, Faith, and Fantasy*, 586. On pre-9/11 plans to invade Iraq, see Lloyd C. Gardner, *The Long Road to Baghdad: A History of U.S. Foreign Policy from the 1970s to the Present* (New York: New Press, 2008), especially 121–129 on Cheney. In *Fiasco*, Ricks notes that Cheney publicly "called for war" against Iraq on August 26, 2002 (49).

84. John McCain, *Faith of Our Fathers*, especially 345–346 on Vietnam as "the first lost war in American history." McCain wrote that Robert McNamara and the other "civilian commanders" were "complete idiots who didn't have the least notion of what it took to win the war" (186).

85. For these and other instances, see Joseph M. Siracusa, "The Munich Analogy," *Gale Encyclopedia of U.S. Foreign Policy*, available at www.answers.com/topic/the-munich-analogy.

86. In *Fiasco*, Ricks notes Wolfowitz's repeated comparisons of Iraq to Nazi Germany and the Holocaust, in which "he had lost most of his Polish extended family" (16, also 386, 24–28). Douglas Feith also "came from a family devastated by the Holocaust" (77). On Shinseki's removal, see 157 and 412. Shinseki had also argued for many more U.S. troops in Iraq. President Obama appointed him as secretary for veterans' affairs. For Kanan Makiya's characterization of Iraq as a "tin-pot little dictatorship," see George Packer, *The Assassins' Gate: America in Iraq* (New York: Farrar, Strauss and Giroux, 2005), 46. For

European allies who told President Johnson that Munich had no relevance to Vietnam, see George McTurnan Kahin and John W. Lewis, *The United States in Vietnam*, rev. ed. (New York: Dell Publishing Company, 1969), 303.

87. Ricks, *Fiasco*, 168.

88. On the lack of planning, despite warning reports, see Ricks, *Fiasco*, 68–84; Chandrasekaran, *Imperial Life in the Emerald City*, 32–42; and Packer, *The Assassins' Gate*, 120–135. Rumsfeld quoted in Ron Suskind, *The Way of the World: A Story of Truth and Hope in an Age of Extremism* (New York: Harper-Collins, 2008), 380.

89. Packer, *The Assassins' Gate*, 454–455; see also 457–458 on Iraq's disintegration.

90. Ibid., 161 (half urban, half bedouin), 461 (Iraq tribal).

91. Kahin and Lewis, *The United States in Vietnam*, especially chapter 5, "The Origins of the Civil War," 99–126; *The Fog of War: Eleven Lessons from the Life of Robert S. McNamara*, documentary film directed by Errol Morris, DVD, Sony Pictures Home Entertainment, 2003.

92. On Wolfowitz's presumption that Iraq had sponsored bin Laden, see Packer, *The Assassins' Gate*, 40. On the fake letter that Tahir Jalil Habbush sent—an impeachable offense—see Suskind, *The Way of the World*, 361–373; see also 374–380 on its uncritical reception.

93. Packer, *The Assassins' Gate*, 65. Packer notes that Bernard Lewis and Fouad Ajami urged the United States to modernize Arab states against their will. Iraq would be "the starting point" for transforming Islamic society from sickness to health (51–53). As Packer concludes, "the neoconservatives saw American power in almost messianic terms" (74).

94. In *Imperial Life in the Emerald City*, Chandrasekaran emphasizes that when Paul Bremer dissolved the Iraqi security forces, he "disrespected" the "honor" of the soldiers and turned most of them into insurgents (88). In *Fiasco*, Ricks states that "personal dignity" is "perhaps the core value of Iraqi culture" (139). See also 192 on "Iraqi pride, and the humiliation Iraqi men felt to be occupied by this Western army." Ricks writes that Iraqis frequently fired "honor shots" not to kill but to take a stand, thus restoring honor, though Americans concluded "that the Iraqis were bad shots" (252).

95. Packer, *The Assassins' Gate*, 45. Melani McAlister suggests that in 1980, the Iran hostage crisis made Islam a synecdoche for racialized external threats; McAlister, *Epic Encounters*, 275.

96. John B. Kelly, quoted in Huntington, *The Clash of Civilizations*, 116.

97. Amy Kaplan, "Black and Blue on San Juan Hill," in *Cultures of United States Imperialism*, edited by Amy Kaplan and Donald E. Pease (Durham, N.C.: Duke University Press, 1993), 231. Alexander Saxton discusses Roosevelt's

changing assessment of black soldiers in Cuba in *The Rise and Fall of the White Republic: Class Politics and Mass Culture in Nineteenth-Century America*, rev. ed. (London: Verso, 2003), 375–376.

98. The two secretaries of state were Colin Powell and Condoleezza Rice, the commanding general was Ricardo Sanchez, and the deputy director of operations and public military spokesman was Brig. Gen. Vincent K. Brooks.

99. For two fine studies of the Middle East and Asia in American popular culture after World War II, see McAlister, *Epic Encounters* and Christina Klein, *Cold War Orientalism: Asia in the Middlebrow Imagination, 1945–1961* (Berkeley: University of California Press, 2003).

100. Evelin Lindner, *Making Enemies: Humiliation and International Conflict* (Westport, Conn.: Praeger Security International, 2006), 172. See also Bertram Wyatt-Brown, "Honor and American Diplomacy," 81; and Thomas Friedman, "The Humiliation Factor," *New York Times*, November 9, 2003, WK11.

CHAPTER 6 — THE 2008 CAMPAIGN

1. Brian Williams pointedly summed up the story's significance for the campaign on his October 24, 2008, *NBC Nightly News* report: "The McCain campaign steered reporters' attention to the story. John McCain even called the 20-year-old woman. Sarah Palin called her family."

2. Van Jones, "Shirley Sherrod and Me," *New York Times*, July 25, 2010, WK10. In 2009, Jones—a black man—was forced to resign from his position as a White House special adviser for environmental jobs because he had made a vulgar statement about Republicans and because he was falsely accused of signing a statement blaming President Bush for the 9/11 attacks. Shirley Sherrod, a black employee in the Department of Agriculture, was fired in July 2010 because a doctored video showed her as a racist instead of as someone who talked about overcoming her racism.

3. For the LBJ quotation, see Timothy Noah, "Forget the South, Democrats," *Slate*, January 27, 2004, See also Elizabeth Drew, "The Truth about the Election," *New York Review of Books*, December 18, 2008, 94. William Leuchtenburg notes the rage of southern whites during the 1964 campaign. The five states were Georgia, South Carolina, Alabama, Mississippi, and Louisiana. Despite Johnson's lingering prejudice against black people, he gave an extraordinary speech in New Orleans on October 9, 1964. He quoted an old southern senator who told a young Sam Rayburn that he wanted to give a speech arguing for doing social good, but "all they ever hear at election time is '*Nigra, Nigra, Nigra*.'" After a shocked pause, there was tumultuous applause. Leuchtenburg notes that even the president's critics called it "Johnson's finest hour"; Leuchtenburg, *The White House Looks South: Franklin D. Roosevelt, Harry S.*

Truman, Lyndon B. Johnson (Baton Rouge: Louisiana State University Press, 2005), 314–322, quote at 321. See also David Remnick, *The Life and Rise of Barack Obama* (New York: Alfred A. Knopf, 2010), 478–480.

4. The Quayle Vice Presidential Learning Center in Huntington, Indiana, celebrates Quayle's first campaign. On linking "starve the beast" to the "black-beast rapist," see Ivan Evans, *Cultures of Violence: Lynching and Racial Killing in South Africa and the American South* (Manchester: Manchester University Press, and New York: Palgrave Macmillan, 2009), 257. Robert J. Norrell's essay-review, "Modern Conservatism and the Consequences of Its Ideas," *Reviews in American History* 36 (September 2008): 456–467, considers several books highlighting the Southern Strategy; see 447 for Reagan. Norrell agrees with Matthew Lassiter and Kevin M. Kruse, whose books argued that the new conservatism reflected the insulation of white suburbanites. See Lassiter, *The Silent Majority: Suburban Politics in the Sunbelt South* (Princeton, N.J.: Princeton University Press, 2006); and Kruse, *White Flight: Atlanta and the Making of Modern Conservatism* (Princeton, N.J.: Princeton University Press, 2005). See also Norrell's fine book, *The House I Live In: Race in the American Century* (New York: Oxford University Press, 2005); and Julian E. Zelizer, "Rethinking the History of American Conservatism," *Reviews in American History* 38 (June 2010): 367–392, which emphasizes the close ties between the conservative resurgence and racial backlash, first in the South, then in the suburbs (368–369).

5. See Bob Herbert, "Impossible, Ridiculous, Repugnant," *New York Times*, October 6, 2005. When Alexander P. Lamis interviewed young Reagan staffer Lee Atwater (who was not identified by name) in 1981 for *The Two-Party South* (1990), Atwater credited Harry Dent for inventing the Southern Strategy. Atwater ran George H. W. Bush's 1988 campaign, after which he became chair of the Republican Party. He died of a brain tumor in 1991 at the age of 40. Lamis revealed Atwater's name some years later. Atwater's quote continues, "And subconsciously maybe that is part of it. I'm not saying that. But I'm saying that if it is getting that abstract, and that coded, that we are doing away with the racial problem one way or the other. You follow me—because obviously sitting around saying, 'We want to cut this,' is much more abstract than even the busing thing, and a hell of a lot more abstract than 'Nigger, nigger.'" See "Atwater on the Southern Strategy" in Wikipedia's entry for Lee Atwater. Ironically, in the 1960s Atwater briefly played backup guitar with Percy Sledge, and he liked to hang out with James Brown and B. B. King. See *Boogie Man: The Lee Atwater Story*, 2008 documentary film produced by Stefan Forbes, distributed by Interpositive Media LLC, available from PBS.

6. On the subtext of tax cuts, I'm indebted to a conversation with Anne Rutledge.

7. The first debate took place on September 26, 2008.

8. David Grann, "The Fall: John McCain's Choices," *The New Yorker*, November 17, 2008, 61; Evan Thomas et al., "How He Did It, 2008: The Inside Story of an Epic Election," *Newsweek*, November 17, 2008, 83. Surprisingly, McCain ruled out any attacks on Obama's lack of military service as well as directly race-based attacks (108).

9. Grann, "The Fall," 61, quoting Robert Timberg's biography of McCain.

10. John McCain with Mark Salter, *Faith of My Fathers* (New York: Perennial, 2000), 63 and 94 (military service of father and grandfather), 51 (mother), 70 (absences), 51 (relationship between sailor and his children metaphysical). McCain's father worked until 8:00 P.M. every day, including weekends, and prayed for an hour twice a day (70–71).

11. Ibid., 95 (driven by desire to honor father's name), vii (father and grandfather McCain's first heroes), 66 (life ransomed to duty), 269–270 (father testifies at Senate).

12. Ibid., 67 (dishonorable conduct a shame), 254–255 (obligations of honor).

13. Ibid., 57 (father expelled from dormitory), 56 (young McCain notoriously undisciplined), 19 (quick tempers a McCain family trait). On the stature of the McCain men, see 52–53, 107. Stories about McCain's frequent episodes of disobedience as plebe, young officer, and prisoner pepper the book. On his migrant childhood, see 21, 100, 107–108. As he writes on viii, "First made a migrant by the demands of my father's career, in time I became self-moving, a rover by choice."

14. Ibid., vii (balancing liberty and honor), 267 (McCain's criticism of military leaders during Vietnam War), 277 (father makes decision to bomb Hanoi, also 337–340), 342 (father declines to meet McCain when he returns from war).

15. Ibid., 278–279 (McCain searches in father's letters for information), 287 (custom of withdrawing).

16. McCain with Salter, *Faith of My Fathers*, 76 (racism of McCain's grandfather), 71–74 (alcoholism of McCain's father, quote at 74), 336 (McCain's shame at breaking under torture), and 348 and 253 (McCain's "failings" and "remorse").

17. George Lakoff, *Moral Politics: How Conservatives and Liberals Think*, 2nd ed. (Chicago: University of Chicago Press, 2002).

18. Ibid., 244 (McCain's despair while a POW), 245 (McCain seen as the Crown Prince of prisoners).

19. Ibid., 233–238 (McCain refuses offers of early release), 286 (quote). What he most "dreaded" happened; the admiral heard the tape, McCain learned

after his release. McCain writes that he "would have been distressed beyond imagination" if he had known that while he was in prison (286).

20. Ibid., 287 (faith of my fathers).

21. Drew, "The Truth about the Election," 94; Maureen Dowd, "Tao of Lee Atwater," *New York Times*, October 8, 2008, A31. On the fact that Obama did not serve in the military, see Thomas et al., "How He Did It, 2009," 83. On McCain's "internal struggle" about using race, see Remnick, *The Bridge*, 541–542.

22. Grann, "The Fall," 65.

23. In "How He Did It," Thomas et al. write that McCain blocked the campaign's use of explicitly racial issues because in 2000 the Bush campaign had scurrilously called North Carolina voters to say that the McCains' adopted daughter was McCain's "love child" with a black prostitute. I think his sense of honor and his admiration for the historical progress that Obama's campaign represented were at least as important. John Heilemann and Mark Halperin note McCain's instructions to "steer clear" of racism but also discuss Obama's belief that "McCain is playing the race card by accusing me of playing the race card"; Heilemann and Halperin, *Game Change: Obama and the Clintons, McCain and Palin, and the Race of a Lifetime* (New York: HarperCollins, 2010), 331, 333.

24. The Obama campaign staffers' shorthand for white working-class voters was "bitter people"; Heilemann and Halperin, *Game Change*, 251. Bill Ayers and Bernadine Dohrn note examples of "white code talk for 'he's not one of us'": Obama doesn't share blue-collar, mainstream, small-town, hockey-mom values. Racial recoil constituted part of Hillary Clinton's appeal for white Democrats, too; Ayers and Dohrn, *Race Course against White Supremacy* (Chicago: Third World Press, 2009), 219–220; see also 197–201, 210–215 on the Clintons' angry responses to the charge that race played a role in her campaign. See also Remnick, *The Bridge*, especially 496–516. Michael Tesler and David O. Sears emphasize that voters' attitudes about Muslims were probably more important than their attitudes about American blacks in their decisions to vote for or against Obama; Tesler and Sears, *Obama's Race: The 2008 Election and the Dream of a Post-Racial America* (Chicago: University of Chicago Press, 2010), especially chapter 7.

25. Jim Rutenberg and Julie Bosman note McCain's hiring of Steve Schmidt, who in 2004 "relentlessly painted" Senator John Kerry as "effete, elite, and equivocal"; Rutenberg and Bosman, "McCain Is Trying to Define Obama as Out of Touch," *New York Times*, July 31, 2008, A15. According to Ryan Lizza, the ads had a huge impact on the Obama campaign. The central staffers were "spooked by the Paris Hilton ad" and for months tried to block any evidence of

"presumption," including the staging of big rallies. But field organizers needed those rallies "to help identify Obama voters." Eventually the organizers won, and Obama drew huge crowds in the last two months of the campaign; Lizza, "Battle Plans: How Obama Won," *The New Yorker*, November 17, 2008, 46–55, quotes on 53. According to Heilemann and Halperin, the ads also implied that Obama was "the affirmative-action nominee." Soon the polls were in "a dead heat"; Heilemann and Halperin, *Game Change*, 333–334.

26. Adam Nagourney, "Campaigns Shift to Attack Mode," *New York Times*, October 7, 2008, A21; Dowd, "Tao of Lee Atwater," A31. The lead editorial in the *Times* on the day of Dowd's column noted that according to the *Washington Post*, when Governor Palin linked Obama to "terrorists" at a Florida rally, a man yelled "Kill him!" and "others shouted epithets at an African-American member of a TV crew"; "Politics of Attack," *New York Times*, October 8, 2009, A30. Palin was particularly eager to link Obama to Muslims; see Tesler and Sears, *Obama's Race*, 140.

27. See Andrew Hacker, "Obama: The Price of Being Black," *New York Review of Books*, September 25, 2008, 12, 14, 16; and William Safire's etymological exploration in his "On Language" column for the *New York Times Magazine*, September 28, 2008, 20. Safire notes a 2008 study by Daniel Hopkins, who finds that what he calls "the Wilder effect . . . was significant only through the early 1990s." For Hacker, the 2006 Michigan election counters Hopkins's conclusion. Ironically, as Safire also notes, the term "Bradley effect" was first used in 1984 to refer to Senator Bill Bradley of New Jersey. Remnick notes that the Bradley effect seemed most relevant after the New Hampshire primary; Remnick, *The Bridge*, 506, 556.

28. Ron Fournier and Trevor Tompson, "Poll: Racial Views Steer Some White Dems away from Obama," AP story, September 20, 2008.

29. See, for instance, Jim Rutenberg, "Pinpoint Attacks Focus on Obama," *New York Times*, September 24, 2008, A1, A20.

30. For a balanced portrait of Rev. Wright, see Remnick, *Bridge*, 468–472, 518–520, 527–533.

31. Bill Ayers and Bernadine Dohrn end *Race Course* with a section on the Republican campaign's racism and the abuse of Ayers (219–226). One example: when Michelle Obama said "For the first time in my adult life, I am really proud of my country," Bill O'Reilly responded, "I don't want to go on a lynching party against Michelle Obama unless there's evidence, hard facts, that say this is how the woman really feels"; *MediaMatters for America*, February 20, 2008, mediamatters.org/research/200802200001.

32. For example, see Matt Bai, "Obama the Other, Deployed as Election Tactic," *New York Times*, September 16, 2010, A21. See also Nicholas D. Kristof,

"The Push to 'Otherize' Obama," *The New York Times*, September 21, 2008, WK9.

33. Brent Staples, "Barack Obama, John McCain and the Language of Race," *New York Times*, September 22, 2008, A22.

34. Tim Wise, "White Privilege, White Entitlement, and the 2008 Election," The Buzzflash Blog, September 30, 2008, available at *www.buzzflash.com/articles/contributors/1755*.

35. Remnick, *The Bridge*, 542–543; M. A., M. M. B., and M. W., "Media Denounce Corsi's Anti-Obama Book," *MediaMatters for America*, August 15, 2008, mediamatters.org/research/200808150015.

36. Jerome R. Corsi, *The Obama Nation: Leftist Politics and the Cult of Personality* (New York: Simon & Schuster, 2008), xii–xiii (1968 Chicago gun battle), (Obama's schooling in Indonesia).

37. Ibid., 50–62. Ironically, William H. Grier and Price M. Cobbs, the two black psychiatrists who wrote *Black Rage* (New York: Basic Books, 1968), promoted the notion of therapy for blacks who were mentally ill. See Obama, *Dreams from My Father: A Story of Race and Inheritance*, rev. ed. (New York: Three Rivers Press, 2004), 72–91, on the rage of several black high school friends.

38. Corsi, *The Obama Nation*, 69, 83, and 88 (on black anger), 79 (Fanon), 94–97 (Obama a "Kenyan Tribal Elder").

39. Nicholas Kristof, 'What? Me Biased?' *New York Times*, October 30, 2008, A39.

40. Remnick uses Jarrett's remark for the title of chapter 13 of *The Bridge* (466–495, quote at 477–478), which includes a succinct history of how "racial appeals gradually shifted from the explicit to the implicit" (479). Candidate Richard Nixon said after filming a 1968 commercial, "It's all about law and order and the damn Negro–Puerto Rican groups out there" (479). In *The New Jim Crow: Mass Incarceration in the Age of Colorblindedness* (New York: The New Press, 2010), Michelle Alexander quotes Nixon aides H. R. Haldeman and John Erlichman, who said that Nixon's 1968 campaign used anti-black innuendo to "go after the racists" (43–44, Erlichman quote 44, and 43–55 on the Southern Strategy). Alexander concludes, "In the 1968 election, race eclipsed class as the organizing principle of American politics" (46).

41. Douglas MacArthur, *Reminiscences* (New York: McGraw-Hill, 1964), 33. MacArthur greatly admired Roosevelt's "prophetic vision of Asian politics" as well as his "abounding vitality" and his achievement in establishing the United States as a "first rank" world power.

42. On John Lewis's criticism of McCain, see Grann, "The Fall," 57; Evan

Thomas et al., "How He Did It, 2008," 108, 110; and Remnick, *The Bridge*, 546–547.

43. Later that week, Rev. James L. Bevel—the man who had delivered the impromptu sermon about Shadrach, Meshach, and Abednego when Lewis and Bevel were being fumigated in that Nashville fast-food restaurant (chapter 1)—was sentenced to fifteen years in prison for incest with his daughter that had taken place in the early 1990s. The one-paragraph story in the *New York Times* (October 15, 2008, A25) noted that Bevel was dying of pancreatic cancer. He had helped organize the 1963 Children's Crusade in Birmingham. On November 26, Bevel was released on bond—ostensibly for his appeal, really to die; see "Virginia: Ill Civil Rights Figure Released from Jail," *New York Times*, November 27, 2008, A26. See also Bruce Weber, "James L. Bevel, Advisor to Dr. King, Is Dead," *New York Times*, December 23, 2008, B10.

44. A Chicago strategist told David Remnick, "The rule was: no radioactive blacks." That meant Harold Ford and Jesse Jackson Jr., yes; Sharpton and Jackson Sr., no. See David Remnick, "The Joshua Generation: Race and the Campaign of Barack Obama," *The New Yorker*, November 17, 2008, 76–77. Even when Obama spoke about not looking like other presidents on dollar bills, his poll numbers went down (78). As Colin Powell put it admiringly, Obama didn't run as a postracial candidate. Instead he ran "as an American who's black, not as a black American" (80). Tim Wise indicts Obama for that strategy and champions angry black men such as Jackson, Sharpton, Jeremiah Wright, or even Barry Bonds; Wise, *Speaking Treason Fluently*, 146–147, 251–263, 307–317.

45. Obama, *Dreams from My Father*, 94–95.

46. Grann, "The Fall," 60.

47. Lizza, "Battle Plans," 54.

48. Rachel L. Swarns, "Vaulting the Racial Divide," *New York Times*, November 5, 2008, P7. On Obama's steady though small lead in the electoral college, see Drew, "The Truth about the Election," 95. The judge told that remark to me. It complicates the argument of Michael Tesler and David Sears that race-based support balanced race-based opposition. Their book shows ample polling evidence of "racial resentment," which they call "Symbolic Racism." They rightly argue that "race is probably the most visceral issue in American public life" and that the campaign was the most racialized in American history. But they oversimplify both sides by implying that voters decided primarily because of their racial attitudes. That good old boy wasn't a liberal on race. See Tesler and Sears, *Obama's Race*, 17–28, 43–48, 80–88, 92, 199, quote on 92.

49. Heilemann and Halperin, *Game Change*, 429. Two days after the elec-

tion, a *Times* story by Kate Zernike stated that race was a factor for 17 percent of white voters and that McCain gained most of their votes. But Obama lost only 16 percent of white male voters, well under Gore's 24 percent and Kerry's 25 percent. The Bradley effect had never existed, Zernike declared, since it didn't include absentee ballots. She argues that in the 1990s the Wilder effect did exist, but only until white concerns about crime and welfare faded. Even in Pennsylvania, where longtime congressman John Murtha had called his western Pennsylvania constituents "racist" near the end of the campaign, the polls predicted only a 7 percent victory for Obama, but he won by 10 percent. Murtha was comfortably reelected with 58 percent of the vote. Zernike, "For Pollsters, the Racial Effect That Wasn't," *New York Times*, November 6, 2008, P8.

50. John Harwood, "Level of White Support for Obama a Surprise," *New York Times*, November 3, 2008, A20. Harwood notes another change: in 1984, when Reagan won his second term, whites constituted 86 percent of the electorate. In 2004, they constituted 77 percent.

51. Krauthammer caustically compares Obama's lack of experience to McCain's "Hail Mary" passes—the surge, Palin, suspending his campaign while the government attended to the bailout. At the end of his article, Krauthammer turns to what Oliver Wendell Holmes Jr. said after meeting young Franklin Delano Roosevelt: "a second-class intellect, but a first-class temperament." Perhaps Obama's first-class intellect and temperament will be enough to elect him, Krauthammer wearily concludes. See Krauthammer, "Hail Mary vs. Cool Barry," *Washington Post*, October 3, 2008, A23.

52. See, for instance, "Barack Obama's Speech on Race," *New York Times*, March 18, 2008. For other analysis of Obama and race in the 2008 election, see Thomas J. Sugrue, *Not Even Past: Barack Obama and the Burden of Race* (Princeton, N.J.: Princeton University Press, 2010), 108–111; and David Remnick, *The Bridge*, 18, 537–564, 586.

53. On dignity as an alternative mode of working-class black manhood in the late 1960s to counter white stereotypes of black rage or acquiescence, see Mitchell Duneier, *Slim's Table: Race, Respectability, and Masculinity* (Chicago: University of Chicago Press, 1992). Duneier's study of older black men who frequent a South Side Chicago cafeteria brings out their caring and sensitivity as well as their reserved manliness.

54. Alex Kotlowitz, "Wrong Side of History," episode 376 of NPR's *This American Life*, aired March 13, 2009, part 4. Epton died while visiting his son, Jeff Epton, a Democratic Socialist, in Ann Arbor. At that point his father clearly "didn't want to live," his son said. See also Remnick, *The Bridge*, 157–160.

55. Jackie Calmes and Megan Thee, "Voter Polls Find Obama Built a Broad

Coalition," *New York Times*, November 5, 2008, P9. Among white Protestants, who constituted 42 percent of the voters, only 34 percent supported Obama; only 26 percent of evangelical voters supported him. Among white Catholics, 47 percent supported Obama. Obama won 62 percent of Asian American voters, 67 percent of Hispanic voters, and 95 percent of black voters. See Joseph Woodward, "How Historic a Victory?" *New York Review of Books*, February 12, 2009, 49. On Lee Atwater and the Southern Strategy, see also Marc Ambinder, "Race Over?" *The Atlantic*, January/February 2009, 64.

56. My wife, Anne Rutledge, vividly recalls the moment in 1967 when she drove into southern Indiana for the first time and saw a big billboard that said "Martin Luther King Is a Communist." Residual Cold War fear and contempt may have pushed many white voters to think that Obama would be a "socialist" or a "Marxist."

57. A week after the election, Adam Nossiter highlighted the constriction of southern support for Republicans to "poorer, less educated and whiter" counties; Nossiter, "For South, a Waning Hold on National Politics," *New York Times*, November 11, 2008, A1, A20. A few days later, Frank Rich noted that McCain won only 38 percent of the southern white vote. Rich sarcastically suggests that Republicans might continue to avoid confronting the failure of their 40-year-old Southern Strategy by focusing on the threat of same-sex marriages as a way to lure conservative African Americans and Hispanics. See Rich, "The Moose Stops Here," *New York Times*, November 16, 2008, WK 12.

58. "McCain's Concession Speech," *New York Times*, November 5, 2008. McCain had highlighted that contrast at the end of his speech at the Alfred E. Smith Memorial Dinner in New York half a month earlier by saying "the crude and prideful bigotry"; "Transcript of McCain's Comedy Roast at Al Smith Dinner," http://politicalhumor.about.com/od/johnmccain/a/mccain-al-smith_2.htm. On southern rage in reaction to Teddy Roosevelt's dinner with Booker T. Washington (and on the president's subsequent betrayals of the black leader), see Robert J. Norrell, *The House I Live In*, 43–44, 53–56. Norell notes that in 1906 Roosevelt said that black men who were lynched were rapists (57). See also Marc Ambinder, "Race Over?" especially 62–65.

59. As an Obama adviser told Elizabeth Drew, the goal was to "build the comfort level" by having Obama avoid "grievance politics" and talk about aiding the middle class, not the poor; Drew, "The Truth about the Election," 94. Drew suggests that the length of the campaign helped build that comfort level.

60. Hua Hsu, "The End of White America?" *The Atlantic*, January–February 2009, 48, 50–52, 55. Hsu notes that the McCain-Palin campaign relied on white identity politics "almost to the point of absurdity" (54).

61. On Lewis's life, see Remnick, *The Bridge*, 5–11, 574–576, 579. Gwen Ifill makes a similarly optimistic argument for the differences between an older generation of black people accustomed to humiliation and a younger generation whose lives reflect access rather than denial; Ifill, *The Breakthrough: Politics and Race in the Age of Obama* (New York: Doubleday, 2009). Werner Sollors recounts the history of the word "multicultural," which first appeared in a 1941 novel by Edward F. Haskell, *Lance: A Novel about Multicultural Men*. See "The Word 'Multicultural,'" in *A New Literary History of America*, edited by Greil Marcus and Werner Sollors (Cambridge, Mass.: Harvard University Press, 2009), 757–761.

62. Orlando Patterson, "The New Mainstream," *Newsweek*, November 10, 2008, 40–41; Tavis Smiley, commentary on NBC during election night. Smiley had criticized Obama for months on his TV show. In February 2007 and February 2008, Obama declined to appear at Smiley's annual State of the Black Union forum in New Orleans, probably because he didn't want to get branded as the black people's candidate. Smiley resented the slight, but the black backlash against Smiley convinced Obama's campaign that the candidate didn't have to make white people nervous to win black votes. (Smiley eventually supported Obama.) See Marc Ambinder, "Race Over?" 63–64; Remnick, *The Bridge*, 472–475, 535.

63. Drew, "The Truth about the Election," 95.

64. Among many other calls for the renewal of moral imperatives, see Anthony Appiah, *Honor Code: How Moral Revolutions Happen* (New York: Norton, 2010); and Ron Suskind, *The Way of the World: A Story of Truth and Hope in an Age of Extremism* (New York: HarperCollins, 2008).

65. In late spring of 2009, after the release of memos detailing the Bush administration's advocacy of torture, Philip Gourevitch wrote, "There can be no restoration of the national honor if we continue to scapegoat those who took the fall for an Administration—and for us all." Gourevitch, "Interrogating Torture," *The New Yorker*, May 11, 2009, 34.

66. Drew, "The Truth about the Election," 98.

67. Junot Diaz, *The Brief Wondrous Life of Oscar Wao* (New York: Riverhead Books, 2007), 264. The hero continues: "the same charge of gleeful sadism that he remembered from his youth still electrified the halls." But now "the chief tormentors" are "kids of color who performed the necessaries" (ibid.)

68. Nicholas Kristof suggests that the campaign made racial bias "a teachable moment"; Kristof, "What? Me Biased?" *New York Times*, October 30, 2008, A39.

69. Michael Cooper and Dalia Sussman, "Growing Doubts on Palin Take a

Toll, Poll Finds," *New York Times*, October 31, 2008, A1, A18. Tesler and Sears make a similar argument in *Obama's Race*.

70. David Remnick, "Joshua Generation," 81; also Remnick, *The Bridge*, 553.

CHAPTER 7. TO THE TEA PARTY—AND BEYOND?

1. Michelle Alexander argues that since 1982, the War on Drugs has rein-stituted slavery in its third phase, after explicit slavery and Jim Crow. The United States is the only country in the world that disenfranchises former prisoners in the millions, not in the dozens or hundreds, as in some European nations, where laws that restrict voting sanctions against former prisoners are constructed very narrowly. Alexander notes, "Practically from cradle to grave, black males in urban ghettos are treated like current or future criminals." Alexander, *The New Jim Crow: Mass Incarceration in the Age of Colorblinded-ness* (New York: The New Press, 2010), 154, quote on 157.

2. Elise Lemire, *"Miscegenation": Making Race in America* (Philadelphia: University of Pennsylvania Press, 2002), 147; Susan Saulny, "Black and White and Married in the Deep South: A Shifting Image," *New York Times*, March 20, 2011, A1, A4. Saulny writes, "In North Carolina, the mixed-race [black and white] population doubled. In Georgia, it expanded by more than 80 percent, and by nearly as much in Kentucky and Tennessee. In Indiana, Iowa and South Dakota, the multiracial population increased by about 70 percent" (A1)

3. Michael Tomasky notes that before Santelli's rant, Michelle Malkin had been agitating on her blogs for tea party revolts against the stimulus bill and the bank bailouts; Tomasky, "Something New on the Mall," *New York Review of Books*, October 22, 2009, 4.

4. Jill Lepore, *The Whites of Their Eyes: The Tea Party's Revolution and the Battle over American History* (Princeton, N.J.: Princeton University Press, 2010), 95. The nostalgia Lepore writes of isn't new; Scott L. Malcomson writes that "white Americans in the 1890s pined for a lost world where their own dominance . . . made sense." They felt "a nostalgia not for whiteness or power but for the legitimacy of white power"; Malcomson, *One Drop of Blood: The American Misadventure of Race* (New York: Farrar Straus Giroux, 2000), 362.

5. On Beck's and Limbaugh's charges of stealth reparations, see Tim Wise, *Colorblind: The Rise of Post-Racial Politics and the Retreat from Racial Equity* (San Francisco: City Lights Publishers, 2010), 141–150. Wise advocates repa-rations and vehemently faults Obama's allegedly colorblind liberalism for placating whites by minimizing the effects of white racism (36–61, 119). See also Tim Wise, *White Like Me: Reflections on Race from a Privileged Son* (Brooklyn: Soft Skull Press, 2005), 99. Henry Louis Gates Jr. has argued against repara-

tions because European Americans were not entirely at fault, since 90 percent of Africans who became slaves overseas were sold by other Africans. See Gates, "Ending the Slavery Blame Game," *New York Times*, April 23, 2010, A27.

6. David Barstow, "Lighting a Fuse for Rebellion on the Right: Loose Alliances of Protesters Join under Tea Party Umbrella," *New York Times*, February 16, 2010, A1, A14–A15. Richard Mack told Barstow that people who are trying to understand foreclosures or joblessness or lost retirement funds "just do not trust" statements by government officials anymore and see elite conspiracies and incipient tyranny everywhere. Riché Richardson emphasizes the theatricality of the Tea Party's dress; supporters often dress in Revolutionary War–era styles; Richardson, "Black Masculinity and New Precedents," postscript to *Fathers, Preachers, Rebels, Men*, edited by Timothy Buckner and Peter Caster (Columbus: Ohio State University Press, 2011).

7. Sean Wilentz, "Confounding Fathers: The Tea Party's Cold War Roots," *The New Yorker*, October 18, 2010, 37; Kate Zernike, *Boiling Mad: Inside Tea Party America* (New York: Times Books, 2010), 51–52; Will Bunch, *The Backlash: Right-Wing Radicals, High-Def Hucksters, and Paranoid Politics in the Age of Obama* (New York: HarperCollins, 2010), 11, 337–342. The NAACP's report finds the Tea Party "permeated with concerns about race"; Kate Zernike, "Report Raises Concerns about Racism in Tea Party Groups," *International Herald Tribune*, October 22, 2010, 2. Zernike faults the report for not examining the local groups that constitute the decentralized party. For the report, see Devin Burghart and Leonard Zeskind, *Tea Party Nationalism* (Kansas City, Mo.: Institute for Research & Education on Human Rights, 2010). Jill Lepore emphasizes the Tea Party's ahistorical erasure of slavery and anger about the government using "our" money for "bums"; Lepore, *The Whites of Their Eyes*, 96, 100, 129. Will Bunch emphasizes the movement's coded statements and fears of the Other. The implicit racism acts as "a purification tool . . . to promote an ugly but powerful brand of unity, the 'white culture'"; Bunch, *The Backlash*, 341. Zernike acknowledges overt and subtle racism among earlier conservatives who opposed using tax money for people defined as "them"; Zernike, *Boiling Mad*, 56–60. She notes, however, that the Tea Party officially disowns racists (137).

8. Julian E. Zelizer, "Rethinking the History of American Conservatism," *Reviews in American History* 38 (June 2010): 375–379, 388.

9. Robin Einhorn argues that "American mistrust of government . . . comes from slaveholding elites." Therefore "the antigovernment rhetoric that continues to saturate our political life today is rooted in slavery rather than liberty"; Einhorn, *American Taxation, American Slavery* (Chicago: University of Chicago Press, 2006), 7.

10. On Rush Limbaugh and Glenn Beck, see David Bromwich, "The Rebel Germ," *New York Review of Books*, November 25, 2010, 4, 6, 8.

11. Christopher Edley Jr., a Harvard Law School professor, claims to have first used "preternatural calm" to describe Obama. David Remnick, *The Bridge: The Life and Rise of Barack Obama* (New York: Alfred A. Knopf, 2010), 217.

12. Charles M. Blow, "Lady BlahBlah," *New York Times*, January 16, 2010, A17. Whites' approval ratings for Obama were lower than their ratings of previous presidents by "10 to 36 percentage points." According to a July 13, 2010, Quinnipiac University poll, "A plurality of whites even said that Obama has been a worse president than George W. Bush." In mid-April 2010, a New York Times/ CBS News poll found that the 18 percent of Americans who declare themselves Tea Party supporters "tend to be Republican, white, male, married and older than 45"; they are also "better educated and wealthier than the general public." Kate Zernike, "Discontent's Demography: Who Backs the Tea Party," *New York Times*, April 15, 2010, A1. As conservatives, they feel "that the country is being run by people who do not share their values, for the benefit of people who are not like them"; Kate Zernike, "Doing Fine, but Angry Nonetheless," *New York Times*, April 18, 2010, WK1.

13. In "Hamlet and His Problems" (1919), T. S. Eliot argues that Gertrude's guilt is an inadequate "objective correlative" for Hamlet's "disgust." In Eliot, *Selected Essays*, rev. ed. (New York: Harcourt, Brace, 1950), 124–125.

14. Maureen Dowd, "Boy, Oh, Boy," *New York Times*, September 13, 2009, WK17. Two weeks later, after interviewing white people at rallies against health care reform, Philip Weiss reported that they felt "anger, upset, a sense of dispossession." He concluded that "Obama was, quite literally, their nightmare." See "Who Is Barack Obama?" *New York*, September 28, 2009, 25–26.

15. Jimmy Carter, NBC interview on September 15, 2009. Carter used the phrase "radical fringe" in a CNN interview and Georgia town hall meeting on September 16, 2009. See also Jeff Zeleny, "Obama Addresses the Opposition on Health Care," *New York Times*, September 19, 2009, A10. As she introduced Toni Morrison at Cornell University on October 2, 2009, Riché Richardson noted "the resurgence of neo-Confederacy in the public sphere"; transcript in author's possession.

16. *The Brian Lehrer Show*, WNYC, September 16, 2009.

17. Bertram Wyatt-Brown, *Southern Honor: Ethics and Behavior in the Old South* (Oxford: Oxford University Press, 1982), 307. See also 154–155 on aggressiveness to fend off "shame" at "weakness and inferiority" and 157 on submissiveness "based as much on fear as on love of the father." Even the earliest codes of honor uneasily mixed aggression and obedience. Karen Armstrong notes that among sixth-century Bedouins, a man "had to be ready

to leap to the defense of his kinsmen at a moment's notice and to obey his chief without question"; Armstrong, *Muhammad: Prophet for Our Time* (2006; repr., London: Harper Perennial, 2007), 24.

18. Rush Limbaugh quoted in Michael Tesler and David O. Sears, *Obama's Race: The 2008 Election and the Dream of a Post-Racial America* (Chicago: University of Chicago Press, 2010), 142; see also Tim Wise, *Colorblind*, 149. Tesler and Sears cite polls suggesting that Obama's links to Muslim culture made him seem more "other" (127–141, 8–9, 152). Gordon Liddy, a former Watergate co-conspirator, made his charge that Obama might be an "illegal alien" on July 23, 2009, on Chris Matthews's MSNBC show *Hardball with Chris Matthews*. Matthews responded by showing Liddy a photocopy of Obama's Hawaiian birth certificate. Brian Stelter, "A Dispute over Obama's Birth Lives on in the Media," *New York Times*, July 25, 2009, B2.

19. Tomasky, "Something New on the Mall," 4, 8. Tomasky notes that the "ferocity" of the town hall meetings and demonstrations was "something new in our political life" (8, 4). He concludes that the anger has "ideological rather than racial roots and causes," even though he concedes that "everything these folks say about 'their' country being taken away from them has an inevitable racial overtone'" (8).

20. Chris Stigall quoted in James C. McKinley Jr. and Sam Dillon, "Obama's Plan for School Talk Ignites a Revolt," *New York Times*, September 4, 2009, A1, A17.

21. Obama has a Hawaiian birth certificate, which he released on April 27, 2011, because the furor hadn't abated. In addition, there were birth announcements in two local newspapers. After investigating the possibility that Obama had not been born in the United States, the McCain campaign discounted the rumors, not least because in the 2000 and 2008 campaigns McCain was accused of not being a legal citizen. He was born in the Panama Canal Zone.

22. See Frank Rich, "Small Beer, Big Hangover," *New York Times*, August 2, 2009, WK8. Rich notes that both O'Reilly and right-wing writer Ann Coulter condemned the birther movement. He predicts "a 30-year struggle" before angry white citizens "accept the reality that America's racial profile will no longer reflect their own."

23. Joan Walsh, "The Blackening of the President," *Salon.com*, September 14, 2009. The woman was echoing Rush Limbaugh and Glenn Beck. By 2010 the phrase had become a ubiquitous Republican mantra. Ironically, in his 2002 speech opposing the second Iraq War, Obama spoke of the Bush administration's "weekend warriors" who want to "shove their own ideological agendas down our throats"; quoted in Remnick, *The Bridge*, 347.

24. Keith Olbermann, "Special Comment," *Countdown*, MSNBC, aired

February 15, 2010. As early as April 16, 2009, a guest on Olbermann's show, Janeane Garofalo, called the movement "racism straight up." Meghan McCain spoke of Tom Tancredo's "innate racism" when she guest hosted *The View* on ABC on February 9, 2010. Tancredo is a former Colorado congressman and Tea Party leader who advocates literacy tests for voters. See also Will Bunch, *Backlash*. When Obama released his birth certificate, Jerome Corsi's new book, *Where's the Birth Certificate? The Case That Barack Obama Is Not Eligible to be President* (New York: WND Books, 2011) was already a best seller, though it wouldn't be officially published until May 17.

25. Leonard Pitts, "On Race and the Tea Party," *Dallas Morning News,* March 3, 2010. Paul Krugman and Frank Rich pointed to the real or imagined erosion of white supremacy as the basis for anxiety and anger as well as the Republican strategy of Just Say No. See Krugman, "Fear Strikes Out," *New York Times*, March 22, 2010, A25; and Rich, "The Rage Is Not about Health Care," *New York Times*, March 29, 2010, WK10. See also Nicholas Kristof, "America's History of Fear," *New York Times*, September 5, 2010, WK10.

26. Frank Rich, "The Guns of August," *New York Times*, August 23, 2009, WK8; Michael Rubinkam, "Darts Shot at Obama Likeness," AP, August 4, 2010. The head of the amusement park company said, with ambiguous ruefulness, that he had voted for Obama. Rich finds parallels with "the simmering undertone of violence" before Timothy McVeigh's Oklahoma City bombing in 1995, during President Clinton's administration. Over a month after the amusement park incident, Thomas Friedman compared the "poisonous political environment" to the atmosphere in Israel right before Prime Minister Yitzhak Rabin was assassinated in 1995; Friedman, "Where Did 'We' Go?" *New York Times*, September 30, 2009, A31. Friedman cited the Facebook poll. Titled "Should Obama be killed?" it offered four choices: "No, Maybe, Yes, and Yes if he cuts my health care."

27. Michelle Malkin, *Culture of Corruption: Obama and His Team of Tax Cheats, Crooks, and Cronies* (Washington, D.C.: Regnery, 2009), 1, 289.

28. Dinesh D'Souza, *The Roots of Obama's Rage* (Washington, D.C.: Regnery Publishing, 2010), 130 (credibility of the color-blind ideal), 9 (contrived black identity), 137–140 (Fanon's lactification strategy), 151–158 (Afrocentric drive to reduce the American standard of living), 159–160 (ACORN), 204 (reducing the American arsenal), 200–202 (converting NASA to a community outreach program for Muslims), 196 (wants his country to go the way of Britain), 198 (Obama a time machine), 207–210 (Africa needs colonialism).

29. Katon Dawson quoted in Alexander Burns, "What's the Matter with South Carolina?" *Politico*, September 11, 2009. On John L. Perry's public ruminations about a coup to forestall Obama's "Marxist" transformation

of the United States, see Alex Koppelman, "Newsmax Explains Decision to Take Down Coup Column," *Salon.com*, September 30, 2009. On the New York rally against Holder, see Jane Mayer, "The Trial: The Right's War on the Attorney General," *The New Yorker*, February 15–22, 2010, 52. Others shouted, "Communist!" "Traitor!" A woman told Mayer that Holder is "a Marxist mole. . . . Holder wants to help the terrorists." Holder later reversed his decision to try Mohammed in New York. After Holder's "cowards" charge in his January 2009 speech, the Obama administration repeatedly tried to control Holder's tendency to make decisions without thinking through the political consequences. See Jodi Kantor and Charlie Savage, "Getting the Message: After 9/11 Trial Plan, Holder Hones Political Ear," *New York Times*, February 15, 2010, A1, A12.

30. See Matt Bai, "Obama the Other, Deployed as Election Tactic," *New York Times*, September 16, 2010, A21. Writing shortly before the election, Bai suggests that the Republican campaign strategy isn't meant to appeal to general voters but is instead designed to unite three conflicting Republican constituencies: advocates of free enterprise, proponents of neoconservative foreign policy, and social conservatives. Communism had provided a similarly powerful unifier in the Cold War years, Bai says, and now Obama gives "a reason to fear."

31. In 2010 two black Republicans were elected to Congress: Allen West from south Florida and Tim Scott from a mostly white district in South Carolina. An admirer of Strom Thurmond, Scott was endorsed by Sarah Palin. His opposition to Obama's alleged policies of "bankruptcy and socialism" reflects the politics of a white man who became his mentor and rescued him from a difficult childhood and imbued him with a Christian self-help philosophy. The mentor's death when Scott was seventeen sparked his ambition "to have a positive effect on the lives of one billion people" (A14). Katharine Seelye, "Candidate Shrugs Off History's Lure: South Carolinian Tries to Keep Focus on G.O.P. Issues, Not Race," *New York Times*, June 26, 2010, A8, A14.

32. On the Know-Nothing Party and nativism, see John Higham, *Strangers in the Land: Patterns of American Nativism 1860–1925*, 2nd ed. (New York: Atheneum, 1973).

33. In his interview with Dayo Olopade for *The Root*, Gates speculated that his lock had been "damaged" by an intruder, since the door seemed "jimmied" and he saw a footprint. See "Skip Gates Speaks," *The Root*, July 21, 2009, available at www.theroot.com/views/skip-gates-speaks.

34. For these details, which are more complex than in the initial reports, see Don Van Natta Jr. and Abby Goodnough, "An Unlikely Meeting That Led to a National Talk about Race," *New York Times*, July 27, 2009, A13.

35. Gates later denied the vernacular language attributed to him in the

police report. See the police transcript, reprinted in Charles J. Ogletree Jr., *The Presumption of Guilt: The Arrest of Henry Louis Gates Jr. and Race, Class, and Crime in America* (New York: Palgrave Macmillan, 2011), 21–25. Ogletree notes that Gates lives in "a predominately [*sic*] White neighborhood" (17).

36. On June 30, 2010, an independent Cambridge report on the incident faulted Crowley for not adequately explaining why he was there and Gates for using a confrontational tone. It concluded that fear, class, race, and police authority all played a part. It also noted that "both men told the panel they would not have acted differently now." Katie Zezima, "Officer and Professor Faulted for Confrontation at Home," *New York Times*, July 1, 2010, A18.

37. The first three quotes in this paragraph are from Van Natta and Good-nough, "An Unlikely Meeting," A13. In his interview with Olopade, Gates said that he first said, "Officer, can I help you?" The last quote is from Maureen Dowd, "Bite Your Tongue," *New York Times*, July 26, 2009, WK11. The original 9-1-1 call did not specify race.

38. Frank Rich, "Small Beer, Big Hangover," WK8.

39. Glenn Beck, guest appearance on *Fox & Friends* morning show, July 28, 2009. By February 2010, 31 percent of over 2,000 self-identified Republicans believed that Obama was a "Racist who hates White People" and 33 percent weren't sure. See Markos Moulitsas, "The 2010 Comprehensive Daily Kos/Research 2000 Poll of Self-Identified Republicans," February 2, 2010, available at www.dailykos.com. Beck was responding to the Gates arrest. As Frank Rich pointed out in "Small Beer, Big Hangover," Obama's alleged hatred for white people would include his mother. On Beck's ambiguous relation to white nationalism, see Alexander Zaitchik, "Glenn Beck's White Nationalist Fans," *Salon*, November 20, 2009. Zaitchik quotes from two white nationalist websites, one run by David Duke, the other by "Don Black." The bloggers agree that though Beck isn't a white nationalist, he's a "useful" prompter.

40. Obama's interview with Eugene Robinson quoted in Brent Staples, "President Obama, Professor Gates and the Cambridge Police," *New York Times*, July 24, 2009, A18. See also Ogletree, *Presumption of Guilt*, 47–53, on Obama's address and his first press conference. Thomas J. Sugrue emphasizes that Obama's speeches often balanced calls for responsibility with mentions of racial inequality; Sugrue, *Not Even Past: Barack Obama and the Burden of Race* (Princeton, N.J.: Princeton University Press, 2010), 85, 117–126, 136. Sugrue writes that "Obama's call for responsibility seemed new" to whites, but not to blacks, since "the everyday world of black politics and religion remained—and remains—invisible to most of white America" (90).

41. Here I disagree with Ogletree, who vigorously defends Gates, a close friend, and faults Obama for not choosing to "teach others" about racial

profiling; Ogletree, *Presumption of Guilt*, 122–127, quote on 127. To me, Obama made it a teachable moment about how to get beyond mutual humiliation.

42. When Gates first shook hands with Crowley, he said, "I would have sworn you were six feet eight inches tall." Crowley responded, "I used to be, but I've lost two to three feet over the last two weeks." Speaking to a sympathetic crowd at the Martha's Vineyard book fair a few days later, Gates joked—maybe—that he could help get Crowley's children into Harvard.

43. Gates quoted in Helene Cooper and Abby Goodnough, "Over Beers, No Apologies, but Plans to Have Lunch," *New York Times*, July 31, 2009, A10. Another good sound bite came the day before, from Lucia Whalen's lawyer, Wendy Murphy: "The three highly trained guys who acted badly are getting together for a beer tomorrow at the White House, and that's a good thing. The one person whose actions were exemplary will be at work tomorrow here in Cambridge." Katie Zezima, "Caller Says Race Wasn't Mentioned to Officer in Gates Case," *New York Times*, July 30, 2009, A18. On Whalen's "two gentlemen," see Kelefa Sanneh, "Discriminating Tastes," 21. In late October, Crowley and Gates got together for another beer at a Cambridge pub, and in early 2010, Crowley gave the handcuffs to Gates, who gave them to the Smithsonian.

44. Mike Barnicle, "Barnicle's View on WTTK: The False Arrest of Henry Louis Gates," July 22, 2009, audio file available at www.mikebarnicle.com. Barnicle also said that Gates was arrested for disorderly conduct "because he yelled at the cops. And who could blame him?"

INDEX

9/11. *See* September 11th, 2001
2004 presidential election, 135, 136, 139
2008 presidential election, 6, 142–143, 150–166; Southern Strategy and, 144–145; voting map of post-election, 162–163. *See also* McCain campaign; Obama campaign

abolitionism, 33, 51, 106, 169. *See also* slaves/slavery
abortion, 57, 176
Abu Ghraib prison, 133–137, 240n74
Adams, Henry, 124
Adams, John, 65, 120, 235n26
Adams, Robert M., 65
Adas, Michael, 223n69, 230n6, 231n9
Addison, Joseph, 67
Adventures of Huckleberry Finn (Twain), 5, 85, 86, 94–97, 226n28; honor and, 101, 103–104, 105, 107; regional consciousness in, 106
affirmative action, 25, 153
Afghanistan, 22, 136
Africa, 18, 80, 178, 192n29; Huntington and, 126–127; Kenya, 174, 225n8; Liberia, 33; Libya, 117. *See also* Barbary Wars (1783–1815)
agonistic sports, 2, 60, 72–73, 167–168
Alexander, Michelle, 28–29, 253n1
Algerine Captive, The (Tyler), 115, 118, 122, 233n16, 237n39
Algiers, 234n24
"Alien Attack" (amusement park game), 177, 257n26
Almost All Aliens (Spickard), 114
amalgamation, 40, 80. *See also* miscegenation
American Anthropological Association, 20

American Dictionary of the English Language, An (Webster), 66
American Dilemma, An (Myrdal), 35, 42
American honor. *See* national honor
American identity, 81, 114, 189n10
American Negro Slavery (Phillips), 35
American Revolution, 65–66, 68–69
American Slavery, American Freedom (Morgan), 17, 67
American South. *See* South, the
Anderson, Benedict, 50, 51–52, 54, 70, 76
anger, 14, 26, 110, 121, 141; black, 29, 32, 42, 56, 82, 154, 156, 158, 165; at Obama, 169, 170–171, 174–176; shaming and, 3, 5, 9, 24, 29; Tea Party and, 169, 177; Wright and, 32–33
"Anglo-Saxon" (term), 17, 80, 222n66
anthropology, 20, 71
anti-Semitism, 26, 211n97
Appiah, Kwame Anthony, 21–22, 56, 76–77, 165, 190n19
Appleby, Joyce, 27
Arab Americans, 114
Arabic language, 120–121, 214n8
Arab Mind, The (Patai), 133–134
Arab protests, 109
Arafat, Yasser, 159
Arendt, Hannah, 210n88, 222n65
aristocracy, 21, 39, 70, 75; pseudo-, 17–18, 23, 76, 105
Armstrong, Karen, 61, 255n17
Arnold, Benedict, 112
"Aryan" (term), 17, 51, 80, 222n66
Asian Americans, 177, 251n55
Asians, 76
Assassins' Gate, The (Packer), 242n93
Atlantic, The (magazine), 163–164
Atta, Mohammed, 139
Atwater, Lee, 145, 244n5

Smiley, Tavis, 164, 252n62
Smith, Mark, 40
social groups. *See* group honor
socialism, 2, 28, 144, 258n31; black
 male beast image and, 176; McCain
 campaign and, 157; Obama seen as
 supporter of, 251n56; Tea Party and,
 169, 171
Social Security, 169
social segregation. *See* segregation
solipsism, 100, 108
Somalia, 22, 93, 225n6
Sombart, Werner, 28
Song of Solomon (Morrison), 39
Soul by Soul (Johnson), 23
Souls of Black Folk, The (Du Bois), 6, 29,
 36–37, 42, 49, 198n24
"Souls of White Folk, The" (Du Bois), 5,
 81–84
South, the, 27, 66, 75, 206n68, 221n63,
 233n16; 2008 presidential election
 and, 162–163; chivalry and, 48; "cult of
 honor" and, 78, 234n23; nationalism
 and, 76; North and, 23, 43–44, 76, 78,
 204n56; Wyatt-Brown on, 23
South Africa, 43, 80, 189n16, 204n55,
 221n63, 222n65
South Carolina, 35, 58, 68, 173–174, 178,
 243n3
Southern Honor (Wyatt-Brown), 22–23
Southern Strategy, 144–145, 157, 171,
 244n4, 244n5, 251n57
southern white elites, 219n47
Spanish-American War (1898), 110–111,
 140–141, 146
Specter, Arlen, 176
Spickard, Paul, 114, 232n11
Stampp, Kenneth, 35
Staples, Brent, 154–155, 158
"Star-Spangled Banner, The" (Key),
 119–120, 236n34
"states' rights," 144, 145
status, 18, 19, 24, 39–40, 51, 190n19; competition for, 59; slaves as marker of, 70;
 wealth and, 75; white anxiety about
 provincial, 17, 21, 25
Steele, Michael, 171
stereotyping, 12, 56, 208n78
Stewart, Frank Henderson, 190n18,
 191n22, 192n28, 214n8, 218n34
Stewart, Jon, 143, 171
Stigall, Chris, 174
stimulus plans, 169

Stowe, Steven, 220n58
Strange Career of Jim Crow, The (Wood-
 ward), 48
Strangers in the Land (Higham), 81, 124
Sugrue, Thomas, 44
suicide bombings, 133
Sula (Morrison), 38–39
Sumner, Charles, 68, 173, 217n26
Supreme Court, U.S., 34, 35, 56, 80
Suskind, Ron, 139, 165
Sweet, Ossian, 46
Sweet Land of Liberty (Sugrue), 44
swimming, 44–45, 95
swimming pool contamination, 1, 9–10,
 30, 31, 53, 195n3; odor of people and, 40,
 200n38, 225n8
swimming pools, integration of, 44–45,
 204n58

Tademy, Lalita, 196n11
Taibbi, Matt, 12, 15–16
taxes, 66, 145; Barbary wars and, 117;
 Boston Tea Party and, 70, 168; Obama
 and, 157; Tea Party and, 168–171
Tea Party, 2, 6, 168–171, 179, 254n6; demo-
 graphics of, 255n12; fear and, 176–177;
 Malkin and, 253n3; NAACP and, 254n7;
 Santelli and, 16, 168
Tea Party Nationalism (NAACP report),
 170
television, 4, 132, 252n62; 2008 presi-
 dential election and, 151, 153, 157; civil
 rights movement and, 54, 133, 135–136,
 211n96; *Hardball* and, 3, 12–16, 174;
 Obama and, 163, 174–175, 179; shoe-
 throwing incident and, 129–130
terrorism, 8, 27, 35, 206n68, 241n82;
 Guantánamo prison and, 135, 136;
 Obama and, 113, 152, 159, 247n26. *See
 also* lynching
Tesler, Michael, 256n18
"Teuton" (term), 17, 80, 222n66
Texas, 111
Their Eyes Were Watching God (Hurston),
 20, 38
"Them" and "Us." *See* othering
There Goes My Everything (Sokol), 177
This American Life (radio program),
 161–162
Thoreau, Henry David, 93
Thucydides, 63–64, 215n16
Thurmond, Strom, 40, 173, 258n31
Till, Emmett, 55–56, 103, 135–136

ABOUT THE AUTHOR

David Leverenz is a professor of English emeritus at the University of Florida. He has written *Paternalism Incorporated* (Cornell University Press, 2003); *Manhood and the American Renaissance* (Cornell University Press, 1989); and *The Language of Puritan Feeling* (Rutgers University Press, 1980), along with many articles and essays. He has received four teaching awards.